History along the Way

ATM travel guides

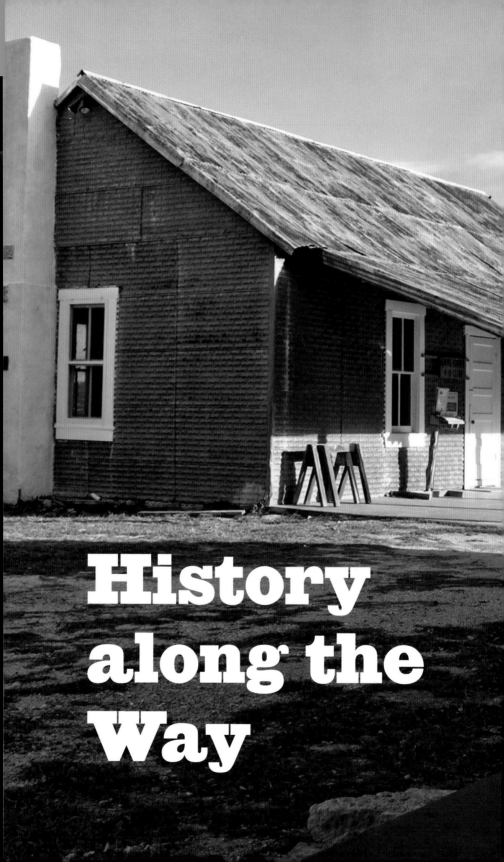

History along the Way

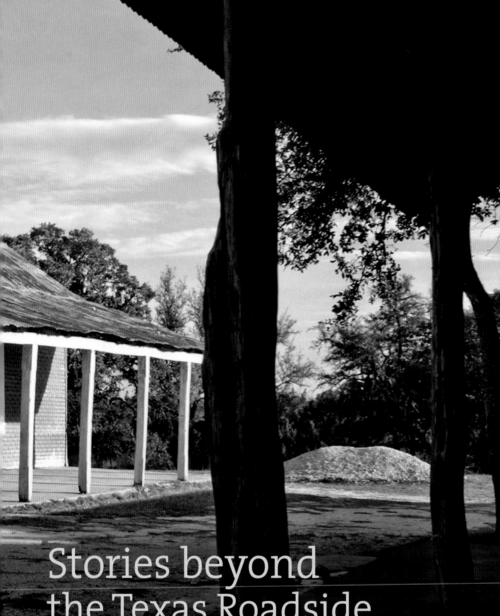

Stories beyond
the Texas Roadside
Markers

Dan K. Utley & Cynthia J. Beeman

TEXAS A&M UNIVERSITY PRESS College Station

Copyright © 2013 by
Dan K. Utley and Cynthia J. Beeman
Manufactured in China by Everbest Printing Co.,
through FCI Print Group
First edition

This paper meets the requirements
of ANSI/NISO, z39.48–1992
(Permanence of Paper).
Binding materials have been
chosen for durability. ♾

Library of Congress
Cataloging-in-Publication Data
Utley, Dan K.
History along the way : stories beyond the
Texas roadside markers / Dan K. Utley and
Cynthia J. Beeman. — 1st ed.
p. cm. — (Texas A&M travel guides)
Includes bibliographical references and index.
ISBN-13: 978-1-60344-769-0 (flexbound : alk. paper)
ISBN-10: 1-60344-769-5 (flexbound : alk. paper)
ISBN-13: 978-1-60344-818-5 (e-book)
ISBN-10: 1-60344-818-7 (e-book)
1. Historical markers—Texas. 2. Texas—History.
3. Texas—History—Anecdotes. 4. Texas—Description
and travel. 5. Texas—Biography. I. Beeman, Cynthia J.
II. Title. III. Series: TAM travel guides.
F387.U86 2013
976.4—dc23
2012013080

Dedicated to the county historical commissions of Texas, who, with little support or praise but with great energy and devotion nonetheless, tirelessly, unselfishly, and persistently preserve the diverse heritage of the Lone Star State. We are all in their debt.

Contents

Acknowledgments ix

Introduction 1

PART ONE. TEXAS ORIGINALS

Chapter 1. A Chance Encounter of the Great Procession 5

Sidebar: Dr. Sellards and the Malakoff Men 15

Sidebar: A Good Place to Hunt 17

Chapter 2. John Ben's Critters 19

Sidebar: Standing for Health 32

Chapter 3. A Life in Ragged Time 35

Sidebar: Maple Leaf Rag 44

Sidebar: Oakwood's Founder 45

Chapter 4. Turn East to Texas 47

Sidebar: The Abert Context in the Texas Panhandle 60

Sidebar: Replacing Historical Markers 61

Chapter 5. Illumined by Truthful Artistic Ideals 63

Sidebar: El Paso High School 76

Chapter 6. Her Lonely Way Back Home 78

Sidebar: Rainbow Bridge 93

PART TWO. THE TEXAS CULTURAL LANDSCAPE

Chapter 7. And the Cars Keep Rolling By 99

Sidebar: East Mound Cemetery 111

Sidebar: Granbury's Town Square Service Station 112

Chapter 8. "To Have What We Must" 115

Sidebar: Landmark Schoolhouses of Gillespie County 127

Chapter 9. A Journey back to Nature 134

Sidebar: The Invasion of Lampasas County 145

Chapter 10. Lift High the Water 148
    Sidebar: Dam, Ditch, and Aqueduct 160
Chapter 11. The Normal on Chautauqua Hill 162
    Sidebar: Northcraft's San Marcos Churches 172
    Sidebar: Orlando Newton Hollingsworth 174
    Sidebar: Remembering Old Main on Capitol Hill 178
Chapter 12. History on the Grounds 183
    Sidebar: Capitol Markers—The Rest of the Story 197
    Sidebar: The Littlest Dreadnought 199

PART THREE. TEXANS REACHING OUT
Chapter 13. Justice Is the Corporate Face of Love 205
    Sidebar: Christ Church Cathedral 217
Chapter 14. A Light on the Path of Wisdom 220
    Sidebar: Fairly Flying from Terrell to Dallas 232
Chapter 15. Two Generations Striving for Civil Rights 235
    Sidebar: Huston-Tillotson University 248
    Sidebar: Wiley College 250
Chapter 16. A Citizen with Work to Do 252
    Sidebar: Women First 266
Chapter 17. Here I Am in Palestine 271
    Sidebar: From Cotton Field to Factory 283
Chapter 18. The Three Graves of Judge Baylor 286
    Sidebar: A Gift in the Hour of Need 300

Notes 305
Index 323

Acknowledgments

The process of writing is in a sense like striking out on a long journey without a highly detailed road map. The authors may have a strong sense of where they started and maybe a vision of where they are headed, but along the route they often have to stop and ask directions or ask for the best local places to visit. Those stops along the way often make the journey memorable and even more meaningful, and such is the case with this endeavor. Having traveled the roads that led to the first installment in this series, we had some idea of who might be able to serve as guides along the way, and there are a number of dependable ones we contact on a regular basis, whatever the trip. There are those, however, who are unknown when the journey begins, but who somehow become an indispensible part of the project. Together, though, whether old friends or new acquaintances, they all formed a sort of support team that kept us headed in the right direction. Our intent here is to give credit to as many as we can and to thank them publicly for their invaluable and unselfish assistance.

First and foremost, we offer great thanks to the staff of the Texas Historical Commission, a place we used to call our second home. It is always comfortable to work with our former colleagues, who we know to be professional, capable, and dedicated. Although we have known many of them for years and consider them our friends, we received no special attention in our pursuit of historical materials. The kindness they showed us differs in no way from that they convey to the general public. They are a remarkable group of public servants, and we could not have completed this manuscript without their direction and insight. In particular, we want to thank Bratten Thomason, director of the History Programs Division, and Bob Brinkman, marker program coordinator. Other THC staff members who provided valuable assistance included Charles Sadnick, Anne Shelton, and Annette Bethke of the History Programs Division, Mark Cowan of the Division of Architecture, and Brett Cruse of the Historic Sites Division. A very special thanks goes to our friend, Kimberly Gamble, the gatekeeper of the marker records, who was always there with a smile and a good word when we went in search of files.

In terms of general historical research assistance, we are indebted to Terry Shults of the University of Texas of the Permian Basin in Odessa; Sam Monroe, president of Lamar State College–Port Arthur; Monteel Copple and Yvonne Sutherlin of Port Arthur; brothers Clyde L. Hall of Sherman and Hugh E. Hall Jr. of Winchester; Ann Morris of Carthage; the Reverend Chris Hines of Bastrop and Nancy Hines Smith of Austin; Ali James of the Texas State Preservation Board in Austin; Gene Preuss of Houston; Jana Beck and Bernice Weinheimer of Gillespie County; Kay Wolf of Hidalgo; the Reverend Jenna Heart of San Marcos; James Patton, Patrick Nolan, and Cheryl Spencer of Huntsville; Barbara Armstrong of Motley County; Matt Renick and Eileen Johnson of Texas Tech University, Lubbock; and Kris Toma, Margaret Vavarek, and Tanesa Scott of Texas State University, San Marcos.

Special thanks are owed to a team of interested individuals who provided excellent background information on the field of archeology, and they include William G. Reeder of Wisconsin, Bob Mallouf of Alpine, Solveig Turpin of San Antonio, Carl Williamson of Roberts County, and Vance T. Holliday of the University of Arizona, a valued friend and a former Prather Rat from the distant collegiate past who served as a trusted guide through the world of mammoths and mammoth hunters, not the usual hangout for historians. Archeological assistance and related photographic assistance came from two trusted sources, Carolyn Spock and Darrell Creel of the Texas Archeological Research Laboratory at the University of Texas at Austin.

While we valued the assistance of each and every person who guided us along the journey, we want to offer special thanks to a few who went far beyond the call of duty to make sure we had the right resources. These are extraordinary people who gave freely of their time and energy, and we appreciate them more than they can possibly know. In Motley County, our enthusiastic assistant was

Marisue Potts Powell, with whom we worked years ago on various marker projects, including the one for Bob's Oil Well, which became the focus of a chapter in this book. In Gillespie County, our new friend is Dr. Jim Lindley, who is a medical specialist, a local history enthusiast, an oral history practitioner, and a ham radio operator extraordinaire. We enjoyed riding through the Hill Country with him to locate some of the most impressive rural schoolhouses in the state. There are times when our work seems like play, and that was one of those occasions. In Hidalgo County, down in the Rio Grande Valley, we enjoyed hooking up again with longtime friends George and Virginia Gause. If there are any nicer people who enjoy life to the fullest, we have yet to meet them.

At the University of Mary Hardin–Baylor in Belton, we met a delightful and dedicated museum curator named Betty Sue Beebe. She is a proud graduate of the institution she now serves, and her enthusiasm, great spirit, and passion serve it well. At another fine collegiate institution, Sam Houston State University, we were fortunate to be guided through archival records by Barbara Kievit-Mason, who gave freely of her time and knowledge for background information on the school's beloved Old Main, sadly destroyed by a fire several decades ago. Another collegiate representative we must mention is Jennifer Helgren, of Pacific University. She is the foremost authority on the history of programs for young women, and we are indebted to her for sharing her research on the Camp Fire organization prior to its publication. Special research assistance also came from an unexpected source: Mr. Dana Wegner of the US Naval Surface Warfare Center in Bethesda, MD. He has the job that must be the envy of young people and the young at heart everywhere; he is the Curator of Ship Models, and it is his task to ensure there are accurate, three-dimensional reminders of the great ships of the US Navy for research purposes. We enjoyed getting to know him through email correspondence.

And finally, we want to recognize the good nature and committed research assistance of two longtime friends, Jimmy and Kathy Odom of Palestine, Anderson County. Mr. Odom—or Catfish Jimmy as we know him—grew up in Anderson County and has likely covered every road and trail of that area in his lifetime.

His reverence for the past is broad, and he has worked with count-less people to place historical markers for schools, churches, ceme-teries, industries, and a special place known as the Palestine Ser-vice Men's Club. He is always quick with a quip, and his assistance always comes with a wink and a nod, and we consider him a land-mark in his own right. Truth be known, though, Kathy keeps him between the ditches, and for that she is a saint.

Those people who helped us gather photographs for this book are myriad, and we want to thank them all for their assistance on our behalf. In addition to some already mentioned, we want to include Aminatta Kamara, of the Museum of the Gulf Coast, Port Arthur; Nancy Wells, Odessa Main Street Program; Randy Yan-dell, University of Mary Hardin–Baylor; John Anderson, Texas State Library and Archives Commission; Anne Cook, Texas Department of Transportation; Susanne Golden, Shreveport, Louisiana; Patrick Lemelle, Institute of Texan Cultures, San Antonio; and Vanessa Adams, Nancy Canson, and Leta Kay, Caddo Lake National Wildlife Refuge.

There is one final person who deserves credit for her exem-plary work, and that is artist and cartographer Molly O'Halloran of Austin. We consider her a part of our team, and if anyone can get us to the right place by way of a map, it is she. Molly is the consum-mate professional and a delight to work with, and we always en-joy drinking coffee with her at Progress Coffee while we exchange ideas and wander off into less meaningful, albeit enjoyable, con-versation. Here is how we work with Molly: we give her dim photo-copies of maps cluttered with our notes and arrows and bad hand-writing, and in a matter of days she gives us back a set of beautiful maps that make us look like we knew where we are going. She is a remarkable person and a good friend, and she will always be a part of our projects if we need to convey directions.

If there are names we left off our list, we apologize. Any omis-sions are unintended and most likely the result of inadequate note-taking at the appropriate moment. We will try to do better the next time—and we hope there will be a next time, for there are still many stories to tell along the roadsides of Texas.

Introduction

As we prepared to turn in the manuscript for this, the second volume of our work on the stories behind the roadside markers of Texas, there was great uncertainty about the future of the Texas Historical Commission (THC), which oversees the Official Texas Historical Marker Program. Formed in 1953, the THC has, during its relatively brief existence, established a state program unequaled in the nation. Texas has more than fifteen thousand state historical markers, while the closest contenders have no more than four thousand apiece. There are perhaps myriad reasons for the state's preeminence in the field, but a major contributing factor is the inclusive nature of the process. Markers in Texas not only tell big stories, but they also chronicle the bits and pieces that make up the larger picture that we call history. A foundation of the Texas program has always been the work of county historical commissions—to whom we dedicate this book—in partnership with the state, which preserves diverse elements of the past and records history where it happened. It is a unique program, one that brings great pride to Texans and good basic information to those who want to know more about our state.

Sadly, though, as the state legislature pondered its budgetary obligations in the spring of 2011, there was considerable talk of killing the THC or at least cutting it to a point where the marker program could be significantly curtailed. Thanks in large part to an unprecedented outpouring of support from historians, preservationists, county historical commissions, students, and many others interested in the history of Texas, cooler heads prevailed and the THC survived, albeit in a drastically reduced capacity. The Official Texas Historical Marker Program survived, though, and to date there has been no interruption of services. New markers continue to be placed throughout the landscape to interpret history, promote tourism, and enhance community pride. Although the program survived for now, it is perhaps a reflection of our time that history could even be considered at risk. That saddens those of us who see the state markers as part of a public-held trust from past generations to those in the present and future. While we join with those celebrating the agency's continued viability, we are pleased to know there is sufficient stock of public history in place along the state highways—with more on the way—to allow us the privilege of again researching old stories, uncovering new ones, and sharing with others what we found along the way. It is a responsibility we do not take lightly. As all students of history no doubt understand, our past is not static. It is, instead, dynamic and ever-changing based on various influences from generational interpretation to new discoveries. Regardless of budget woes now and in the future, the history remains, and we all share in that inheritance.

The response to our first effort in this series has been both overwhelming and reassuring. History lives in Texas, and it thrives along the roadsides, in the neighborhoods, on the courthouse squares, and up and down Main Street. As we traveled around the state in the past year giving presentations and signing books, we heard countless stories of what makes our state unique. In places like Rockdale, Woodville, San Antonio, Georgetown, Fort Worth, Lake Buchanan, Burnet, Thurber, Dallas, Luling, Houston, Lufkin, and Austin we met proud Texans who not only wanted to know more about their state—and thus thought our book might help in that regard—but also wanted to share their family's piece of the past with us. What a great honor for us to hear those stories.

When all is said and done, history not only lives and remains, it also moves ahead. In that vein, we offer this new collection of stories for those who want to know more about how Texas came to be what it is today. While you are, we hope, enjoying these, we will be working to gather another batch on down the trail.

PART ONE
Texas Originals

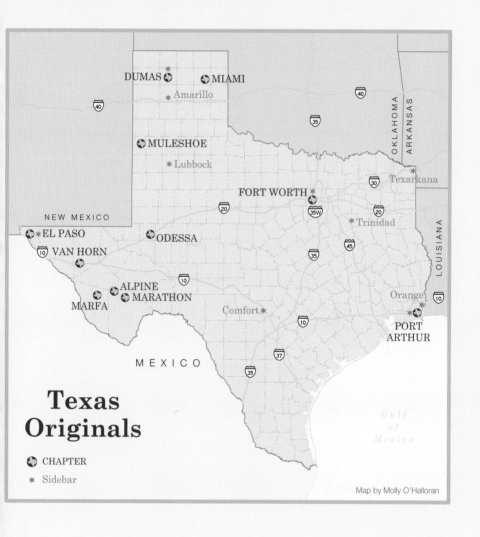

DUMAS ●
● MIAMI
★ Amarillo

● MULESHOE
★ Lubbock

40

35

40

OKLAHOMA
ARKANSAS

30
Texarkana

FORT WORTH ●
20

35W

20
★ Trinidad

NEW MEXICO

● EL PASO
10 ● VAN HORN

● ODESSA

35

45

LOUISIANA

10

ALPINE ●
● MARATHON
MARFA

10

Orange
10

★
PORT
ARTHUR

Comfort ★

MEXICO

10

37

35

Texas
Originals

● CHAPTER
★ Sidebar

Gulf
of
Mexico

Map by Molly O'Halloran

1

A Chance Encounter
of the Great Procession

As the planting season approached in 1933, migrant farm worker Charles Puckett prepared to work the soil on the Charles Ross Cowan ranch nine miles northwest of Miami in Roberts County. It was a time of unprecedented economic downturn in the nation, and the Panhandle of Texas was in the early phases of a drought that would also prove to be unprecedented. In time, the area would come to be known as part of the Dust Bowl, but in 1933 there was still enough hope in the promise of the coming season for farmers to plant wheat, increasingly a dominant crop on the High Plains. That particular season, however, Puckett set the plowshares deep in order to carve out furrows that might somehow manage to resist the destructive, arid winds that had for some time been scouring the farmland, reconfiguring the surrounding landscape with aeolian drifts and deeply incised gullies. Deep plowing, like dust mulching and contouring, were relatively new techniques designed to meet the challenging demands of dryland farming, and it seemed to Puckett to be worth the effort.

As the farmer slowly worked his way across the Cowan lands that season, though, all was not as normal. In one particular area of the vast field, his plow began turning over a series of large, chalky bones. Puckett and Cowan were unsure of what they had encountered, but they knew the bones were something other than the remnants of cows or wild animals. As a result, they shared their findings with County Judge John A. Mead, not out of suspicion of crime, but rather because Mead had earned a reputation in the region as a knowledgeable amateur archeologist. The judge had investigated numerous prehistoric finds in the area around Miami, and it was possible the large bones unearthed on the Cowan ranch might prove to be similar. Although in some respects they were, in one important aspect they were like nothing else discovered to that point. What emerged from the deep furrows of the Roberts County field would eventually prove to be revolutionary, controversial, and nationally significant.

Judge Mead inspected the field and, intrigued by what he found, returned to oversee extensive excavations in 1934. Working with others, he carefully removed the agricultural layer of soil and methodically worked his way down, finding numerous bone fragments along the way. Over time, he came to what appeared to be a bone bed, a sizeable layer of artifacts that lay intact beneath the depth of the plow. Among the artifacts he recovered were the teeth, leg bones, and ribs of an ancient, extinct elephant. On closer inspection, he found amid the massive bones, and on the same plane, a carefully worked spear point. It was then he realized the site held greater scientific potential than any other he had encountered, so he sought outside assistance.[1]

Among those he contacted early on was Floyd V. Studer. A native of Canadian, twenty-four miles northeast of Miami, he was, like the judge, an amateur archeologist with extensive field experience in the region. He was, by profession, a businessman, with interests in banking, ranching, and insurance. A resident of Amarillo by the 1930s, Studer became one of that city's most prominent civic leaders. Throughout his life he maintained a strong fascination with archeology and paleontology, particularly along the Canadian River, which cut a wide swath across the Panhandle. Although he lacked formal training in the disciplines, he had field experience, as well as the investigative and analytical skills to make him a recognized authority at a formative time for the professions in Texas. As a result, he eventually transitioned from a successful business career to one as a museum curator. Joining the staff of the Panhandle-Plains Historical Museum, which opened at Canyon in 1933, he directed the development of that institution's impressive collections of both archeological and paleontological materials.[2]

Studer worked closely with Mead on further investigations at the Cowan site, and he published the first treatment of the information in *Science Service*. Subsequently interviewed for a 1935 issue of *Sci-*

ence News Letter, Studer reflected on the matter of the site's significance, speculating on its relative antiquity: "While I have personally found several true Folsom or Yuma points in this immediate
area, this is the first time one has been reported in direct association with fossil animals. The bones were found in blue-green clay,
which indicates a lake bed. There is no evidence of river or stream
sand. This blue-green formation lies undisturbed about 18 inches
below the present soil level." The article concluded by placing the
Miami site in the context of what were then the earliest known
eras of human existence in the United States: "The discovery site is
not very far from Clovis, New Mexico, where Dr. Edgar B. Howard of
the University Museum, Philadelphia, has made notable discoveries indicating existence of early inhabitants in the region. It is also
not far from Folsom, New Mexico, where one of the first startling
clues suggesting that America was inhabited more than a very few
thousand years ago came to light." Such discoveries were relatively
recent, and the evolving scientific analysis, as well as the concomitant speculation, caution, and controversy, continued to capture
the attention of the archeological community.[3]

Renewed interest in the Cowan Ranch site in 1937 signaled a new
era of scientific analysis. That year, Elias Howard Sellards of the
University of Texas began his intensive investigations. He brought
a new level of professional expertise to the project. A native of Kentucky who earned his doctorate in paleontology at Yale University,
where his dissertation was on "fossil plants and cockroaches of
the Upper Paleozoic in Kansas," Sellards had an extensive career
background in geology. Prior to his association with the University
of Texas, he served as the state geologist in Florida for more than
a decade. Through that position he worked on what proved to be
a controversial project at Vero (now Vero Beach) that he believed
showed evidence of human existence with Pleistocene fauna. Considered a radical departure from existing anthropological norms
of the time, his associated report met with considerable criticism
from members of the scientific community who leveled charges of
inexperience and misinterpretation against him. As his friend and
colleague, the noted archeologist Alex D. Krieger, later wrote: "This
criticism—or rather, the kind of reasoning behind it—affected him

more deeply than he would ever have admitted to anyone; he disliked controversy and avoided it in publications all his life. The Vero experience had aroused in him a consuming interest in the general problem of contemporaneity of man and Pleistocene fauna in America, but it was many years before he could find time to pursue the matter again with field work." Sellards relocated to Texas soon after the Florida controversy as a research geologist at the Bureau of Economic Geology, part of the University of Texas at Austin. In 1932 he became the director. Only six years later he would accept an additional, dual assignment as director of the Texas Memorial Museum on campus.[4]

For the fieldwork he would oversee at the Cowan Ranch site, Sellards called on his trusted bureau colleague, Glen L. Evans, to serve as manager. In Evans, Sellards saw a kindred spirit, someone with impeccable credentials and diverse interests who shared his finely honed observational skills and intensely focused work ethic. The two proved to be a strong team, collaborating through the years on a number of significant archeological sites, and they became fast friends in the process. Writing later of their countless research trips together, Evans noted his supervisor's "wonderful zest" for fieldwork and added that his "way of studying a subject, mountain or anything else, was not by viewing it from afar. He liked details, and always preferred a scientific approach to a problem." Sellards's drive in the field, as Evans noted, often required some personal adjustment to the intense schedule: "Never one to lie abed of mornings, especially when in the field, in his eagerness to get started he occasionally misread his watch and got up at an ungodly early hour. Then he would rout me out of my blankets with his familiar sleep-rupturing call, 'It's hard on daylight, Glen, time to get up.' We would then get breakfast and a packaged lunch at some truck-stop or all-night café, and drive to where we intended to work that day — there to sit shivering and yawning in the automobile until it was light enough to start work."[5]

For the project northwest of Miami, Sellards set the parameters for the scope of the investigations, and Evans oversaw the on-site excavations. Assisting them by providing the labor necessary for moving large amounts of dirt were a number of unskilled workers hired through the Works Progress Administration (WPA), a New Deal agency set up to bolster employment during the Great Depression by means of federally funded public works projects. Such an arrangement between the government and the university was not unusual in the 1930s, and the WPA funded a number of important early archeological projects and related surveys in the state.

Under Evans's careful excavations, the Cowan Ranch site—given the scientific site designator 41RB1—began to yield important new evidence, much of it geological in nature. He showed that the basal feature was, in prehistoric times, a pond or playa lake approximately seventy-five feet in diameter—a watering hole frequented by mammoths, specifically Columbian elephants (*Mammathus columbi*). Evans uncovered the remains of several mammoths, but, curiously, no other animals. All of the remains were in a horizontal plane, an indication they had likely died on their sides rather than being trapped vertically in the thick silt layer of the playa lake. In his examination of the bone bed, Evans found what proved to be a monumental discovery: a fluted projectile point less than three inches from the atlas vertebra (at the base of the skull) of one of the elephants. As Sellards described, the point and vertebra "were removed in a single block." He added, "The point, including the broken base but excluding the extreme tip, which is wanting, is 113 mm. long, 22 mm. wide at the base, and 30 mm. wide above the base. It is made from slightly mottled light chert or flint."[6]

While no doubt concerned about the position and proximity of the point to the skeletal remains, given the earlier criticism of his work at Vero, Florida, Sellards realized this find was different. It was a site separate from any early stream bed or collapsed geological feature that could have resulted in movement or repositioning of the artifact over time. With the discovery, Sellards had his long-sought-after evidence that early man and early mammoth existed contemporaneously. He also believed, as others would later echo, that the site revealed some considerable skill on the part of the ancient hunters, who evidently knew how to disable the massive animals by severing the spinal cords. Sellards remained, however, somewhat cautious in his assessment: "Although the evidence in this connection is meager, the most probable explanation of this

The discovery of this fluted projectile point within inches of a mammoth's atlas vertebra, shown here encased in plaster following excavation, helped make the Cowan Ranch site one of the most important early man sites in North America. Courtesy Texas Archeological Research Laboratory, The University of Texas at Austin. TARL Photographic catalog number 41RB1–27 300.

unusual occurrence of a group of elephants in a water-hole, with associated artifacts, seems to be that disease, starvation, or drought may have caused the death of some of the elephants and that others, enfeebled by disease or otherwise, may have been killed by early man."[7] Because of the design of the projectile point, the discovery also provided some general sense of the site's antiquity. Sellards determined it to be associated with the so-called Clovis people, a Paleo-Indian culture which earlier excavations in New Mexico and other locales had shown to exist roughly 13,000–10,000 years BP (before present). That placed the Roberts County find among the earliest known cultural sites in North America at that time. By comparison, the important benchmark Paleo-Indian discoveries at Folsom, New Mexico, occurred in the mid-1920s, and excavations of an earlier culture near Clovis, also in New Mexico, took place in 1932, the year before the Cowan Ranch site discovery.[8]

Subsequent excavations in the western states showed that the Columbian elephant, among the last of the megafauna to face extinction, was a commonly discovered mammoth species in the North American paleontological record. Several sites in Texas, including most notably the Waco Mammoth Site in McLennan County, discovered in 1978 and only recently opened to the public, have yielded their remains. The larger of the mammoths are believed to have reached twelve to thirteen feet in height and approximately ten tons in weight. Speculation on the era of the megafauna differs considerably, but the Columbian elephants may have faced extinction sometime more than ten thousand years ago. That would place the encounter near Miami near the end of their existence.[9]

When Evans and Sellards closed the project on Cowan Ranch, WPA workers refilled the site, and the land returned to agricultural use, with no evidence remaining of the landmark investigations. The artifacts, carefully encased in plaster, went back to Austin for further analysis. They included numerous elephant bones and teeth, three projectile points, and a scraper. Sellards, a prolific writer, authored several important papers and articles on the finds over the years, and the Miami mammoth collection became one of the most important in the holdings of the Texas Memorial Museum. There, the geologist-paleontologist kept a watchful eye on the materials through his years as director, from 1938 until his retirement in 1957.

In 1952, Sellards completed perhaps his most important and long-lasting work, a broad-based overview entitled *Early Man: A Study in Prehistory.* By the time of the publication he was in his seventies and facing complications associated with long-neglected health concerns. Nevertheless, the book seemed to offer him a personal release at that point in his career, and his colleagues noted a marked change in his demeanor. As Alex Krieger observed: "The indomitable old man, always unsparing of himself, began to mellow and relax; he spent more time with people and took an interest in small talk. He became more interested in the problems of others, and wherever he traveled he showed warmth and charm and a lively sense of humor which had apparently long been suppressed."[10]

Sellards's new persona is perhaps reflected best in his seminal

This photograph of the Cowan Ranch site taken at the time of the 1930s Sellards-Evans excavations shows various artifacts, encased in plaster, awaiting transfer to the Texas Memorial Museum in Austin. Courtesy Texas Archeological Research Laboratory, The University of Texas at Austin. TARL Photographic catalog number 41RB1–9 300.

work *Early Man,* in which he took the time to provide a contextual commentary replete with his own personal perspectives from a lifetime of study and contemplation. The results are an amalgam of philosophy and literature. "It is as though the earth were a stage across which passed an endless succession of changing scenes and changing life," he wrote. "Each succeeding group and kind held the stage temporarily and disappeared to be seen no more." And then making the connection with the present, he added, "We, ourselves, who are now part of the moving scene, are privileged through records of the past to obtain glimpses of the great procession."[11]

Elias Howard Sellards retired from the Texas Memorial Museum in 1957 and passed away four years later. Sadly, in the early 1970s someone stole all but one of the original Clovis spear points that were central to his longtime analysis of the Cowan Ranch investigations. Photographs remain, however, as do meticulously detailed replicas of the points, the latter thanks to a collaborative effort with the University of Missouri in the 1940s. Sellards's beloved and trustworthy coinvestigator, Glen L. Evans, had a remarkable career in his own right through extensive work in both the public and private sectors. Always a man of diverse interests and talents, Evans had an inquisitive mind that led him to explore far afield of the geology that had proven to be his early defining passion. Toward the end of his long life he compiled a collection of nature stories he entitled *Wildness at Risk*. Evans passed away in the summer of 2010 at the age of ninety-nine, remembered by many who worked closely with him as the "dean of Texas paleontology."[12]

Although the materials removed from the Cowan Ranch site continued to generate additional analysis and scholarship for decades following the excavations in the 1930s, the site itself remained unaffected. That changed in 1990, though, when a team of four scientists revisited the area to conduct additional investigations. Drawn by lingering questions about the site and by an interest in exploring additional methodologies with new technologies not available to Sellards and Evans in the 1930s, the team hoped to examine the stratigraphy, gather any remaining evidence, and provide a tighter date for the site radiometrically. Comprising the new investigative team were Vance T. Holliday, of the University of Wisconsin; C. Vance Haynes Jr., of the University of Arizona; Jack L. Hofman, of the University of Kansas; and David J. Meltzer, of Southern Methodist University. In their published report three years later they noted, "Upon arrival in 1990 we found the same situation that greeted Sellards and Evans: a flat field with no topographic indication of the site, but with numerous mammoth bone and teeth fragments at the surface." To verify the site, which had been excavated fully and then backfilled by the University of Texas team, they used hydraulic soil coring equipment to take multiple core samples in a T-shaped pattern. They used resulting playa fill material for accelerator mass spectrometry testing in order to establish dates for various elements of the feature: the Clovis cultural level; an underlying layer of loess, or wind-blown material, thought to be an indicator of severe drought in the region; and then the basal part of the playa. According to their findings, "the Clovis event probably occurred sometime between 11,400 and 10,500 yr B.P., and probably closer to the former." By comparison, they noted, "Other well-dated Clovis sites are between 11,200 and 10,900 yr B.P."[13]

The 1990 investigations confirmed that even after more than half a century following the intensive investigations by E. H. Sellards, Glen L. Evans, and their WPA field crew, site 41RB1 remained one of the signal geoarcheological studies in North America. Providing some of the earliest evidence of cooccurrence of Clovis man and the mammoth, it represented an important benchmark in the ongoing scientific understanding of the ancient past. While it left some questions unanswered, it nevertheless served to move the collective knowledge forward, perhaps toward answers that will only be found as the result of other scholarly encounters. In the interim, though, those seeking to know more about the Cowan Ranch site or to observe the artifacts it yielded can visit the Roberts County Museum in Miami, where examples of the bones are on display. The majority of the artifacts, however, now reside at the Vertebrate Paleontology Laboratory of the University of Texas on the J. J. "Jake" Pickle Campus in north Austin. There, security is high, and access is granted only to recognized scholars with a demonstrated professional interest in the subject matter. While there is no evidence of the excavations on the old Cowan place, an Official Texas Historical Marker in the Roberts County seat now interprets the story of the Miami Mammoth Kill Site. The marker dates to 2003, seventy years after farmer Charles Puckett, hoping for the best but planning for the worst, set his plowshares deep to challenge a Panhandle drought.

MARKER LOCATION: 200 E. Commercial, Miami

DR. SELLARDS AND THE MALAKOFF MEN

Dr. E. H. Sellards was a pioneer investigator of early man sites in the United States, and as a result he was never far from controversies that surrounded his discoveries and related theories. Over time, many of his theories entered the mainstream of archeological studies, but others have remained clouded in conjecture and debate for well over half a century. Some of those debates are now so old they have passed into the realm of lore that surrounds the archeological profession and are rarely brought up in scientific journals. One of those stems from finds near the town of Malakoff in Henderson County. On November 2, 1929, workers from the Texas Clay Products Company, excavating deep gravel deposits along Cypress Creek, a tributary of the Trinity River, uncovered what appeared to be a small boulder "carved to represent a man's head." V. C. Doctorman, a mining engineer with the Malakoff Fuel Company, wrote to Sellards a few days later to tell him of the discovery, and by the end of the month the scientist traveled to the site to conduct his own investigations. Upon examination of the artifact at the mining office, Sellards found that the "rounded, boulder-like rock" exhibited what appeared to be primitively carved but distinct facial features, including eyes, ears, a nose, and mouth. The artifact was approximately sixteen by fourteen inches and weighed ninety-eight pounds. With permission of the landowner, Judge W. R. Bishop, Sellards and his team excavated in the gravel pit around the discovery site but found no evidence of other cultural materials.

As word of the discovery spread, the carved boulder became popularly known as the Malakoff Man, although the site was closer to Trinidad. Sellards, who referred to the artifact even years later simply as a "stone image," prepared a report to *American Anthropologist* on the find but withdrew it, hoping continued excavations at the pit would eventually produce further evidence. His hunch paid off in 1935 when workers at a second pit on the Bishop land uncovered what they believed was a similarly carved boulder. His interest renewed, Sellards planned for intensive investigations in the area that occurred sporadically from 1938 to 1940, with some financial assistance from the Work Projects Administration of the federal government. Through those excavations, another head surfaced in 1939. Workers found it imbedded in gravels at a depth of twenty-two feet, and it measured approximately twenty inches long and weighed 135 pounds. Sellards determined the head did not move to the location by water action, but rather was *in situ* first and then covered by the gravels. Following the third find, the archeologist prepared a detailed study, published by *American Antiquity* in July 1941. Providing analysis of ancient stream bed action, as well as what he observed were contemporaneous faunal fossils, he determined "the geologic age of the images in Pleistocene." Heads number one and three became part of the collections at the Texas Memorial Museum in Austin, where various students and archeologists studied them and even wrote about them through the years. Head number two ended up in a private collection and was therefore never analyzed as closely as the other two.

Dr. Sellards died in 1961, and over time the mystique of the Malakoff heads subsided, although there were subsequent studies and excavations. For the most part, though, the story showed up more commonly in newspaper articles, but also in some minor archeological publications. In an attempt to end the ongoing speculation, which included reports of similar finds in other areas of the state, archeologist Dr. Thomas H. Guderjan revisited the story in the 1980s and applied new analytical techniques to determine the validity of Sellards's claims. He had access only to the first and third heads, though. Determining that the first one exhibited evidence of relatively recent working by stone tools and then subsequent color touch-up, he concluded that "Head No. 1 is a forgery" created most likely at the time of its "discovery" in November 1929. By comparison, though, he found the extant eye feature on the third head was "the result of natural erosion" around crystals within the stone and therefore "an ecofact without any archeological meaning."

Despite such careful and convincing analysis, the Malakoff Men (Malakoff Heads) remain an enigmatic element of the past. If, in fact, the first head was the result of forgery, questions remain about who might have orchestrated the deceit and how they managed to pull it off so convincingly. The answers may well remain unknown and unknowable, but the story of the Malakoff discovery, like early man sites in Vero, Florida, and Miami, Texas—and numerous other locales—continues to fascinate those who follow the colorful pioneering career of Dr. Elias Howard Sellards.

MARKER LOCATION: SH 31 just west of intersection with SH 274, Trinidad

Sources: E. H. Sellards, "Stone Images from Henderson County, Texas," *American Antiquity* 7, no. 1 (July 1941), pp. 29–38; Thomas H. Guderjan, "An Examination and Appraisal of Malakoff Heads No. 1 and No. 3," *Bulletin of the Texas Archeological Society* 60 (1989; published in 1991), pp. 325–33.

A GOOD PLACE TO HUNT

In 1970 the Texas State Historical Survey Committee formally recognized one of the oldest hunting sites in the state when it approved an Official Texas Historical Marker for the Lubbock Lake Site (Lubbock Lake Landmark). Archeological artifacts recorded at the early man site since the 1930s provide evidence that the original hunters who came to the Yellow House Draw of the Brazos River drainage on the northwest side of present-day Lubbock sought mammoths and other game, including bison and camels. The national significance of the Lubbock Lake Landmark stems in part from its deep stratigraphy, with various layers of definable occupational periods dating from a prehistoric era of approximately 11,500 years before the present to the relatively recent historic era of buffalo hunters and frontier commercial traders. Now operated by the Museum of Texas Tech University, which oversees ongoing investigations, analysis, interpretation, and public education pro-

Austin sculptor Mike O'Brien designed the dramatic piece Columbian Mammoth Mother and Calf *which adorns the grounds of the Robert Nash Interpretive Center at the Lubbock Lake Landmark, administered by the Museum of Texas Tech University. Based on nearby scientific excavations conducted over many years, the bronze statues provide a life-sized visual representation of the type of animals uncovered in Roberts County as well.* Courtesy Lubbock Lake Landmark, Texas Tech University.

grams, it is maintained as an archeological and natural history preserve open to the public. In addition to the recognition provided by the historical marker, the site is listed in the National Register of Historic Places and has been designated a National Historic Landmark and a State Archeological Landmark.

MARKER LOCATION: 0.5 mi. northwest of Loop 289 on US 84, Lubbock

Sources: Lubbock Lake Site, Lubbock County, THC marker files; Lubbock Lake Landmark, www.depts.ttu.edu/museumttu/111 /, accessed March 13, 2011; Eileen Johnson and Vance T. Holliday, "Lubbock Lake National Historic and State Archeological Landmark," *New Handbook of Texas*, vol. 4, ed. Ron Tyler (Austin: Texas State Historical Association, 1996), p. 324.

2 John Ben's Critters

Texas is a unique state, and Texans love to make claims of uniqueness. Whether it's the oldest, biggest, richest, first, or only, the claims often owe more to community boosterism than history, although many are at least based on some historical event or connection. The unique claims often come with official titles, mottoes, or nicknames legitimized by action of the Texas Legislature, which has officially named scores of "capitals" throughout the state based on a region's identity as tied to features such as ethnic heritage, arts, culture, and recreation. The town of West bills itself as the Czech Heritage Capital of Texas; Danevang is known as the Danish Capital; Dublin is the Irish Capital; and the Norwegian Capital of Texas is Clifton. Navasota, with its rich music traditions, is the Blues Capital, and Fredericksburg celebrates its German heritage as the Polka Capital.

Some "capitals" of Texas are towns that celebrate their culinary heritage: Lockhart is the Barbeque Capital, Friona is the Cheeseburger Capital, and Caldwell is the Kolache Capital, although the town of West also claims to be "Home of the Official Kolache of the Texas Legislature." Elgin is the Sausage Capital, and Hawkins is the Pancake Capital. The state's natural history is celebrated as well. The town of Ennis is Bluebonnet City, and the counties of Burnet and Llano share the Bluebonnet Co-Capital of Texas title. Sanderson is the Cactus Capital, Weslaco is the Citrus Capital, both Waxahachie and Paris claim to be the Crape Myrtle Capital, and Knox City is known as the Seedless Watermelon Capital of Texas.

In some Texas towns the capital claims extend to local fauna, complete with mascots symbolized in promotional graphics or even in monumental statuary. From dinosaurs and fish, birds, insects, and reptiles to mammals large and small, the animals of Texas claim their share of community identity and promotion. The southeast Texas town of Anahuac is known as the Alligator Capital, West Tawakoni in East Texas is the Catfish Capital, Kenedy in South Texas celebrates the Texas horned lizard, and Midland is the official Ostrich Capital of Texas.

In a few instances in the early days of the state marker program, a town's adoption of an animal mascot also led to placement of an Official Texas Historical Marker, with inscriptions written to explain the connection between the place and the animal and to promote tourism as well as history. A few of those markers, some of which are accompanied by monumental statues of the animals they interpret, can be traced directly to John Ben Shepperd, an early chairman of the Texas State Historical Survey Committee (TSHSC, now Texas Historical Commission).

A native of Gladewater in East Texas, Shepperd (1915–90) was an attorney and civic leader who served on numerous state boards and commissions. Appointed Texas secretary of state in 1950 by Gov. Allan Shivers, he was elected attorney general two years later and served two terms in that office, during which time he presided over a number of controversial legal cases. Retiring from elective office following his second term, he moved to Odessa in West Texas, where he resumed practicing law and became a colorful civic leader and community booster. While simultaneously serving as a member of the TSHSC and as chairman of the Odessa Chamber of Commerce, he began promoting his adopted hometown as the Jackrabbit Capital of Texas, and the often humorous and tongue-in-cheek promotion of the jackrabbit has provided fodder for newspaper writers ever since. To the delight of many citizens and the derision of others, the promotion eventually led to a proliferation of commemorative rabbits, with more than two dozen colorful imitations placed throughout the town for an event known as the Jackrabbit Jamboree.

According to city officials, the town's jackrabbit story goes back to 1932, when the Odessa Sandhills Rodeo staged a jackrabbit roping contest as a publicity stunt to promote the annual community event. As reported years later, "A local cowgirl, Grace Hendricks,

Grace Hendricks won the jackrabbit roping contest at the 1932 Odessa Sandhills Rodeo. Courtesy Permian Historical Society Archives, J. Conrad Dunagan Library, University of Texas of the Permian Basin.

roped the rabbit in five seconds, setting off a hue and cry nation-wide over the cruelty to poor rabbits. Most of the letters came from back east where folks were used to cute little bunnies, not big ol' crop-damaging jackrabbits."[1]

Of course, hunting jackrabbits was nothing new in 1932. In his seminal work *The Great Plains,* historian Walter Prescott Webb wrote, "Some of the animals of the Plains are both significant and important. The jack rabbit [*sic*] is an example. Its marvelous speed is significant, but the animal is important because of its destructive habits with growing crops." He went on to say, "The jack rabbits have certain qualities that well fit them for Plains life. Their long ears, which make them resemble the burro, gave them the name of jackass rabbit, later shortened to the present form."

Pointing out that the jackrabbit is not really a rabbit at all, but a hare, Webb also described the destructive nature of the animal and the resulting adversarial relationship with the settlers that invaded its habitat:

Because of their size the jack rabbits do much harm to growing crops, and it is a common saying in the West that one rabbit will eat as much as a horse. They eat voraciously all young and tender farm and garden plants and strip young fruit trees of bark. Because of this impartial destruction of grain and forage crops, of gardens and nurseries, the farmers have waged constant war against the rabbits. Bounties have been offered for their ears in practically all Western states. . . . They are hunted with long-range guns, poisoned, run with greyhounds, and the farmers and small boys kill the young as they are found in the fields. In spite of such widespread destruction, the rabbits are still innumerable and bring to the farmers in some seasons heavy losses.[2]

John Ben Shepperd viewed the jackrabbit as a talisman of the Old West, so when his friend Tom Taylor, head of the state tourism office at the Texas Highway Department, suggested Odessa adopt the jackrabbit as its mascot, Shepperd made arrangements for the World's Largest Jackrabbit statue to be erected in front of the Odessa Chamber of Commerce office in 1962. Fabricated by a California company, the eight-foot-tall fiberglass rabbit immediately became a tourism draw as Odessans and visitors alike stopped to photograph it, often with their children happily posing alongside.

However, in Shepperd's view, the statue needed more. Within two years of its unveiling, he also spearheaded the effort to place an Official Texas Historical Marker for The Jackrabbit next to the statue. While the text of the marker is fairly straightforward in describing the animal and its significance to the West, it also contains a bit of whimsy, relating that the animal was "the subject of tall tales" and the "actual hero of world's only Jackrabbit Rodeo, in Odessa, in 1932." But that was not the end of Shepperd's fun with the jackrabbit. He also decided the back of the marker should carry a recipe for jackrabbit stew. He wrote to Dallas newspaper colum-

(opposite) *The original Odessa jackrabbit statue later inspired the Jackrabbit Jamboree, a program that added more than three dozen colorful replica jackrabbits around town.* Courtesy Permian Historical Society Archives, J. Conrad Dunagan Library, University of Texas of the Permian Basin.

nist Frank X. Tolbert, saying, "We need your best recipe for a Jackrabbit Stew, starting off with the old folk saying, 'First, you have to catch the rabbit. . . .'" So, sure enough, the marker was cast with a recipe on the reverse side:

First, catch your rabbit.
Dress rabbit. Salt and soak in
brine, then boil till tender.
Add pepper to taste.
Fill pot with dumplings.
Cook until dough is done.

A notation on the order form from the TSHSC staff to the San Antonio foundry reads, "Mr. Shepperd said to remind you that the reverse side of the marker is to be cast free of charge."[3]

Over the years, the citizens of Odessa came to revere their jackrabbit and, in a nod to its creator, nicknamed it Jack Ben Rabbit. But Shepperd took pains to give credit where credit was due and set the record straight regarding his friend Taylor's original suggestion. In a humorous speech to the Texas Travel Counselors Conference in 1985—"Let me say at the outset that I'm deeply appreciative that your august body is providing a forum for me to reach the pinnacle of my legal and political career, appearing as a mouthpiece for a plastic jackrabbit"—he continued, "Odessans are not entitled to all the credit and praise for the jackrabbit. We weren't smart enough to think this up by ourselves; it was really Tom Taylor's idea." He went on to report on the statue's tourism appeal:

The Odessa Jackrabbit hasn't always been so popular. In fact, many laughed when he was lovingly placed on his perch by the chamber of commerce 25 years ago, and laughed even louder when the state recognized his contributions to the West with an official marker. But then some "doubting Thomas" [a tongue-in-cheek reference to his friend, Mayor Dan Hemphill, who was in the audience] began counting the cars—many from out-of-state—that stopped to look him over, and saw the thousands of pictures taken of children climbing over him, and began reading the hundreds of articles about him from all over the country.

The laughing stopped, bragging began, and many started taking credit for Tom's idea. To add fuel to the hutch, a sudo [*sic*] intellectual mayor—seeking the limelight—boldly proclaimed that he was really a "Prairie Hare." This pitted the academic community against the old-timers, resulting in international publicity.[4]

A few years after its initial placement, the jackrabbit became the object of vandalism and pranks. Thieves absconded with it on at least one occasion, but local police quickly recovered it. Citing security concerns, city officials moved the statue and its accompanying state historical marker to a new location in front of the Odessa Independent School District Office on 8th Street. In 1990 the Heritage of Odessa Foundation erected a second marker next to the statue. Entitled World's First Championship Jackrabbit Roping, it further details the story of the 1932 rodeo and the "out-of-town dogooders" who tried to stop the contest. It also tells of a later event that, like its predecessor, engendered controversy and brought an official end to jackrabbit roping in Odessa: "Notorious contest revived in 1977 causing coast-to-coast outcry. Midland animal lover delayed action by liberating captive jackrabbits. Event proceeded on schedule when former prisoners returned at feeding time. Seven ropers competed on foot. Jack Torian placed first with a six second scamper. In 1978 Humane Society blocked all future ropings with court order."[5]

If imitation is the sincerest form of flattery, Jack Ben Rabbit received the ultimate compliment in 2004 when a consortium of arts and civic organizations initiated the Jackrabbit Jamboree, a public art event that brought some thirty-seven six-foot replica jackrabbits to town. The new rabbits, painted in colorful themes chosen by sponsors, appeared at locations throughout the city, and funds from the project benefited a scholarship program at the University of Texas of the Permian Basin Art Department. Many of the statues remain on public view, and the Chamber of Commerce maintains a list of locations, along the "Trail of Tails," on its website.

Perhaps inspired by the success of the jackrabbit marker, Shepperd decided Odessa also needed a historical marker for the prairie dog, another pesky Western Plains animal. The local Rotary Club sponsored the new marker, to be placed in Prairie Pete Playland, a children's playground, previously developed by the club, that included a fenced prairie dog town in the city's Sherwood Park. The marker text explains that the prairie dog is actually a type of squirrel whose name evolved because of the sound of its bark and describes the once-vast territory covered by prairie dog towns: miles of interconnected underground burrows with numerous access holes that proved hazardous to horses and livestock. And like the jackrabbit marker, the one for the prairie dog also contained a recipe on the reverse side, for Prairie Dog Pie, obtained from columnist Frank X. Tolbert.[6]

Calling the prairie dog "the squirrel of the Plains," Webb wrote, "He exemplifies what frequently happened when men crossed the line. In the East men were accustomed to a squirrel that climbed trees; when they struck the Plains they found that the animal no longer went *up* but *down*. The contrast was more than their minds could grasp, and so they made the Plains squirrel a dog!" He related an account of "a prairie-dog town on the Texas plains, between San Angelo and Clarendon, which covered 25,000 square miles and which was estimated to contain 400,000,000 prairie dogs." A 1901 report placed the total number of prairie dogs in Texas at twice that number and claimed that "these would require as much grass as 3,125,000 cattle."[7]

Texans' views of the prairie dog have run the gamut in the past century. Once the source of early settlers' bemused observation, the animal became the target of well-organized extermination efforts at the turn of the twentieth century, but just a few decades later it rebounded as a popular resident of zoos and prairie dog parks and the darling of conservationists. Still promoted as tourist attractions in cities such as Lubbock, which maintains a large prairie dog town in Mackenzie Park, and Snyder, where another state historical marker for the animal was erected in 1968, the prairie dog was reviled by pioneer Texas ranchers and farmers. As crop losses mounted and grazing lands increasingly became overrun by miles of burrows, landowners declared war on the rodent.

By 1898 an official Anti-Prairie Dog Movement, coordinated by a central committee whose members represented affected property owners, began making strides in efforts to eradicate the animal from Texas. Spreading word of its mission through the state's newspapers, and organizing a petition drive aimed at persuading the Texas Legislature to enact laws to address the problem, the movement soon gained widespread support. By 1903 the legislature passed a measure "providing for the extermination of prairie dogs" by allowing counties to enact laws to require landowners to kill the animals on their own property and enabling adjoining landowners to sue if prairie dogs from a neighbor's land migrated over property lines because the neighbor failed to exterminate them effectively.[8]

Going after the pests was easier said than done, however. Once the need for extermination was established, the next step was to find an effective method of eradication. A 1904 progress report distributed to the state's newspapers stated, "A trip to West Texas at this time will convince any one [sic] of the wisdom of the act passed by the last State Legislature providing for the destruction of prairie dogs." Speaking of the ongoing challenges of addressing the problem, the article continued:

> A number of people went West with the idea of developing into prairie dog hunters and profiting by the State's bounty. It did not take any great length of time for these people to find out that the hunting of prairie dogs was about as precarious an occupation as any man could engage in, and that the little animals seemed to bear a charmed life. Prairie dogs live in colonies, like civilized humanity, and a regular system seems to be observed in the posting of sentinels on the hillocks surrounding the burrows in which they abide. These never fail to give the alarm upon the approach of any danger, and upon the sounding of the alarm, the whole colony departs in the direction of China in the twinkling of an eye. It is almost impossible, apparently, to hit one of these animals with a bullet, and cowboys and other old-timers rarely waste any ammunition on them.[9]

Soon both state and federal agricultural agencies entered the fray, and in the next few years government biologists developed a formula and process for a concerted poisoning program, offering

low-cost grain laced with cyanide and strychnine to county officials for distribution in their regions. Other extermination methods
became popular as well, including running hoses from automobile
exhaust pipes into prairie dog burrows to kill entire colonies with
poison gas, or "twisting," an operation that involved inserting a
hook down a hole to latch onto the fur, and then twisting it to hook
the animal in order to bring it to the surface.[10]

By the 1950s newspapers were reporting the prairie dog almost
extinct in Texas. Soon public opinion shifted, and efforts began
to preserve the little mammals and establish self-contained prairie dog towns in several West Texas cities for the amusement of
citizens and tourists alike. And although the prairie dog remains
popular with many, it continues to pose challenges as local governments grapple with how best to maintain urban colonies. Now, instead of resorting to extermination to control growing prairie dog
populations, cities employ hunters who use more modern methods to trap the animals, such as filling their burrows with water to
flush them out or sucking them out of the ground with large vac-
uum hose systems. Once captured, the prairie dogs are then sold to
pet stores or zoos or to other cities or organizations for their own
prairie dog towns. Individual opinions vary, as well. Some people
have successfully tamed the wild animals and kept them as pets.
"There's not anything makes a cuter pet," claimed one resident of
Snyder, who recalled a pet prairie dog named Gip that followed her
mother around the house and hid in a hole in the front yard when
strangers visited. A resident of Lubbock had quite a different view,
however, when the animals kept digging up her yard. "I don't see a
dang thing cute about them," she said. "They're just a form of a rat,
is what they are. All those people who say they love prairie dogs so
much should come out here and get a dozen."[11]

While jackrabbits and prairie dogs both gained fame as obstacles
to settlement of the West, the third animal John Ben Shepperd
helped commemorate with an Official Texas Historical Marker is
revered as one that "made Texas history," according to the marker
text. The mule, celebrated with both a historical marker and a
memorial statue in the town of Muleshoe in Bailey County, certainly receives much kinder treatment. The people of Muleshoe—

Modeled on a mule named Old Pete, the Muleshoe mule statue, along with its historical marker, attracted widespread attention immediately following its dedication in 1965. Courtesy Texas Department of Transportation.

the town named not for the animal but for the brand of a nearby ranch—began talking about erecting a statue to the mule as early as 1961. Under the auspices of the local Mule Memorial Association of America, they instituted a fundraising campaign to finance fabrication and installation of the statue. Gil Lamb, president of the association and manager of radio station KMUL, promoted the idea on his daily "Muletrain News" program, and soon the citizens of Muleshoe got behind the idea and helped spread the news. Indeed, as Deolece Parmelee, director of research at the Texas Historical Commission in the 1960s and 1970s, wrote, "It seems to have required a people with strong civic pride to reach the point of self-assurance where they could kid themselves by erecting a statue to a mule."[12]

"The mule has discovered that he does, after all, have some friends, even if generations of mule drivers may have addressed some pretty vicious words at him," wrote a reporter in 1964 as the years-long fundraising campaign stretched on. "A group of perceptive people in this Far West Texas town, taking the animal on his merits—which are numerous—and not on his disposition—which is generally terrible—are erecting a memorial to the mule at last. They decided an animal which helped build America and over whose stubborn bodies several wars were won deserves a statue." Original plans called for a bronze statue, but when the fundraising efforts failed to generate enough money to cover the anticipated cost, the monument was fabricated of fiberglass by the same California company that built the Odessa jackrabbit statue. Old Pete, an eighteen-year-old mule owned by local citizen Dave Anders, served as model for the statue, a decision that caused a number of people to protest. It seems Old Pete, described by one writer as "a horsey-looking Muleshoe mule with rather small ears," didn't fit some people's image of the perfect mule. One critic said, "I've seen bigger ears on some jackrabbits." Some even went so far as to call Old Pete a "snide," a term used by early mule and horse traders for a mule that looked good and was all right for trading purposes, but worthless as a work animal.[13]

Despite Old Pete's detractors, the statue modeled on him was completed in time for a festive dedication ceremony during Muleshoe's Fourth of July celebration in 1965, and thanks to John Ben Shepperd, the Official Texas Historical Marker for The Mule, erected next to the statue, was unveiled the same day. Texas attorney general Waggoner Carr gave the dedication speech, although his connection to the mule is not revealed in the historical record and is a bit of a mystery, since Mule Memorial Association president Gil Lamb had earlier told a reporter that no "big shot" would be invited to speak at the event. "We want the mule to take the spotlight," he said. "We can't have a politician out here trying to outdo our mule." And although the marker for the mule, unlike the ones for the jackrabbit and prairie dog, does not include a recipe, its inscription is somewhat amusing and a bit dramatic. Beginning with "Without ancestral pride or hope for offspring," and personalizing the topic with use of personal pronouns, the inscription writer seems to have been trying to set a rather romantic Old West atmosphere with such phrases as "His small hooves scaled rock and steep untrod by horse or ox, but big ears endangered him in lake or river. He went fast, endured much, ate sparingly. Since beginning of Christian Era, has helped all over world to bear burdens of mankind."[14]

In the 1980s the Muleshoe Heritage Foundation led a community effort to acquire the town's 1914 Santa Fe Railway depot and renovate it as a museum. Since that time the organization has added other historical buildings to the site, including a log cabin, a two-story ranch house, and a bunkhouse and cookhouse from the Muleshoe Ranch. The entrance to the property is marked by "the world's largest muleshoe," a twenty-seven-foot-tall metal sculpture designed and built by a local teenager as his Eagle Scout project in 1994.

The jackrabbit, the prairie dog, and the mule—all legendary frontier animals—left their marks on West Texas. And thanks to John Ben Shepperd and the citizens of West Texas, their histories and folklore are celebrated with statues, historical markers, and community pride.

MARKER LOCATIONS
The Jackrabbit: corner of W. 8th and W. Sam Houston, Odessa
The Prairie Dog: Prairie Pete Park, in Sherwood Park, 44th St. at
    N. Dixie Rd., Odessa
The Mule: north side of US 84 between Main St. and 1st St.,
    Muleshoe

STANDING FOR HEALTH

Located near Comfort in the Texas Hill Country, an unusual thirty-foot-tall wooden tower stands as one of the few remaining examples of an early experiment to control the spread of malaria. Designed by Dr. Charles A. R. Campbell, a San Antonio native who served as that city's public health officer, it was one of sixteen such structures built in the early twentieth century to house bats. Campbell, noting that bats were natural predators of malaria-carrying mosquitoes, believed locating large colonies of the flying mammals near mosquito-infested areas would help eradicate the disease.

Campbell spent years studying the best way to put his theory into practice. He built his first "Malaria-Eradicating, Guano-Producing Bat Roost" in San Antonio in 1907 on the grounds of the US Department of Agriculture Experimental Farm.

With shelves built into the interior walls of the tower to provide roosts, and a hopper system designed for easy removal of guano (the sale of which Campbell promoted for use as fertilizer), the doctor baited the structure with three sliced hams and waited for the bats to appear, but none came. Discouraged but not defeated after several years of trying to make his first roost a success, Campbell continued his study of bats, observing their habits in a number of Texas Hill Country caves. He concluded they preferred to nest near bodies of water, which provided ample incubation for mosquito larvae, and by 1911 he built a second tower at Mitchell Lake on the south side of San Antonio.

Used for sewage treatment by the city since the turn of the century, Mitchell Lake — now reclaimed as a nature center popular with birdwatchers — was in a notoriously swampy area. At the outset of his experiment there, Campbell tested eighty-seven inhabitants of the area — mostly tenant farmers and their families — and found that seventy-eight of them had malaria. Believing Mitchell Lake to be a good place to test his theory once again, he received permission from the city to build a tower at the site. Soon, the

Dr. Charles C. R. Campbell standing in front of his first "Malaria-Eradicating, Guano-Producing Bat Roost" in San Antonio in 1907. Courtesy Institute of Texan Cultures, UTSA #069–8391, courtesy of San Antonio Express-News.

insect-eating bats took up residence in the structure, and within a few years the experiment was regarded as a success. Four years after the tower's construction, Campbell tested residents of the area once more and found no active cases of malaria. As news of the bat roost experiment spread, medical and scientific organizations endorsed the doctor's work, and requests for his bat roost construction plans—for which he received a US patent in 1914— arrived from as far away as Italy. Several more towers were built in the San Antonio area, including one on the grounds of the Southwestern Insane Asylum and one in Alamo Heights.

Albert Steves Sr., a former mayor of San Antonio, contracted with Dr. Campbell to build a bat roost on his ranch near Comfort in 1918. Coining a new term using the Greek words for health (*hygieia*) and standing (*stasis*), Steves dubbed the structure—the first to be built on private property—the Hygieostatic Bat Roost. Resting on a pier and beam foundation raised seven feet off the ground, the structure features decorative shingle siding, a pyramidal hipped roof capped by an ornamental finial, and elongated louvered dormers that provide egress and ingress for the bats. Carefully preserved and maintained by several generations of the Steves family, the Hygieostatic Bat Roost received the Recorded Texas Historic Landmark designation and an accompanying historical marker from the Texas Historical Commission in 1981 and was listed in the National Register of Historic Places in 1983. It remains a popular tourist attraction and is one of only two Campbell bat towers remaining in existence. The other one, located in Sugarloaf Key, Florida, is also the subject of preservation and interpretive efforts.

MARKER LOCATION: FM 473, 1.5 mi. east of Comfort

Sources: Hygieostatic Bat Roost, Kendall County, THC marker and NR files; Charles A. R. Campbell, *Bats, Mosquitoes and Dollars* (Boston: The Stratford Company, Publishers, 1925); Mari Murphy, "Dr. Campbell's 'Malaria-Eradicating, Guano-Producing Bat Roosts,'" *BATS Magazine* [Bat Conservation International] 7, no. 2 (Summer 1989); Mari Murphy, "A Campbell Bat Tower Restoration Project in Texas," *BATS Magazine* [Bat Conservation International] 7, no. 2 (Summer 1989); Will D. Swearingen, "Dr. Campbell's Remarkable Experiment," *American Heritage* 33, no. 4 (June–July 1982); S. W. Pease, "Campbell, Charles Augustus Rosenheimer," *Handbook of Texas Online*, www.tshaonline.org/handbook/online/articles/fca31, accessed October 27, 2010.

3 A Life in Ragged Time

Not much is known of Euday Louis Bowman, and what little has been written about his life is often limited, repetitive, conjectural, or inconsistent. Available sources disagree on key components of his life, even ones that would seem to be easily documented, and there is little historical analysis of his personal struggles, his motivation, or his reaction to his success. Part of that stems from the quiet and almost reclusive nature of the man himself. More has been written on the outcome of his work and its relative worth within broader contexts than on the process of creation. Even in the field in which he excelled, he remains an enigma, lesser known than a fellow Texan who gained much of his own renown decades following his death. The cycles of history that sometimes shift individuals from relative obscurity to newfound prominence have largely passed him by. Given the nature of his life, though, all of that might have been expected.

The discrepancies surrounding the life of Euday Louis Bowman begin with his birth. While most historical references within larger works list the year as 1887, others show it to be 1886. Census records are inconclusive on the matter, but two important pieces of evidence indicate the earlier date. One is his military registration card (from the World War I era), which he filled out himself. It gives his date of birth as November 9, 1886, and shows him to be a thirty-year-old unemployed musician. At the time, Bowman lived at 707 Arizona Avenue in Fort Worth. An equally compelling record of his birth, although by no means definitive, is the inscription on his mausoleum, which notes the 1886 date.[1]

Census records provide a sketchy glimpse into Bowman's early life. His father, George, was a Kentucky native who listed his occupation in the 1880 census as farming and in 1900 as carpentry. Euday's mother was Olivia Marguerite Graham Este Lembin (shown in other sources as Lamlin and Landin), a native of France. Early census notations give her birthplace as Holland, with France added in parentheses. Bowman had two older siblings: Mary Margaret (b. 1877), who became a music teacher, and Junius (b. 1879), about whom not much is known except that he was a farm worker early in his life. Olivia and George made their family home on Fort Worth's Louisiana Avenue in 1900 but divorced in 1905. Afterward, Olivia moved to the Arizona Street home with Mary and Euday, and in the 1910 census she, too, listed her occupation as music teacher.[2]

Several accounts of Bowman's early life, including some he evidently conveyed himself, relate to his decision to leave home at the age of eleven. A central figure in that decision was an elusive local character known only as Raggedy Ed. Whether Raggedy Ed even existed is open to speculation, but according to a 1942 *Kansas City Times* article by Landon Laird, Bowman and Raggedy Ed knew each other in Fort Worth and reconnected in Kansas City, Missouri. There, Raggedy Ed spoke of his plans to open a pawn shop on 12th Street, and Bowman, already an accomplished musician and arranger even at such an early age, reportedly said he would use the three-ball symbol, then used to denote pawn establishments, to write a musical piece centered on a repeating three-note core. The year was 1897, and ragtime music was the craze, so Bowman drafted a number he dubbed the "12th Street Rag" (also shown as "Twelfth Street Rag"). As one version of the story goes, he perfected his piece with assistance from local theater musicians who frequented a popular restaurant, also on 12th Street. Other variations of the Kansas City story depict Bowman playing piano in brothels and bars of the city's red light district along the same street, as well as a number of other streets he later memorialized in music.[3]

The story of a runaway preteenager making his way in the dark and sinister underworld of Kansas City, relying only on his natural musical wit to survive and even thrive in the wide open, freewheeling era of ragtime, is compelling and almost picaresque in its construction. Such historical backgrounds were essential, it seemed, to the mystique of early ragtime performers. These were, after all, as their music implied to many, social misfits who somehow performed on a different musical plane with a whole new means of communication.

At its origins, ragtime had an African American pedigree, with an emphasis on a steady ground beat rhythm but with equal consideration for melody and harmony. In the vernacular of the time, to rag the music meant to introduce elements of unanticipated rhythmic shifts through the use of syncopation. As music historian Terry Waldo observed, "A *rag*, strictly speaking, is an instrumental syncopated march and follows the same convention as the march. *Ragtime*, however, is a much more eclectic term." The word *ragtime* itself, he ventured, "seems to have come from the phrase *ragged time*—tearing time apart."[4] At the end of the nineteenth century and into the early twentieth century, ragtime represented a radical departure in popular music. In hindsight, it was transitional in nature, helping bridge the gap from marches, cakewalks, gospel songs, minstrel music, and even blues to what eventually became known as jazz. Bowman proved to be an integral part of the transition, writing a number of rags in his musically formative years but also acknowledging later that he was, in fact, a jazz musician.

Bowman's story about coming of age in Kansas City at the end of the nineteenth century provided him with the street credentials for a career in ragtime. It had all the elements of independence, roguery, mystery, and unharnessed talent, and because of those associations it is often repeated in any mention of his past. It may not, however, be true. The alternative story that has been handed down is much more sedate, respectable, and family oriented. It begins with Bowman's growing up east of Mansfield, in Tarrant County, on the farm of his grandfather, Kentuckian and Mexican War veteran Isaac Gatewood Bowman. There, George and Olivia Bowman raised their family until moving into Fort Worth soon after the turn of the twentieth century. According to family members and others, the couple experienced considerable discord in their marriage, but they nevertheless set high expectations for their children. Those who have researched the family indicate that previous generations were well educated, with perhaps some grounding in the arts.[5]

No records of Bowman's scholastic endeavors survive, but he indicated later in life that he attended only grade school, which is consistent with his story of leaving home at age eleven. When he left, though, it may have been to live with his sister, Mary, approximately nine years his senior and an important figure in his life. It was Mary who reportedly taught Euday to play the piano, and she provided stability for her brother through both her assiduous nature and her ability to maintain a steady, albeit limited, source of income as a music teacher. She also helped her brother finalize his magnum opus, and although her name does not appear on the sheet music, she nevertheless received a share of royalties from him in later years.[6]

Whether the "12th Street Rag" had ties to Kansas City—and some writers have conjectured it more likely relates to a red light district along Fort Worth's 12th Street—Euday Bowman had the manuscript ready for publication by 1914, when he began shopping it around to local publishers. At the same time, according to various stories, he played it along with his other tunes in nearby shoeshine parlors and billiard halls. Bowman's hard-charging piano style gained him a strong following in the area, and according to one of his relatives, "He was quite a celebrity, at least in Fort Worth." Bowman was a big man, over six feet in height with broad shoulders, and local newspaperman and Bowman friend Jack Gordon later recalled, "He would strike his piano keys like a blow from a sledge hammer. He did not merely play his piano. He assailed it." Bowman's style and his unquestioned proficiency within a musical genre closely tied to African American culture led some to speculate that he was, in fact, either a black man or a mulatto who passed for white. That was not the case, however. He was Caucasian, with Scots-Irish heritage on his father's side of the family and French ancestry on his mother's.[7]

Despite his local popularity, Bowman's rag failed to garner the type of interest he anticipated, so he ended up selling the rights in 1916 to J. W. Jenkins' Sons Music Company of Kansas City, giving the piece yet another connection with the Missouri town. Through his association with the firm established years earlier by John Wesley Jenkins, whose family had grown it into one of the leading music publishing houses of the Midwest by the early twentieth century,

Early cover art for Euday L. Bowman's "12th Street Rag," the composer's most popular work. Accessed from Wikimedia Commons. Image is in the public domain in the United States.

Bowman hoped to build a career in songwriting. Sources differ on how much he received for the transaction, but all accounts place the sum at no more than one hundred dollars, and possibly much less. While the sum was low, the Fort Worth piano player probably needed the money and certainly the recognition that went along with a published piece, and he had no way of knowing his song would soon become a national hit, eventually spreading world-wide. In the days before radio, sheet music drove national trends in popular music, and "12th Street Rag" caught on quickly because of its simple rhythm, upbeat tempo, and adaptability to improvisation, an essential element of jazz. At the time, and for decades later, it remained the most popular ragtime number in publication, far outselling even the works of fellow Texan Scott Joplin, widely recognized as the King of Ragtime. Joplin's popularity, though, grew from the breadth of his musical repertoire, while Bowman remained in relative obscurity, inextricably tied to one successful piece.[8]

Remaining in Fort Worth, where he continued to reside with his sister—for many years at 818 South Jennings Street—Bowman worked on other musical numbers, including "Fort Worth Blues," "Rockin' Chair Blues," "Shamrock Rag," "Petticoat Lane," and a series of rags named for other streets, including 10th, 11th, and 6th. None of the pieces came close to rivaling the popularity of his first one, however, and without royalties for even that tune, he took on a series of odd jobs for a living, working as a teamster, a jazz teacher, and finally a junk dealer. He also drank heavily and gained a local reputation as a helpless drunkard. He married Geneva Morris in 1920, but the couple separated less than three months later, and he once again lived with his sister. By all accounts Mary and Euday lived frugal lives, but when times got particularly tough they sold some of their cherished belongings, including even the piano on which he had composed his famous rag.[9]

Even as his world continued to unravel, though, his "12th Street Rag" met with unprecedented success through interpretations and recordings by some of the leading musical performers of the era, including Louis Armstrong, Duke Ellington, Fats Waller, Lester Young, and Count Basie. Reshaped and revised by those and many others in the process, it became a jazz standard, a benchmark by which up-and-coming artists proved their chops. No longer considered simply a piano piece as a result, it became a staple for everything from small combos to big bands, with solos on clarinet, saxophone, and trumpet, as jazz continued to evolve in the 1920s and 1930s. Even Bowman himself tried to cash in on the performing success, recording his own version in the 1920s—ironically on the B side of a tune entitled "Baby Is You Mad at Me"—and self-publishing his other works, both with limited return.[10]

Remarkably, "12th Street Rag" was one of those tunes with enough staying power to survive the cultural transition of World War II, living long beyond the end of the ragtime era. An international hit in the twenties and a standard even before the war, the tune enjoyed renewed success in the years afterward. The rebirth came in 1948 with a new recording by bandleader Walter "Pee Wee" Hunt. The Ohio native rose to prominence in the jazz world as a trombonist and singer and as a key member of the successful Casa Loma Orchestra led by Glen Gray. Hunt split with Gray during the war and in 1946 formed his own band in Los Angeles. His decision to record "12th Street Rag" two years later as a nostalgic novelty piece proved prescient; it was an immediate national hit, reaching near the top of the *Billboard* chart and temporarily renewing Hunt's career in the process. It also focused attention once again on the composer, and this time he was ready.[11]

Bowman had never given up his quest to seek royalties for his famous rag, and in 1941 he successfully regained the copyright. Soon after, he struck a deal with Shapiro, Bernstein, and Company, a prestigious New York City publishing house with a rich history as one of the stalwarts of the celebrated Tin Pan Alley. In addition to Bowman's rag, the firm's catalog grew to include such jazz classics as "Cherokee," "In the Mood," "Harlem Nocturne," and "I Can't Give You Anything But Love." It still controls licensing rights to several tracks of "12th Street Rag," including the one made famous by Pee Wee Hunt.[12]

As a result of the renewed popularity of his first piece, Bowman finally began to receive the royalties so long denied him. The timing, however, proved problematic. His health had deteriorated by the late 1940s, and much of his first payout went for medical expenses. He married again in 1949, this time to Ruth Emma Thompson, twenty-seven years his junior, but they separated just forty-two days later. In late May of that year he traveled to New York City on business but contracted pneumonia while there and passed away on May 26. Sadly, Mary, who inherited the bulk of his estate, outlived him less than a year, dying in May 1950. Brother and sister are both interred in Fort Worth's Oakwood Cemetery, north of the downtown area, in an impressive mausoleum. Designed by Cheek Monuments, the mausoleum reflects a modernist interpretation of a classical temple, with stylized references to classical themes through simple vertical and horizontal lines and a central pediment elevated slightly above flanking wings. Incised at the end of the stately mausoleum are the Bowmans' names and vital dates, but no mention of Euday's magnum opus or his complex life. Nearby are the graves of such prominent Fort Worth residents as rancher John B. Slaughter, oilman and businessman Samuel Burk Burnett, Texas governor and US senator Charles Culberson, and rancher and oilman W. T. Waggoner.[13]

In 1953, following a performance in Fort Worth, Pee Wee Hunt visited Oakwood Cemetery to pay his respects to the composer who changed his life but whom he never met. Standing by the Bowman mausoleum, he said, "Me and my band were nothing until we recorded '12th Street Rag.' I owe everything to Euday Bowman. And

The Bowman mausoleum in Fort Worth's Oakwood Cemetery.
Photograph by Thomas L. Charlton.

what I have heard pleases me . . . that my '12th Street Rag' record brought at least one year of plenty to Euday, so long denied the riches he deserved."[14]

Decades after his death, Bowman's historical stock rose again with a ragtime renaissance that grew in part from the popular 1973 movie *The Sting*, which featured, in addition to the dynamic star power of Robert Redford and Paul Newman, a distinctive Scott Joplin piano rag called "The Entertainer." The updated score by Marvin Hamlisch seemed to the movie makers and movie patrons to be poignantly evocative of a wide-open era of the past, although in reality it reflected a time much earlier than the 1930s backdrop of the film. Nevertheless, ragtime began reaching a new generation, as did some of the surviving purveyors of the genre such as James Hubert "Eubie" Blake, who frequently appeared on such national television venues as *The Tonight Show* with Johnny Carson and *The Merv Griffin Show*. The renaissance of the 1970s brought particular attention to the work of East Texan Scott Joplin, and the newfound notoriety finally pushed the cumulative sales of his works past those of Euday Louis Bowman.[15]

The "12th Street Rag" continues to be a historical mainstay of American popular music in general and ragtime specifically. It has outlasted many of the musical landmarks of the era in which it was born and stayed around through a nostalgic revival in the 1940s and a major renaissance in the 1970s. While its syncopated melody line, steady ground beat, and three-note motif may seem dated to some, at least when played in its original form, it somehow remains familiar and comfortable to a wide audience regardless of how it is performed. It is still out there over a century after its inauspicious debut, challenging musicians and awaiting fresh interpretations or perhaps another renaissance. Questions still surround its inception, contributing to its continuing mystery in jazz history, but the composer, enigmatic and inadequately rewarded to the end, evidently took the answers with him to the grave.

MARKER LOCATION: Oakwood Cemetery, 701 Grand Ave., Fort Worth; block 24 of the cemetery, near the intersection of interior roads Ave. VIII and D St.

MAPLE LEAF RAG

The details of Scott Joplin's life, like those for Euday Louis Bowman, are often sketchy and subject to conjecture and inaccuracies. He was probably born near Linden, in East Texas, about 1868, but his family soon moved to Texarkana even before it was formally platted. Growing up there in a family of amateur musicians, he first began his musical experimentation on banjo and piano. Sources differ significantly on the subsequent years, with some having Joplin drifting throughout the Midwest while others indicate he stayed in Texarkana as a teacher. He was in St. Louis by 1890, though, and there he immersed himself in the popular music of the day that came to be known as ragtime. Significantly, he traveled to the Columbian Exposition in Chicago in 1893 as one of countless musicians from around the country attracted by the entertainment potential surrounding the fair. The following year, he moved to Sedalia, Missouri, where he would later enroll as a music student at the George R. Smith College for Negroes. He also formed a band called the Texas Medley Quartet, which traveled a largely regional circuit, and performed in the local Queen City Concert Band as a cornet player.

Sedalia, located east of Kansas City and well known to Texas history enthusiasts for its association with early cattle drives in the days before the Chisholm Trail, enjoyed a robust nocturnal "sporting life" in the 1890s that included more than its fair share of brothels, bars, and gaming parlors. In those venues Joplin enjoyed local renown as a piano player, and he regularly performed at such establishments as the Maple Leaf Club owned by brothers Will and Walker Williams. As Rudi Blesh and Harriet Janis noted in *They All Played Ragtime,* the Maple Leaf Club was an establishment, frequented by both black and white patrons, that consisted of "a large room dominated by a Victorian bar of carved walnut and filled with pool and gaming tables" (p. 14). In such places in Sedalia and nearby Kansas City, musical innovations born of various cultures merged. "Ideas were freely exchanged, and rags, true to one meaning of the name, were patched together from the bits of melody and scraps of harmony that all contributed." In the Sedalia club, Joplin debuted a distinctive number he dubbed the "Maple Leaf Rag." Later, local music store owner and publisher John Stark chanced to hear the piece and purchased it for his company. The sheet music quickly became a national best seller, propelling both Joplin and Stark to fame they could not have imagined when they collaborated in the small Missouri town.

In his later years, Joplin spent much of his time working on a folk opera, *Treemonisha,* and promoting the entertainment "legitimacy" of ragtime. By the time he died in 1917, the distinctive sounds of ragtime had given way to jazz. Joplin's legacy, though, continued, and all of his works received renewed attention in the 1970s, with the composer posthumously awarded the Pulitzer Prize for his grand opera. Now recognized as the King of Ragtime, the East Texan is also regarded as one of the leading pioneers of a musical genre known as jazz. As a result, his "Maple Leaf Rag," like Bowman's "12th Street Rag," lives on.

MARKER LOCATION: 901 State Line Avenue, Texarkana

Sources: Rudi Blesh and Harriet Janis, *They All Played Ragtime: The True Story of an American Music* (New York: Grove Press, 1959); Theodore Albrecht, "Scott Joplin," *New Handbook of Texas,* vol. 3, pp. 1000–1001.

OAKWOOD'S FOUNDER

Few people have contributed more to the development of a community than Kentucky-born John Peter Smith did for his adopted hometown of Fort Worth. Following his 1853 graduation from Bethany College in what is now West Virginia, where he studied mathematics and foreign languages, he made his way to Texas. Settling in Fort Worth late that year, he worked as a teacher and surveyor and studied law. Although opposed to secession at the onset of the Civil War, he nonetheless helped raise a company of local men for Confederate service. He participated in Gen. H. H. Sibley's ill-fated 1861 campaign into New Mexico and the 1863 recapture of

Galveston, and although later severely wounded during fighting in Louisiana, he continued in military service until the end of the war.

Upon returning to Fort Worth, Smith worked diligently on a wide range of projects to help the town chart a new direction of growth. His interests included real estate, banking, utilities, and transportation, and he also donated land for parks and hospitals, one of which still bears his name. In addition, upon the death of his stepson in 1879, he set aside twenty acres on the city's north side for a public burial ground that became the core tract of what is now the much larger Oakwood Cemetery.

In 1882 Smith became mayor of Fort Worth, and under his direction through the early part of the twentieth century the city made significant strides in its continuing development, particularly in education and city services. He was on a promotional trip to St. Louis in 1901 when he died, reportedly from complications he suffered as a victim of assault. His body was returned to his beloved hometown for burial in Oakwood Cemetery.

Spanning three centuries of use as an urban graveyard, Oakwood Cemetery chronicles the diverse cultural and social history of Fort Worth. Three distinct burial grounds—Oakwood, Calvary, and Trinity—make up the complex, which has grown in size over the years. A cemetery association formed in 1908 to provide direction for expansion and maintenance, and a chapel was added a few years later. In 1966 the Texas State Historical Survey Committee (now the Texas Historical Commission) approved a marker for the cemetery. Another marker there for founder John Peter Smith dates to 1981.

MARKER LOCATIONS: The marker for Oakwood Cemetery is at the entrance in the 700 block of Grand Avenue. A subject marker entitled, "John Peter Smith, Founder of Oakwood Cemetery," is also located on the grounds. Additionally, there is a similar marker for Smith at a city park in the 1100 block of Throckmorton Street.

Sources: Oakwood Cemetery, Tarrant County, THC marker files; Kristi Strickland, "John Peter Smith," New Handbook of Texas, vol. 5, p. 1104.

4 Turn East to Texas

People have been moving into or passing through Texas for millennia, but only a relative few have left behind records of their travels. Some left evidence inadvertently through archeological remains and artifacts, cemeteries, public records, or family stories. Others, however, took the time to document their travels with great detail through personal reminiscences, photographs, pictographs and petroglyphs, recorded stories, scientific investigations, or other media. The limitations of those resources are clearly evident; only a small number have retained their historical integrity over the years, and of that group even fewer have been preserved or are now accessible for research and analysis. Given the odds, the collective story of Texas travelers is highly vulnerable, subject to losses and gaps that interrupt the flow of recorded history. For myriad reasons, not all travel accounts stand the test of time, but the reasons are not always clear why some survive while others that are perhaps more important are forgotten and even lost. This is at one level simply the story of a small group of travelers and their remarkable journey across Texas and at another an account of how vulnerable the past can be. In the end, it is also a celebration of how two separate generations focused on the same objectives connected across the years and made the transition from near oblivion to the mainstream, a trip that took almost a century to complete.

James William Abert was born in 1820 at Mount Holly, New Jersey, south of Trenton and due east of Philadelphia. His father, John James Abert, who attended the US Military Academy at West Point, New York, was a career officer who became chief of the Corps of Topographical Engineers when it became a separate unit of the US Army in 1838. That same year, James Abert entered West Point.

There, his classmates included a number of young men who would later distinguish themselves in military service, including Abner Doubleday, Earl Van Dorn, Napoleon J. T. Dana, and James Longstreet. James Abert was not a standout in his class, and scholarship was not his strong suit at the time, although he excelled in art. He persevered with his general studies, though, graduating in 1842 near the bottom of his class just behind Longstreet.[1]

Upon graduation, Abert served with the Fifth Infantry at Detroit, but the following year he followed in his father's footsteps by transferring to the Topographical Engineers for an extensive lakes survey in the north. Soon after, he served with the corps in Washington, DC, presumably under the watchful eye of his father. In 1845, James Abert joined the third expedition to the west headed by the noted military explorer John C. Frémont. Known as the Pathfinder of the West, the Georgia-born Frémont was a complex and enigmatic figure who held both deep-seated expansionist views, not unusual in the era of Manifest Destiny, and national political aspirations. He managed to cultivate both through friendship with the powerful US senator from Missouri, Thomas Hart Benton, who became his father-in-law when Frémont married Benton's daughter Jessie in 1841.[2]

Frémont and Benton forged a unique and at times uneasy military, political, and personal alliance that furthered the expansionist interests of both men while at the same time clouding the chain of command and occasionally bypassing the authority of Col. John Abert. Despite some friction in that regard, the commander valued Frémont's leadership ability and often overlooked his slights of military protocol. There could be no denying the young engineer's early successes in western exploration, and Abert realized the future of his fledgling corps depended not only on such daring and determination, but also perhaps on political support from a key senator as well.[3]

By 1845 the young Frémont was already a seasoned explorer of the west. Seven years earlier, in the first major expedition of the newly independent Corps of Topographical Engineers, he began a two-year exploration of present-day Minnesota and the Dakotas with the French-born scientist and recent émigré Joseph Nicolas

James W. Abert, military topographical engineer, explorer, artist, and chronicler of the Texas frontier. This image is a work of a US Army soldier or employee, taken or made during the course of the person's official duties. As a work of the US federal government, the image is in the public domain.

Nicollet. While there, he experienced what he termed his "prairie education," viewing such game as buffalo and antelope and experiencing contact with the Sioux, at the same time learning the value of scientific documentation. Frémont's first major western expedition as the leader came in 1842, when, with guide Kit Carson, he reached the South Pass of present-day Wyoming, an area that would prove vital to fur trappers and the other travelers who soon followed. Frémont's second expedition, 1843–44, took him even deeper into the West, down through what was then northern Mexico and the present states of Utah, Nevada, and California and on north to the Oregon region. Designed to build on the successes of the Lewis and Clark expedition of 1804–6 and to enhance subsequent surveys, including ones conducted by sea along the Pacific coast, Frémont's second expedition was grand in scope and daring in its execution. With it, the Pathfinder set a course that, unknown to others, and maybe even to himself at the time, would serve as a focal point for the following expedition—one marked by untold danger and international intrigue. It would be an expedition destined to ensure his iconic place in the unfolding saga of Manifest Destiny while also perhaps relegating James W. Abert to a secondary position in the annals of exploration for the decades to follow. Speculation surrounding the controversy in which Frémont found himself embroiled continues to the present and may never be resolved completely.[4]

In 1844 and 1845 the matter of Texas's annexation to the United States and its concomitant ties to overarching issues of slavery, international relations, the political balance of power, westward expansion, and the nation's long-term economic sustainability reached a dramatic conclusion. Pres. John Tyler, embattled on all political sides, abandoned by his own party, and fearful of British intervention if the United States failed to act decisively, pushed forward on the "Texas question" by introducing a joint resolution for annexation near the end of his term in office. In February 1845, as Congress debated the matter, Col. John Abert issued an order setting the objectives for Frémont's third expedition to the West. In it, the commander called for the contingent to:

> strike the Arkansas as soon as practicable, survey that river, and if practicable, survey the Red River within our boundary line, noting particularly the navigable properties of each, and determine as near as practicable, the points at which the boundary line of the United States, the 100th degree of longitude west of Greenwich, strikes the Arkansas and the Red River. It is also important that the Arkansas should be accurately determined. Long journies [sic] to determine isolated geographical points are scarcely worth the time and expense which they occasion; the efforts of Captain Frémont will therefore be more particularly directed to the geography of the localities within reasonable distance of Bent's Fort [present eastern Colorado], and of the streams which run east from the Rocky Mountains, and he will so time his operations that his party will come in during the present year.[5]

Within days, Congress passed the joint resolution on annexation, and in April, Abert further clarified his orders to Frémont, noting, "On arriving at Bent's Fort, if you find it desirable, you will detach a lieutenant and party to explore the Southern Rocky Mountains and the regions south of the Arkansas under such instructions as your experience shall suggest." Once again emphasizing the political ramifications of the survey and referencing what he and others believed would be the inevitability of war with Mexico, Abert added, "It is extremely desirable that you should be in before the adjournment of the next session of Congress in order that if operations should be required in that country the information obtained may be at command." The month before his clarification, Col. Abert sent a communiqué to his son, James, appointing him as Frémont's assistant on the expedition.[6]

Outfitting of the operation began in June, and the party left Missouri the same month, following the Santa Fe Trail west to Bent's Fort, where it arrived on August 2. There, the expedition resupplied and waited for Kit Carson, who arrived two weeks later. During that time at the fort, and for reasons not fully known to this day, the broader objectives of the expedition changed, and apparently without the prior consent of the corps commander. Rather than follow the original instructions, Frémont instead turned the Canadian River survey over to Lieutenant Abert and prepared to head west to California.[7]

While the strategic security of California was a matter of utmost concern to the United States, given the certainty of war with Mexico and strained relations with Britain, which had an interest in the Pacific region, there was no indication that Frémont had the official sanction of his government. As biographer Ferol Egan noted, "A careful reading of Colonel Abert's letter showed no go-ahead to strike across the Rocky Mountains and head for California. There was an implied suggestion that part of the reason for the expedition was to check out any probable paths Mexican troops might take if they headed north, but even this suggestion was terribly vague and had to be read into what was written." And, he added, "If there ever was any validity to Frémont's later claim that he had been given oral instructions to strike out for California . . . then either Colonel Abert had no knowledge of these things, or he wanted his written order to appear as innocent as possible."[8]

Equally confusing, according to Egan, was the fact that the stated purpose of the expedition was strangely limited in scope and included areas already surveyed by others, including Frémont. Despite what Colonel Abert noted in his charge, the corps already knew that both the Red and Canadian Rivers were not navigable to the points included in the survey. As Egon further noted, "If the instructions were ever put down on paper for the expedition to proceed to California, that paper has never been issued." He concedes the possibility, however, of oral communiqués. Regardless, the Pathfinder felt he had the government's support when he left

Bent's Fort, and while his revised route seemingly surprised many, the new president, James K. Polk, and other top political officials were not among them.[9]

What Frémont and his party endured after leaving Bent's Fort is the basis of both legend and controversy, involving accusations of espionage, massacre, revolution, murder, military conquest, and, for the Pathfinder personally, a court-martial. Regardless, he subsequently managed to revive his career as an explorer and eventually became a national political figure as well. He remains a seminal character in the context of westward expansion, but despite his many exploits and his enduring influence on the history of the American Southwest, he is not the subject of any Official Texas Historical Marker. That distinction remained for his colleague, Lt. James W. Abert, who drew the assignment to continue the expedition's original objectives—at least as delivered in writing by his father.

Abert's second-in-command for the journey from Bent's Fort was Lt. William G. Peck, a Connecticut native who graduated from West Point at the first of his class in 1844 and immediately received appointment with the Topographical Engineers. Peck's strengths were in physics and mathematics, disciplines that would guide his later career as a college professor. Abert and Peck were the only military men on the expedition; the others, numbering just over thirty, included several with French surnames and two unnamed African Americans. Serving as guide was Irishman Thomas Fitzpatrick, a celebrated mountain man who had traveled with both Frémont and Jedediah Smith. Two other seasoned mountain men, Caleb Greenwood and John Hatcher, signed on as hunters for the first part of the trip. Abert outfitted the expedition with four supply wagons, fifty-six mules, seven horses, and eight head of cattle. Scientific instruments included only a sextant and chronometer, but no barometer.[10]

In his journal entry for August 16, 1845, Abert wrote, "All our preparations being completed, we began to descend the Arkansas, having bid adieu to the gentlemanly proprietors of Fort William (Bent's Fort). Our route lay along the right bank of the river; one continued series of hills and sand plants." With the next sentences the minute detail of Abert's observations is clearly evident: "We noticed a profusion of prairie sage, '*artemisia tridentata*,' being about the only shrub that grows in these sandy regions. This plant seems to love a dry and arid soil, covering, as it does, millions of acres of the great desert at the eastern base of the Rocky mountains." Even the expected but unseen elements of the natural landscape warranted his observations, as he added, "We were disappointed in not seeing even one specimen of the sage cock, '*tetrao upophrasianus*,' which is so extravagantly fond of feeding on this plant that its flesh becomes so embittered as to render it perfectly uneatable." Food supply from the land was a particular concern of Abert, as evidenced by his continued observations of that first day. "One of the men killed a fine fat doe," he wrote, "which furnished us with a grateful meal, after having lived so many days on tough beef." Such descriptions, as historian H. Bailey Carroll noted, set the young explorer apart from other chroniclers of the era and region. "As an early recorder of the Texas and Southwestern scene Abert displays an insatiable thirst for information which must characterize the true naturalist and scholar. He had a great eye for detail." His details were not restricted solely to plants and animals, but included his fellow travelers and those they encountered along the way as well.[11]

Upon leaving Bent's Fort, Abert's detached command moved generally in a southerly direction and soon crossed over into what was then northern Mexico, proceeding down through Raton Pass, keeping Santa Fe to the west, before turning east toward what is now the Texas Panhandle. Scientific expeditions' practice of crossing international boundaries was not uncommon at the time and rarely challenged along sparsely settled frontiers, but the Abert party traveled during a time of heightened tension between the United States and Mexico and thus had to take care to avoid undue contact. Crossing into the Republic of Texas, though, was a different matter for a variety of reasons. First, although the US Congress had earlier approved the joint resolution for annexation of Texas, the Republic of Texas had yet to finalize a state constitution as required, so it remained an independent country with sovereign rights, albeit with unclear boundaries. Second, the republic's harsh

Indian policy had angered many Native American groups within its borders, including those who frequented the Canadian River valley. And third, Mexico continued to view its former state of Texas as a land in dispute, although it had recently offered recognition of the independent republic as a means of thwarting annexation and thus blocking the westward expansion of the United States along the border.[12]

On September 5 the Abert expedition entered the present-day Texas Panhandle, camping along Minneosa Creek in what is now Oldham County, and the following day it reached the Canadian River farther to the east. In his journal Abert noted that travel through ravines and extensive sand deposits proved particularly difficult on September 11 and included "a plain strewed with agates, colored with stripes of rose and blue, and with colors resulting from their admixture." Describing what is today known as the Alibates Flint Quarries in Potter and Moore counties, he wrote that the stones "were coarse and of little value, but so numerous that we gave the place the name of Agate bluffs."[13]

September 12 and 13, when the expedition moved through southeastern Moore County, the travel remained difficult and slow, and Abert and Peck seriously considered abandoning the wagons at that point. It was this part of the journey that proved particularly critical to the success of the operation for another reason, though, as the explorers successfully made contact with local Kiowas, who had shadowed them for days. As the members of the group later learned, the Indians had elected not to attack only after their close observations indicated the party consisted of Americans and not their enemies, the Texans.

As members of the expedition made camp on September 13, three Indians came forward to join them, asking for a place to set up their wigwam. The leader was a young man named "Tiah-na-zi," Abert noted, adding, "He who accompanied him told us that the Spaniards called him 'Cassalan,' and the little squaw was an 'Up-sah-ro-kee,' his wife." Tiah-na-zi, in particular, enjoyed the hospitality and friendly treatment of the Americans, and he offered his own form of protection in return, climbing to a high hill to deliver what Abert called a "long harangue in a stentorian voice" to inform

This recent photograph along Ranch Road 1913, near the Abert marker site, shows the area's drainage network of the Canadian River system, which features broad, shallow expanses as well as deeply incised arroyos. By this point in the expedition, rough going along the river valley prompted Abert to consider abandoning his wagons. Photograph by Dan K. Utley.

all Indians within hearing distance that the members of the party were not Texans. "Tiah-na-zi," the lieutenant observed, "was a man of very happy disposition, and amused us as he sprang around while constructing his rude shelter for the night, by repeating the words 'how d'ye do,' 'yes,' in playful mimicry of the whites."[14]

On September 15, Hatcher and Greenwood left the party for Bent's trading post on the Canadian, a site later called Adobe Walls. The Kiowa guides left the following day when the party turned farther south to reach what they believed were the headwaters of the Washita (in reality, the North Fork of the Red River). A day later the explorers moved onto the flatland known as the Llano Estacado, and over the course of the next few days they continued at a steady pace, encountering various Native American groups and detailing the landscape, fauna, and flora along the way. On the afternoon of September 22 the contingent crossed into present-day Oklahoma, and eventually it made its way to St. Louis, arriving there in November 1845. In its journey across Texas, Abert's expedition passed through parts of seven future counties: Oldham, Potter, Moore, Hutchinson, Roberts, Gray, and Wheeler.

Lieutenant Abert's final report of his 1845 expedition along the Canadian and Red Rivers provided what Texas historian Frederick W. Rathjen called the first "trustworthy representation" of the region, recording in both detailed writings and illustrations "the best description of the primeval Panhandle . . . replete with observations of the land and its native human, animal, and vegetable contents."[15]

Given the depth of the investigations and their significance within the broader context of US expansion in the decades before the Civil War, it is difficult to comprehend the limited impact Abert's report actually had during its day. Quickly overshadowed by myriad national events, most notably the Mexican War, during which Abert served under Gen. Stephen W. Kearny and rejoined William Peck for surveys in New Mexico, it remained a primary source for explorers and travelers for only a short time. After the Mexican War, Abert's role in the army took him in new directions. From 1848 to 1850 he taught drawing at West Point. He later participated in a series of western river surveys and served in the Third Seminole War in the 1850s, attaining the rank of captain. He was on a leave of absence studying fortifications in Europe when the Civil War broke out, and he quickly returned to serve with the US Army and saw action in the Shenandoah Valley and northern Virginia, participating in eighteen battles. Injured severely in a fall from his horse at South Mountain during an advance on Frederick, Maryland, in September 1862, he convalesced until July 1863 and then saw limited service at Morris Island, South Carolina. Brevetted a lieutenant colonel on June 25, 1864, for meritorious service, he resigned from the army the same day.[16]

Following his military service, Abert worked as a merchant in Cincinnati, Ohio; as an examiner of patents in Washington, DC; and as an English literature professor at the University of Missouri. Something of a renaissance man, he wrote and lectured on a variety of topics, including natural history, and he enjoyed translating Spanish, German, and French works into English. He also liked to sing, play music, and write poetry. He ended his professional career as president of the examining board of public school teachers in Newport, Kentucky, where he died in 1897.[17]

Abert's report of his 1845 expedition languished in government files until the 1930s, when Amarillo oilman Earl Vandale, a bibliophile and prodigious collector of Texana, came across a copy and made it known to his friend, historian H. Bailey Carroll, who immediately recognized its value in Texas history. As Vandale related, "For some unearthly reason, Abert is a 'Forgotten Man.'"[18] Carroll meticulously documented Abert's work over the ensuing years, adding background information and annotations to clarify places, names, events, species, and tribal references included in the report. In 1941, almost a century after Abert, Peck, and Frémont left Missouri for Bent's Fort, the Panhandle-Plains Historical Society published Carroll's edited version of the report in its journal and also as a separate book, in association with the US Army Corps of Topographical Engineers, entitled *Gúadal P'a: The Journal of Lieutenant J. W. Abert, from Bent's Fort to St. Louis in 1845.*

Historians, bibliographers, collectors, and others familiar with the available literature of Texana and western exploration welcomed the important new contribution. Like Carroll and Vandale, they appreciated its place within broader contexts, and they marveled at the detail and breadth of the accounts and the beauty and clarity of the drawings. At the same time, quite understandably, they also wondered about the circumstances that caused the report to lie virtually hidden in plain view for so many years. Clearly, this was a significant window to the past, a vital link to a transitional time of frontier exploration that merged politics, science, geography, and military preparedness. How could it have been overlooked for so long by so many?

The answers proved to be complex and varied, as well as situational and speculative. In his introductory remarks to the 1941 piece, Carroll carefully avoided his personal thoughts on the topic, opting instead to justify the report's relevance within the literature while admitting his own lack of understanding of its postexpedition past. "Perhaps had he been somewhat egotistical he might have achieved greatness at a time when many had greatness thrust upon them; but, no matter how modest, Abert does not deserve the oblivion that is his. By any standard Abert deserves a place among the pathfinders, trail makers, and explorers of the Southwest." In a sense echoing Carroll, the noted Texas historian Walter Prescott Webb offered his own speculation about the matter when, through his role as editor of the *Southwestern Historical Quarterly,* he wrote, "A possible explanation of the neglect of Abert's journal is that historians have been in the habit of following expeditions from east to west. Abert went from the west to the east, and so almost marched into oblivion."[19]

Historian William H. Goetzmann was among the first national historians to place the Abert expedition in its proper context, and by so doing he, like Carroll, ensured the formerly overlooked topographical engineer would avoid any historical brush with oblivion. In his seminal 1959 work, *Army Exploration in the American West, 1803–1863,* Goetzmann gave due credit to Abert for his attention to detail, his diverse interests, and his familiarity with current scientific studies of the day, adding: "he brought to his western survey a kind of enlightened, almost pragmatic, common sense, in that he noted the regional geography with an eye to everything that would contribute toward the possible solution of the problem of settlement and national development in the particular area. . . . By the time he submitted his report, however, the question of settlement had yielded to the preoccupation with war, and Abert's information could be put to immediate practical use in the military campaigns in the Southwest."[20]

With changing perspectives of historical thought in the 1960s and 1970s, Abert began to emerge from the shadows of the past to take his place among the leaders in the era of western exploration, including even his former commander, John C. Frémont. In the Texas Panhandle in particular, Abert also entered the historical mainstream as a new hero whose story played out on the local landscape, which in some places had changed little since the 1840s. His story could have been interpreted for the traveling public along a number of highways in any of the seven counties he crossed, but members of the Moore County Historical Commission took the initiative in 1976 during the nation's bicentennial. Upon approval of its application, the Texas Historical Commission placed an Official Texas Historical Marker for the exploration route southeast of Dumas along FM 1913. The site selected by the local commission is in the general vicinity of what are believed to be two of the expedition's campsites. Isolated, remote, and off the beaten path, with sweeping vistas of the Canadian River valley, it is a location appropriately befitting the contributions of the expedition it honors.

MARKER LOCATION: 19.5 mi. east of Dumas to FM 1913, then south 5.3 mi. to intersection with Plum Creek Road

THE ABERT CONTEXT IN THE TEXAS PANHANDLE

An Official Texas Historical Marker north of Amarillo briefly mentions the survey work of Lt. James W. Abert but places his contributions in a broader context that commemorates efforts of the US Army Topographical Engineers on the Texas High Plains. The marker text pays tribute to three topographical explorations across present-day Potter County in the antebellum era: the one led by Abert in 1845 along the Canadian River; one reconnoitered by Lt. James Hervey Simpson in 1849, under command of Capt. Randolph B. Marcy (who was not a topographical engineer and therefore not mentioned in the inscription), for a wagon trade route from Fort Smith, Arkansas, to Santa Fe, New Mexico, and beyond; and a third under the direction of Lt. Amiel Weeks Whipple in 1853 that investigated a proposed railroad route to the Pacific Ocean. Recognizing the engineers as successors to earlier explorers and mountain men, the inscription noted, "Barometer, compass, sextant, and pencil were their instruments for handling data on climate, geographical features, soil, feasible routes for wagons or railroads, and sites for towns and industrial developments."

While the information gathered by such topographical expeditions did much to document the Southwestern frontier and identify viable trade and immigration routes through the West, the Civil War and subsequent Reconstruction disrupted the continuation of a systematic national approach to explore the area. The war also had its effect on the US Topographical Engineers, which merged into the US Corps of Engineers in 1863 for the sake of efficiency. All three engineers mentioned in the marker near Amarillo—Abert, Simpson, and Whipple—served in the Union Army during the war. Abert, as noted earlier, was wounded in action in Maryland. New Jersey native Simpson was captured at Gaines Mill, Virginia, in June 1862 but released for continued service only two months later. Breveted a brigadier general during the war, he retired from the US Army as a colonel in 1880 and died three years later at St. Paul, Minnesota, where he is buried. Whipple, born in

Massachusetts, participated in the 1861 Battle of Bull Run (First Manassas) and drew some of the earliest maps used by the Union Army in Northern Virginia. At Chancellorsville, Virginia, on May 4, 1863, a sniper's shot felled him while he supervised construction of defensive earthworks. Removed to Washington, DC, he died there three days later following promotion by President Abraham Lincoln to the rank of major general of volunteers. He is buried in Portsmouth, New Hampshire, where he first lived in the years before his survey across the Texas Panhandle.

MARKER LOCATION: nineteen miles north of Amarillo on the west side of US 87

Sources: United States Topographical Engineers in the High Plains of Texas, Potter County, THC marker files; H. Allen Anderson, "Amiel Weeks Whipple," *New Handbook of Texas*, vol. 6, pp. 922–23; James Grant Wilson and John Fiske, eds., *Appleton's Cyclopedia of American Biography* (New York: D. Appleton and Company, 1888); US Corps of Topographical Engineers website, www.topogs.org, accessed December 25, 2010.

REPLACING HISTORICAL MARKERS

As of June 2010, the historical marker for the exploration route of Lt. James W. Abert is missing. Only a metal post now remains along the road where the Moore County Historical Commission dedicated the marker in the 1970s.

While the original application materials are on file with the Texas Historical Commission in Austin, the replacement of markers is not simply a matter of submitting a new order to the supplying foundry. In Texas, the marker process begins at the county level, and that includes funding of any necessary replacements, whether they are called for as a result of damage, theft, deterioration, or factual errors. Official Texas Historical Markers represent a unique partnership between counties and the state, with counties responsible for the basic research and securing funds for foundry costs, while the state provides for program oversight, content review, inscription writing, processing, and promotion. Isolated markers, such as those for the Abert expedition, are often more vulner-

All that remained of the Exploration Route of Lt. James W. Abert marker in 2010. Unfortunately, historical markers in remote rural areas are sometimes subject to vandalism or theft, with replacement costs coming most often from local sources. Photograph by Dan K. Utley.

able, and as a consequence, counties and states sometimes compromise on location in preference for nearby sites that are more secure and also more accessible to the general public.

To report a missing or damaged marker, or to donate funds for replacements, contact the appropriate county historical commission. To obtain contact information for the commission chair, check the Official Texas Historical Marker information on the Texas Historical Commission website, www.thc.state.tx.us, or contact the office of the county judge.

5

Illumined by Truthful Artistic Ideals

Writing in 1907 about the Great Southwest in an advertising pamphlet distributed by his El Paso, Texas, architectural firm, Henry C. Trost explained in a rather romantic fashion the allure of the region that drew him to make it his home: "The atmosphere of the southwest is wonderfully clear. The mountain masses are rugged and their shadows and contrasts are sharply defined. The sunset tints are primary colors, illuminated with wonderful gold and purple. The horizons are infinite—long, distant, level lines, broken only by the far-off mountains or the scrubby desert vegetation against the sky. The dominant characteristics of the arid southwest are: plenty of elbow room, sharply defined contrasts, long unbroken lines, low firm masses, and vivid colors. With accurate instinct, the old Spanish builders adapted their structures to the requirements of environment." Appealing to potential clients, Trost went on to state, "Trost & Trost bring to the working out of each new problem in design or construction, a virile creative power, steadied by sound professional training, and illumined by truthful artistic ideals."[1]

Dubbed the Architect of Arid America by one historian, Ohio native Henry Charles Trost (1860–1933) is recognized as one of the most prolific architects of the American Southwest. With a career that spanned more than half a century, his legacy remains in the hundreds of buildings he designed in Colorado, New Mexico, Arizona, Texas, and northern Mexico. The majority of his work can still be seen in West Texas, particularly in El Paso, which boasts commercial, institutional, and residential structures he designed in a vast array of architectural styles. Drawing inspiration from the desert Southwest that surrounded him, he often designed buildings that celebrated the region's unique environmental context.[2]

63

As children growing up in Toledo, Ohio, Trost and his siblings gained an early appreciation of the building trades from their father, Ernst Trost, a carpenter, building contractor, and grocer who immigrated to the United States from Germany in the 1850s. Henry attended art school in his hometown and following graduation worked as a draftsman for a number of local architectural firms. He left Toledo for Denver, Colorado, in 1880, and after a short stint as a draftsman there he opened an architectural practice in Pueblo in partnership with Frank A. Weston. The firm, Weston & Trost, enjoyed moderate success, but within a few years a restless Trost, while maintaining his legal partnership with Weston, moved to Texas. He briefly spent time in Dallas, Fort Worth, and Galveston—where he worked for noted local architect Nicholas J. Clayton—before relocating to Dodge City, Kansas, to rejoin Weston in a new office there. The two men dissolved their partnership in 1887; Weston remained in Kansas, but Trost, drawn by the exciting and innovative era of architectural design then centered in Chicago, moved to the Windy City.[3]

Trost spent the next eight years in Chicago, where he worked primarily as an ornamental metal designer. Heavily influenced by the work of preeminent architects Louis Sullivan and Frank Lloyd Wright, he was an active member of the prestigious Chicago Architectural Sketch Club, an organization of draftsmen who worked in many of the most important architectural offices in the city. He was particularly taken with the Mission Revival style after its introduction at the 1893 World's Columbian Exposition (Chicago World's Fair), and its influence would inform much of his later work. He returned briefly to Colorado, settling in Colorado Springs in 1897, but by 1899 the lure of the Southwest beckoned and he moved to Tucson, Arizona, and established his own architectural office.[4]

Drawing on the strong Spanish Colonial stylistic influences of the region, Trost designed a number of landmark buildings in Tucson, and while he continued to work on commissions there, he soon joined his brother, Gustavus Adolphus Trost, and their nephew, George Ernest Trost, to form the Trost & Trost architectural firm in El Paso in 1903. Gustavus's twin, structural engineer Adolphus Gustavus Trost, also joined the family firm in 1908. Trost

& Trost, with Henry C. Trost as its principal architect, enjoyed a sterling reputation that brought many important commissions to the firm in the early years of the twentieth century. Scores of Trost buildings, including many in downtown El Paso and in several historic neighborhoods there, are listed in the National Register of Historic Places and are commemorated with Official Texas Historical Markers. Of particular interest to tourists are Trost-designed hotels in El Paso and several smaller West Texas communities, many of which the Texas Historical Commission has recognized with official historical designations.[5]

Located a scant mile from the United States–Mexico border, the Hotel Paso del Norte (now Camino Real Hotel) stands at the northwest corner of West San Antonio and South El Paso Streets in downtown El Paso. Completed in late 1912, it has been described by one source as a fine example of the many pre–World War I "urban luxury" hotels built around the country at that time: "They set a new standard of elegance for the hotels of the world, and an architectural vocabulary was developed to signal to travelers which ones were luxury hotels. They were tall blocks, rectangular in shape, with one or more light wells beginning at the third floor and opened toward the street or toward the rear. Detailing was based on fashionable European palaces and mansions of the past, generally English or French, with walls of brick trimmed with stone, concrete and terra cotta."[6] Prominent El Paso businessman and promoter Zach T. White provided financing for the new hotel, which he believed would be an important element in the city's growth and development. Known locally at the time of its construction as White's "dream hotel," the nine-story structure (a recessed tenth story, also designed by Trost, was added later) soon became a popular gathering place for the city's social elite as well as the traveling public. White, who had arrived in El Paso in 1881 and quickly established himself as a business and civic leader, reportedly engaged Trost & Trost, in consultation with civil engineer J. E. Lewis, to design a building according to structural specifications that mirrored those of buildings in San Francisco that had survived that city's massive 1906 earthquake. The hotel's steel and concrete building materials also incorporated the latest in fireproofing precautions.

The interior walls, constructed of gypsum from White Sands National Monument in New Mexico, added an extra level of fire protection.[7]

The hotel's red brick twin towers, with a light well facing onto San Antonio Street, are set above a white marble–clad two-story base. In describing Trost's design for the hotel, one architectural historian wrote: "It has been suggested that Henry Trost sought to 'synthesize' many prevalent turn-of-the-century architectural concepts with other contemporary nineteenth and early twentieth century architectural genres. If this is so, then the Hotel Paso del Norte may be understood as one of the better examples of this effort. The finely cast Chicago School terra cotta work around the entablature is masterfully combined with numerous allusions to the Beaux Arts Style, both of which are amalgamated within the context of a modern reinforced concrete and brick 'high rise.'"[8] The exterior detailing includes arched windows on the second-floor primary facade as well as a band of arched windows and carved terra cotta ornamentation on the eighth floor, topped by a Neoclassical frieze and cornice along the ninth-floor level. A balustrade surrounds the recessed tenth floor. A seventeen-story addition built immediately to the north in 1986 overshadows much of the 1912 building, but the Trost design is still evident on the original portion of the hotel.[9]

The interior spaces reveal a number of original design elements that contributed to the hotel's reputation for elegance and beauty. The original two-story lobby, now incorporated into a lounge and bar area, features a magnificent stained glass dome attributed to the famed Tiffany Studios of New York as well as geometrically patterned stained glass windows. Also featured are original European chandeliers and a carved sculpture depicting a Spanish friar, the Spanish royal crest, and a Native American. Although no solid documentation exists for the claim, it is said to be the only sculpture signed by Henry Trost.[10]

In the early twentieth century the Hotel Paso del Norte was the scene of many local social events, including an annual Christmas celebration for which White imported a large tree from his ranch in Cloudcroft, New Mexico. Guests enjoyed gourmet meals in the

Gold leaf accents in the lobby of Henry Trost's Hotel Paso del Norte (Camino Real Hotel) in El Paso contributed to the hotel's reputation for elegance and beauty. Courtesy Texas Department of Transportation.

elegant dining room and danced to the music of orchestras playing in the tenth-floor roof garden ballroom. According to some sources, the rooftop terrace also provided a vantage point from which curious onlookers observed skirmishes between revolutionary forces and Mexican soldiers during the Mexican Revolution, and bullet holes from stray shots could be seen along the balustrade for years afterward. Famed revolutionary Pancho Villa is counted among the list of famous guests who stayed in the hotel over the years. The list also includes such notables as humorist Will Rogers, Gen. John J. Pershing, Hollywood actress Gloria Swanson, opera star Enrico Caruso, Pres. Lyndon B. Johnson, and former first lady Eleanor Roosevelt. The hotel remained in White family ownership until 1971, after which time it was acquired by a succession of corporate owners. Still considered a premiere hotel in El Paso, it was listed in the National Register of Historic Places in 1979 and received an Official Texas Historical Marker from the Texas Historical Commission in 1985.[11]

In the 1920s Trost & Trost undertook a number of hotel projects in the Trans-Pecos region of Texas. In addition to more commissions in El Paso, including the Hotel Cortez (1926; now an office building) and Hilton Hotel (1929–30; renamed Plaza Hotel in 1963), Henry Trost also designed hotels for clients in Marathon, Alpine, Marfa, and Van Horn. Each of the settlements had grown up along the railroad lines that crossed the region in the 1880s, and by the 1920s they were established towns. As more people moved to the railroad hubs, the communities developed and soon boasted homes, businesses, and local government facilities, including, in the cases of Alpine, Marfa, and Van Horn, handsome new county courthouses.[12]

Several of the hotels Trost designed in the region were built as part of the Gateway hotel chain based in El Paso, where he remodeled a five-story former bank building into the flagship Gateway Hotel for owner Charles Bassett. Other inns in the chain, particularly El Paisano Hotel in Marfa and Hotel El Capitan in Van Horn, differed significantly in style from the El Paso Gateway property, as did the Gage Hotel in Marathon and the Holland Hotel in Alpine.[13]

Vermont native Alfred S. Gage came to Texas in 1878, at age eighteen, to work on a cattle ranch in Shackelford County. After a brief but unsuccessful attempt at establishing his own cattle ranch in Archer County—his entire forty-head herd was lost to rustlers—he joined with his brothers, Seth and Edward, to form the Alpine Cattle Company and operate a ranch south of Marathon in the Big Bend region. By 1912 Edward Gage had died, and Alfred owned controlling interest in the company, which became highly successful under his shrewd management. He moved to San Antonio with his wife and children in 1920 and became a business and civic leader there while still maintaining his West Texas ranching operations.

In 1926, in part to have a comfortable local residence and office to use when he returned to the Trans-Pecos to supervise his ranching operations, Gage purchased land on the main road—now US Highway 90—adjacent to the railroad line in Marathon and commissioned Trost & Trost to design a hotel. The two-story brick hotel opened in April 1927 and soon became a central gathering place for area ranchers and travelers.

Its simple style features an entry porch with a steeply pitched gable, an arched central parapet, and an attached one-story wing. As described by one observer, its appearance reflects the design principles Henry Trost wrote about in his 1907 advertising pamphlet: "Textured buff-colored brick aesthetically and symbolically

The two-story Gage Hotel opened in April 1927 and soon became a central gathering place for Marathon-area ranchers and travelers. Courtesy Texas Historical Commission, National Register of Historic Places files.

connect the hotel to the semiarid landscape, creating a dramatic effect."[14]

Sadly, Alfred Gage did not live long enough to enjoy his new hotel; he died in San Antonio within a year of its opening. Ownership of the property changed hands numerous times in the years after his death, and by the 1960s it stood abandoned and deteriorating. In 1978, J. P. and Mary Jon Bryan of Houston, strong supporters of historic preservation in Texas, purchased the building and undertook a major restoration project to return it to use as a hotel. The Texas Historical Commission designated it a Recorded Texas Historic Landmark in 1981.[15]

The Holland Hotel in Alpine has a colorful and tragic history reminiscent of stories of the Old West. As a young man, John R. Holland (1852–1922) moved from his native Wharton County in Southeast Texas to the central Texas town of Brady to become a rancher. By 1884 he had moved farther west with his wife, Mary, and children, Crystal and Clay, and established a ranch near Murphyville (later renamed Alpine). As the town grew, the Hollands became prominent citizens, and in 1907 John Holland bought property in the center of town on which he built the first Holland Hotel in 1912.

Following an extensive restoration project, the Texas Historical Commission designated the Gage Hotel a Recorded Texas Historic Landmark in 1981. Courtesy Texas Department of Transportation.

A tragic event four years later generated headlines as far away as Washington, DC, and New York City and captivated citizens of the region, who followed the story in the *El Paso Times* and other local news outlets.

John and Mary Holland's daughter, Crystal, attended Baylor University in Waco, and during her time there she fell in love with her music teacher, Harry J. Spannell. Crystal's parents and the university's administration disapproved of the romance, and Spannell, when told by Baylor officials to choose either his job or Crystal, left the university under a cloud of controversy. Eventually, however, the couple married, and Spannell regained his position at Baylor. John Holland, meanwhile, in a move designed to convince his daughter to move back to Alpine, offered to give the young couple the Holland Hotel, which he did in 1914. Spannell thus became manager of the hotel, and the couple and their young daughter, also named Crystal, lived in an apartment there.

In early 1916, Lt. Col. M. C. Butler, with the Sixth Cavalry, arrived in Alpine. He lived at the hotel for about two months and was soon joined by his wife and young son. According to local sources, the Spannells and Butlers were friends who spent a great deal of time together. On July 20, reportedly in a case of misunderstanding and misplaced jealousy, Harry Spannell picked up his wife and the officer at the front of the hotel and drove a short distance away into a residential neighborhood, where he shot and killed them both. In a series of trials over the next three years, Spannell was eventually acquitted in his wife's death but received a five-year prison sentence for killing Butler.[16]

Ownership of the hotel reverted to John Holland after the tragic events of 1916. Upon his death in 1922, the property passed to his son, Clay Holland, who in 1927 hired Trost & Trost to extensively remodel the original building and design a three-story addition. The renovated hotel, built according to plans drawn by Henry and Gustavus Trost, featured an entry porch supported by two columns and a series of decorative terra cotta lion's head medallions placed between the third-story windows. Reporting on its grand reopening in March 1928, the *Alpine Avalanche* called it "a modern structure with beauty, comfort and conveniences" and added, "The hotel is surpassed in appointments by none in the area. The kitchen is the latest. No expense has been spared to make the hotel the very latest and most modern that could be built and it is believed that this important hostelry will be the means of attracting many people of wealth to the area for their vacation in the wonderful climate." Clay Holland sold the hotel to an East Texas hotel consortium in 1946, and the property changed hands several more times during the next two decades. It eventually closed in 1969, and most of the interior furnishings and some of the architectural fixtures were removed and sold. After being renovated for office use in the 1970s, it once again became an active hotel in the late twentieth century and continues to serve the traveling public. The Texas Historical

Commission placed an Official Texas Historical Marker at the site in 1980.[17]

Located at the corner of Highland Avenue and Texas Street in Marfa, virtually in the shadow of the historic Presidio County Courthouse, El Paisano Hotel also has a colorful past. Designed by Trost & Trost and built in 1929–30 for the Gateway hotel chain, the two-story Spanish Colonial Revival building features a red tile roof parapet, carved plaster ornamentation, wrought iron balcony and entry gate details, and an interior courtyard formed by the U-shaped intersection of the central lobby and two guest room wings. Interior design elements, including decorative tile work, plaster walls, and exposed wooden ceiling rafters, also convey the Spanish Colonial Revival style. Considered "one of the finest small hotels in the Trans Pecos region," El Paisano was built in anticipation of an area oil boom that never materialized, but it nevertheless quickly became "a pivotal point in the social and commercial life of Marfa and the larger County of Presidio."[18]

The most famous chapter of the hotel's history dates to the middle of the twentieth century, when Hollywood came to town. The Warner Brothers film studio chose Marfa as the location for filming the motion picture version of Edna Ferber's novel *Giant*. For several months in 1955, some of the movie's stars, which included Elizabeth Taylor, Rock Hudson, James Dean, Dennis Hopper, Carroll Baker, and Sal Mineo, either lived at El Paisano or used the hotel as a central gathering place. George Stevens, the film's director, famously presided over an open set, encouraging active participation—in the form of bit parts and behind-the-scenes employment, as well as casual observance of the filming process—by local residents.[19] The cachét of Hollywood still pervades the town today, with residents and visitors alike celebrating the landmark film and its stars at various special events. In the summer of 2005, on the occasion of the film's fiftieth anniversary, hundreds of visitors gathered on Highland Avenue in front of El Paisano Hotel to watch

(opposite) *Spanish Colonial Revival features of Marfa's El Paisano Hotel include carved plaster ornamentation and wrought iron balcony details.* Photograph by Dan K. Utley.

Interior design elements of El Paisano Hotel include decorative tile work, plaster walls, and exposed wooden ceiling rafters. Photograph by Dan K. Utley.

the movie on a giant outdoor screen brought to Marfa especially for the event by Austin's Alamo Drafthouse Cinema.

Although the hotel fell on hard times soon after the initial Hollywood hoopla of the 1950s faded, a renovation project in the late 1970s resulted in the property's listing in the National Register of Historic Places in 1978 and designation as a Recorded Texas Historic Landmark the following year. Following a failed attempt to convert it to condominium use in the 1980s, the building remained vacant for a time until purchased in 2001 by Joe and Lanna Duncan, who had earlier bought and renovated the historic Limpia Hotel in Fort Davis. Now restored and once again welcoming guests, El Paisano Hotel continues to be a prime West Texas tourist destination.

The Duncans also purchased and renovated another hotel Henry Trost designed for the Gateway chain, the Hotel El Capitan in Van Horn. Built about the same time as El Paisano, the two-story El Capitan is similar in many ways to the Marfa hotel, with its U-shaped form, interior courtyard, and Mission-style features, including balconies, exposed vigas (wooden roof beams), and arched parapets. Its setting, on a downtown corner lot, also mimics that of El Paisano. Patronized primarily by cattle ranchers during its first four decades, El Capitan also served as a social center for a large area of West Texas and as a base of operations for tourists visiting Carlsbad Caverns and Guadalupe Mountains national parks. The hotel closed in the 1970s, and new owners converted the building into the Van Horn State Bank. Sold to the Duncans in 2008, it underwent a major restoration project and reopened as a hotel in 2010.[20]

Henry Trost has been primarily described as a regional architect. While some architectural historians would disagree with that limiting portrayal, believing him instead to be a gifted artist whose work should be evaluated on a national level, he is most closely identified with what he called Arid America—the rugged, open, colorful Southwest that he described in his 1907 essay. For twenty-first-century travelers his work, as exemplified in the unique hotels of the Trans-Pecos region of Texas, offers an opportunity to experience the beauty of his talents and appreciate the character of buildings that clearly exhibit his "truthful artistic ideals."

MARKER LOCATIONS

Henry C. Trost: 333 N. Dregon St., El Paso

Hotel Paso del Norte (Camino Real Hotel): W. San Antonio and
    S. El Paso St., El Paso (in hotel lobby)

Hotel Cortez: 310 N. Mesa, El Paso

Gage Hotel: US 90 and Ave. C, Marathon

Holland Hotel: 207 W. Holland Ave., Alpine

El Paisano Hotel: N. Highland Ave. and W. Texas St., Marfa

Hotel El Capitan: 100 E. Broadway, Van Horn (not currently
    marked with a historical marker)

EL PASO HIGH SCHOOL

Designed by Trost & Trost in 1914 and completed in 1916, El Paso High School has been called one of the finest examples of Classical Revival architecture in Texas. Carefully planned for its site at the base of the Franklin Mountains, it seems to grow organically from the earth and stands as a monument to the ideals Henry C. Trost espoused regarding placing buildings within an environmental context. As Lloyd C. and June-Marie F. Engelbrecht wrote in their 1981 book *Henry C. Trost: Architect of the Southwest,* "The whole complex is carefully fitted to natural contours, and several vantage points for viewing near and distant features of the landscape are incorporated."

Perched above a concrete athletic stadium that is incorporated into the overall site plan, the school building, with its central pedimented entry portico supported by elaborate Corinthian columns, evokes the Greek and Roman ideals of healthy minds and healthy bodies. Terrazzo steps lead up from the athletic field to the school's main entrance, accessed through the highly decorated portico, and into the central portion of the building, which houses a large auditorium, cafeteria, library, and administrative offices.

Flanking the central bay are two classroom wings that carry forward Classical design elements with details such as terra cotta pilasters, paired windows, and pedimented entries on each end. As originally envisioned by the architect, separate boys' and girls' gymnasiums occupied each end of the wings on the ground floor. Also on the ground floor were industrial arts facilities, a four-room apartment for the domestic arts department, and an armory for use by the school's corps of cadets. Classrooms, study halls, and locker rooms occupied the second floor. The third floor, in accordance with Trost's innovative design, contained skylights and special ventilation systems installed above rooms used for science laboratories and mechanical arts instruction. And finally, a roof garden covered the entire building.

Still in use as the oldest high school in the city, El Paso High

Perched above a concrete athletic stadium that is incorporated into the overall site plan, El Paso High School, with its central pedimented entry portico supported by elaborate Corinthian columns, evokes the Greek and Roman ideals of healthy minds and healthy bodies. Courtesy Texas Historical Commission, National Register of Historic Places files.

School is an important local landmark. It was listed in the National Register of Historic Places in 1980, and the Texas Historical Commission placed an Official Texas Historical Marker at the site in 1982.

MARKER LOCATION: 1600 N. Virginia St., El Paso

Sources: El Paso High School, El Paso County, THC marker and NR files; Lloyd C. and June-Marie Engelbrecht, *Henry C. Trost: Architect of the Southwest* (El Paso: El Paso Public Library Association, 1981); Troy Ainsworth, "Henry C. Trost: Architect of 'Arid America,'" *Journal of Big Bend Studies* 21.

6

Her Lonely Way
Back Home

January 19, 2008, was a cold, drizzly day in Port Arthur, Texas. A large crowd gathered that morning in a Baptist church fellowship hall on 32nd Street and sat reverently listening to recordings of a couple of Janis Joplin songs — "Mercedes Benz" and "Me and Bobby McGee" — and many began singing along as they warmed to the familiar tunes from their past. It was a diverse crowd — children, old-timers, local politicians, curious neighbors, and visitors — some wearing leather motorcycle garb and the beads, tie-dyed clothing, and feather boas favored by Joplin, a local girl. It was not a typical gathering in a church fellowship hall, but then that somehow seemed appropriate. The occasion was the dedication of an Official Texas Historical Marker on what would have been Joplin's sixty-fifth birthday. Few in attendance could picture her as a senior citizen. In their minds she would forever be in her twenties — the queen of rock and roll, flamboyantly performing on stages around the world, her wild hair, colorful costumes, and feather boas flying as she belted out song after song in front of cheering audiences.

Those in attendance that day in Port Arthur, including the authors of this book, heard from Jefferson County Historical Commission officials and several local citizens who shared memories of their famous childhood friend. The event was pleasant, well planned, and orderly, and everyone who spoke, it seemed, had good memories of their friend and neighbor. With the remarks and other formalities out of the way, the crowd slowly moved outside and crossed the street to the site of the marker, located in front of the home where Janis lived as a child. There, as local police blocked the road, the current owner of the house ceremoniously unveiled the marker, and the crowd erupted into applause as one dedicated fan appropriately yelled out, "Janis Joplin lives! Woo!"[1]

The event's celebratory mood represented a marked contrast from the town's attitude toward its most famous native daughter just a few decades earlier. Janis Joplin's relationship with her hometown was complicated. By most accounts, she enjoyed a normal, happy early childhood in a middle-class family in the blue-collar refinery town, but her experiences as an outcast—some would say of her own making—in her high school years set the stage for rebellion and outrageous behavior that colored both her own memories and her legacy. As her fame in the 1960s hippie counterculture movement grew, she simultaneously wrote sentimental letters to her family and made disparaging remarks about her hometown to reporters covering her meteoric rise in the music business. Lyrics written by her friend, lover, and fellow musician Kris Kristofferson in 1971, a year after her death (although not written for her, and paraphrased here), convey a sense of the complex journey toward her evolving legacy in Port Arthur: "[She's] a walkin' contradiction, partly truth and partly fiction, takin' every wrong direction on [her] lonely way back home."[2]

Janis Joplin's parents, Seth Joplin and Dorothy East, moved from Amarillo to the small Southeast Texas town of Port Arthur in 1935. Seth worked at a Texaco container plant, and Dorothy found employment in the credit department of a local Sears store. They married in 1936, and just over six years later, on January 19, 1943, Dorothy gave birth to their first child, Janis Lyn. A second daughter, Laura, was born in 1949, followed by a son, Michael, in 1953. The family lived in a small house on Procter Street until about 1947, when they moved to a larger residence on Lombardy Drive (now 32nd Street) in the Griffing Park neighborhood. "Kids were everywhere," Laura Joplin later recalled. "The streets were laid out like spokes on a wheel, and the hub was . . . Tyrrell Public School."[3]

Childhood friend Monteel Copple remembered riding bicycles around the tree-lined neighborhood streets with Janis and other playmates. "We would always somehow meet up and ride around, and oftentimes go back to the schoolyard and play," she said. "We used to hang upside down on the monkey bars. We did not wear shorts — that was not heard of at the time — we all had dresses, and so we just would struggle to hold our dresses up to our knees while we were hanging upside down, and it would produce fits of insane giggles as we did that, you know, as only five- and six-year-olds can giggle. And that's what I remember so much about her, is the glee in her giggle. Just absolute unabandoned glee."[4]

Seth and Dorothy Joplin instilled in all three of their children the joy of reading and the importance of a good education. One family tradition involved rewarding them for learning to write their names by taking them to the local library to obtain their first patron cards. That early experience stayed with Janis for the rest of her life, and she often spoke to reporters and friends about the books she read. Seth Joplin built stilts, seesaws, tightropes, and other outdoor play equipment for his children and their friends, who often gathered at the Joplin home. The Joplin children did well in school and participated in various club and extracurricular activities. Janis sang in the elementary school glee club and joined a Bluebirds troop. She showed early talent as an artist, as well, and some of her drawings and paintings survive in both private and museum collections. During her junior high school years she participated in community theater and volunteered at the local library. Calling her a "Versatile Miss," the *Port Arthur News* ran a story about the artwork she drew for the library's summer reading program, saying she was "one of the top artists in the ninth grade."[5]

Life began to change for Joplin soon after she entered Thomas Jefferson High School in 1957. At first she maintained a B grade average, and her high school yearbooks reveal she joined clubs such as the Future Nurses of America, the Future Teachers of America, the Art Club, and even the Slide Rule Club. She also joined the choir at Port Arthur's First Christian Church. "She sang in the adult choir because she had perfect pitch," remembered Yvonne Sutherlin, former chair of the Jefferson County Historical Commission. "She would sing any part at the last minute if someone didn't show up, or whatever the choir directors needed. She could sing it right that minute. She was very, very talented." As was the case with many teenage girls, she earned money by babysitting, including for

Sutherlin's family. "The kids always had a really good time because she would sing and play with them. She was a great artist, and she would draw them pictures of different characters—a pumpkin head, a skeleton, a scarecrow."[6]

About the time Joplin turned fourteen, she began to feel apart from those around her. Adolescent weight gain and a severe case of acne presaged a deep insecurity. In Port Arthur in the 1950s, physical appearance and adherence to social norms determined popularity and acceptance among high school students. As Joplin's standing among the school's in crowd deteriorated, her response became one of defiance. According to one biographer, "Janis could have chosen to be inconspicuous, but she decided to fight what other girls accepted as fate."[7] She embraced her outsider image in overt ways: dressing in tights and oversized men's shirts instead of the demure dresses or skirts worn by other girls, dying her hair orange, defying teachers who decried her behavior problems, and arguing with her parents. She read books by emerging Beat Era writers such as Jack Kerouac, Lawrence Ferlinghetti, and Allen Ginsberg and openly questioned and challenged the conservative values of her family and community, particularly criticizing the town's racial segregation.

Joplin became friends with what her sister described as "a group of intellectuals"—boys she met in a community theater group who also questioned authority and the social status quo—and with them she began to push ever widening boundaries. One of her friends, Dave Moriaty, said, "Everybody began to realize she was fun to have around because she raised so much hell. By the time we were in mid–high school, she was one of our favorite characters." She became what he described as a sort of court jester, whom they often used to shock their conservative classmates. "When Janis was outrageous, she was totally outrageous," he said. "We used it to our advantage when we wanted to freak people out.[8]

Joplin's growing rebellion "left an ocean-sized wake of chaos in the house," according to Laura Joplin, who described her sister's last two years of high school as "periods of peace broken by instances of outrageous behavior that led to confusion, panic, and yelling at home." Janis and her friends drove around town, built campfires on the beach, and gathered at an abandoned lighthouse to drink and talk. They climbed to the top of most of the water towers in the area and clambered around on the girders underneath the top of Rainbow Bridge, a 176-foot-high span over the Neches River. Another of her friends, Jim Langdon, recalled it as a symbolic action: "None of us planned on staying in Port Arthur. Whatever lay ahead, it was 'out there' somewhere. From a couple hundred feet above the Neches River . . . you could see there actually was a far horizon to reach toward."[9]

But most significantly, Joplin and her friends listened to music— not the pop ballads and crooners popular on Top 40 radio, but folk music, especially zydeco, and the blues and jazz that culturally migrated across the Sabine River from the juke joints and dives in Louisiana. As their late-night forays to bars on the other side of the river grew more frequent, they became enmeshed in the soulful music of artists such as Huddie "Leadbelly" Ledbetter, Willie Mae

Janis Joplin's high school graduation photo from The Yellowjacket, *Port Arthur High School yearbook, 1960.* Photograph by Cynthia J. Beeman.

"Big Mama" Thornton, Bessie Smith, and Odetta, and soon Janis began singing in imitation of many of her musical inspirations. The more she sang, the more she seemed to find herself, although it was also at that time she began drinking to excess, a precursor of the addictive behavior that later defined her public persona.

The group of friends found trouble along with their musical excursions, and soon Joplin's reputation worsened and her relationship with her parents became more strained. She skated through her senior year in high school as a girl on the edges of acceptable behavior, on the outs with most of her classmates but still finding creative expression through music and painting. She graduated with her class in the spring of 1960, and although some of her friends remembered it differently, after she became famous she told a number of interviewers her high school years were miserable because of cruel treatment by her classmates. In an oft-repeated quote, she told television talk show host Dick Cavett, "They laughed me out of class, out of town, and out of the state, man."[10]

Following the path of many of her Port Arthur contemporaries, Joplin briefly attended Lamar State College of Technology (now Lamar University) in nearby Beaumont and Port Arthur College (now Lamar State College–Port Arthur). She spent time with two aunts in California in 1961, and her brief foray there broadened her horizons. Enthralled by the coffeehouses and art galleries in Los Angeles and Venice Beach, she managed to arrange a few singing gigs and at one point hitchhiked to San Francisco, where she first experienced the waning beat movement and burgeoning hippie scene. In the spring of 1962 she left Port Arthur and enrolled at the University of Texas at Austin as an art student.

Joplin quickly fell in with a beatnik crowd and spent most of her time at the off-campus apartments on Nueces Street, where many of them lived. Nicknamed the Ghetto, the ramshackle building was a haven for writers, artists, and musicians, and its freewheeling lifestyle suited Joplin's temperament. Captivated by folk music, she joined Lanny Wiggins and Powell St. John in the musical group the Waller Creek Boys, playing often at a café in the student union and at Threadgill's, the former gas station/beer joint on the old Dallas Highway run by country yodeler Kenneth Threadgill. "She Dares to Be Different!" proclaimed a headline in the university newspaper. The story portrayed an autoharp-playing Joplin as a campus oddity but also praised her singing. Having found her calling, Joplin became less a student and more a musician in Austin, and with that change came a headlong dive into the counterculture movement, complete with alcohol abuse, drug use, and sexual experimentation. By January 1963 she was only too willing to leave Austin behind and hitchhike to California to begin the next phase of her life.[11]

Joplin's friends in San Francisco in the early 1960s included a number of fellow Austin émigrés, such as Jack Jackson, an innovative artist (and later award-winning historian) widely credited with creating the underground comics movement, and Chet Helms, band manager and later owner of the Avalon Ballroom music venue. With Helms's assistance, Joplin found jobs singing in coffeehouses and a few concert halls. By May 1965 she was dangerously underweight as a result of out-of-control drug use, and her worried friends put together a bus fare party to raise funds to send her home. She returned to Port Arthur intending to straighten out her life and reenroll in college, and she made an effort to do so for a while. But in the spring of 1966, when Helms summoned her to the West Coast to become the "chick singer" for Big Brother and the Holding Company, a band he managed, she left home for the last time and made her way back to California.[12]

Joplin's performances with Big Brother and the Holding Company quickly drew widespread attention. Their appearance at the

Monterey International Pop Festival, a three-day outdoor music event in June 1967, catapulted the band—and especially Joplin—to international fame. Reviews of the concert singled her out for praise and solidified her status as a rock-and-roll star. A *Time* magazine reporter wrote of the first major rock festival: "50,000 members of the turned-on generation celebrated the rites of life, liberty and the pursuit of hippiness." Describing the psychedelic scene and on-stage theatrics of musicians including The Who and Jimi Hendrix, the reporter went on to say, "But what emerged beyond question as the mainstream of pop music today was the 'soul' sound.... Among the high points: Janis Joplin, backed by a San Francisco group called Big Brother and the Holding Company, belting out a biting alto and stamping her feet like a flamenco dancer."[13]

The band, with an increasing focus on lead singer Joplin, exploded onto the rock scene following the Monterey festival and with the release of its first album, *Cheap Thrills*. Robert Shelton, reviewing the band's east coast debut in the *New York Times* in early 1968, wrote, "The lines can start forming now, for Miss Joplin is as remarkable a new pop-music talent as has surfaced in years. There are few voices of such power, flexibility and virtuosity in pop music anywhere."[14]

As Joplin's star rose, her relationship with the members of Big Brother deteriorated, and creative differences caused a parting of the ways by the end of 1968. She struck out on her own as a solo performer backed by a new band of musicians, which she christened Kozmic Blues. Still hugely popular, and increasingly fueled by drugs and alcohol, she remained a favorite topic of music journalists. San Francisco–based writer Michael Lydon, in a lengthy *New York Times* feature story, wrote about her reputation as a blues singer and as a hard-living rock star in early 1969. Saying "she consumes vast quantities of energy from some well inside herself that she believes is bottomless," he related her response to his questions concerning her lifestyle: "Yeah, I know I might be going too fast. That's what a doctor said. He looked at me and said my liver is a little big, swollen, y'know. Got all melodramatic—'what's a good, talented girl doing with yourself' and all that blah. I don't go back to him anymore. Man, I'd rather have 10 years of superhypermost than live to be 70 sitting in some chair . . . watching TV." She also spoke about her hometown, and in one of the many harsh statements that later complicated her legacy in Port Arthur, said, "I always wanted to be an artist. Port Arthur people thought I was a beatnik, and they didn't like beatniks, though they'd never seen one and neither had I. I read, I painted, I thought. There was nobody like me in Port Arthur. It was lonely, those feelings welling up and nobody to talk to. I was just 'silly crazy Janis.' Man, those people hurt me. It makes me happy to know I'm making it and they're back there, plumbers just like they were."[15]

By 1970 Janis Joplin was arguably the most famous female rock-and-roll singer in the world. That summer, as she traveled the United States and Canada on concert tours and made plans to record a new album with her latest group of musicians, the Full Tilt Boogie Band, she also returned to Texas for two special events: a birthday concert honoring Kenneth Threadgill in Austin in June and the tenth anniversary reunion of her high school class in Port Arthur in August. At the Austin event she reunited with old friends, some of whom later recalled the changes they noticed in her. "She could still bust a gut laughing, but she'd changed," Jack Jackson told a biographer in the early 1990s. "At the Ghetto, she had been a restless spirit, a good-humored person of unbridled enthusiasm. Now, she had a cynical, frantic edge."[16]

Accompanied by an entourage of hippie friends sure to stand out in her hometown, Joplin arrived in Port Arthur on August 13, 1970, met by her parents and siblings, as well as the local press, at the airport. Her former classmates on the reunion committee, concerned the entire event would be overshadowed by her arrival, met with her the next morning and asked if she would agree to a press conference before the dinner and dance that evening, in part to stave off some of the harried press attention.

Joplin readily agreed, telling Sam Monroe, "Yes, I'll do all of it. I want to be treated like everybody else." As Monroe recalled later,

And of course she wasn't. I mean she was a celebrity, and she was treated that way by her classmates. I was the emcee, and it was my job to make a report on what had happened in the de-

Joplin's attendance at the tenth anniversary reunion of her high school graduating class caused quite a stir in Port Arthur, and she agreed to hold a press conference at the request of the reunion's organizing committee. Courtesy Museum of the Gulf Coast, Port Arthur, Texas.

cade since we had graduated from high school . . . and I had to cut it short because of all the commotion around Janis. There was just constant talk and laughter, and people were having fun. Everything was being filmed or written about, so she was a distraction to that portion of the program. But she couldn't help it; she wasn't generating it, it was the people around her.[17]

One of Monroe's duties as emcee involved giving awards to people for various accomplishments, and in what was intended to be a humorous part of the program he presented an automobile tire to Joplin for having traveled the farthest to attend the reunion. Joplin, however, who by then was in a fragile emotional state— having burst on the scene earlier in the day with her trademark bravado, only to be left subdued and quieted by questions from the hometown press—failed to appreciate the tongue-in-cheek effort at humor and felt disappointed to be given such a lowly token.[18]

What Joplin hoped would be a triumphant homecoming, one in which she intended to flaunt her celebrity and importance to the town she felt had rejected her, instead turned bittersweet as her old feelings of insecurity resurfaced. Joplin biographer Alice Echols described the filmed press conference, which appears in several documentaries about the singer: "The interview . . . is significant for the way it shows—more clearly perhaps than any other document of Janis's life—how very thin her armor was, how close she felt to the hurt and scorn of her high school years. Back among her classmates, Janis found her tough-girl carapace shattering within minutes."[19]

Joplin returned to California, where plans for a new record with the Full Tilt Boogie Band began to take shape. By September they were recording at Sunset Sound in Los Angeles, with everyone involved pleased with and encouraged by the quality of the sessions. Despite the positive turn in her professional life, however, it soon became apparent to her dismayed friends that she was once again using heroin. On October 3 the band worked in the recording studio, laying down the instrumental track for a song on which Joplin would record vocals the following day. After the gathering broke up about eleven o'clock in the evening, she briefly stopped at a bar on the way back to her room at the Landmark Hotel. At about one in the morning, apparently after injecting herself with a dose of heroin, she went to the lobby to get change to buy cigarettes and spoke briefly with the desk clerk. Returning to her room, she sat on the edge of the bed and almost immediately collapsed to the floor. When she failed to appear at the recording studio the following day, her road manager went to the hotel and discovered her body, the change still clutched in her hand. The song she planned to record that day appeared on her final album, *Pearl,* in its unfinished, instrumental form. The title was "Buried Alive in the Blues."[20]

News outlets around the world reported the death of the twenty-seven-year-old singer. Her hometown newspaper conveyed the news with the terse headline "Singer's Death Laid to Drugs" and said her parents had traveled to California to make funeral arrangements. The *Houston Post* said "she lived like there was no tomorrow . . . and then suddenly there wasn't," and a *Time* magazine reporter wrote she "died on the lowest and saddest of notes." The *Dallas Morning News* editorialized, "Janis Joplin did not have 10 years of 'superhypermost.' She literally exhausted herself to death, whether from drugs or simply from her pace of living, after only three years of stardom. But she seemed aware of all the odds. Whatever her flaws, she leaves behind her the work of a dedicated artist and the memory of a volatile but very human individual." According to Joplin's wishes, her friends and family spread her ashes along the coast of Northern California and later attended a wake to celebrate her life. She left funds for the party in her will and the invitation simply read, "The drinks are on Pearl."[21]

For many years, although her fame grew elsewhere, Joplin's memory in Port Arthur reflected the negativity of her harsh words about her hometown and the disgrace associated with the manner of her death. Gradually, however, as appreciation of her musical legacy began to eclipse disapproval of her lifestyle, opinions started to change. Monteel Copple credits the changing times: "Well, you know, time passes, the edge goes off. I think the notoriety that she received because of the drug overdose factored in. . . . Perhaps the music, the genre, was not well received. Who knew it would never die, who knew?"[22]

By the mid-1980s, spurred on by her former classmates and friends, members of the local historical society and chamber of commerce began reassessing Joplin's legacy. As plans for a museum exhibit at Gates Memorial Library started to take shape, Sam Monroe—at the time the president of Lamar State College in Port Arthur—corresponded with Dorothy Joplin, then living in Arizona. Janis's mother provided letters, photographs, original artwork, scrapbooks, and numerous other artifacts for the exhibit and consulted with Monroe regarding how to display the items properly.[23] About the same time, John Palmer, a high school classmate, commissioned sculptor Doug Clark to create a multifaced bronze bust of Joplin he intended to put on display in the Port Arthur Civic Center. City leaders rejected that idea, according to Monroe, so he suggested adding it to the museum exhibit, with the official unveiling—ironically to be held at the civic center—set for January 19, 1988, Joplin's forty-fifth birthday. What happened from that point is best told in Monroe's own words:

> National Public Radio got interested and . . . did a feature on the Joplin bust unveiling. The people here were opposed to recognizing Janis. One Saturday morning—*Port Arthur News* would do an "on the street" interview; they would ask opinions of maybe ten people about some topic of the day—my wife called me and said, "They've asked ten people on the street if we should honor Janis Joplin. They all said no." So we knew we had a big, big problem.
>
> I'm not sure [the local people] really thought of her as an international celebrity. Perhaps they gave it more credibility when they saw the *Houston Chronicle* take an interest in it [with a front page story]. Calls were coming from all over the United States and the United Kingdom for radio interviews, from television, and daily newspapers. I got concerned because of the way the local people were accepting this—it contrasted so dramatically with the way the national people were following this story. I thought, my god, the city's going to get a black eye. We're going to unveil this bust . . . to an audience of no local people, probably some national news people, that'd be about it. So we broadened the concept to say we were going to honor all of Southeast Texas' legendary musicians, including Janis. That was effective because it brought more people into the picture, and then the music community got behind this. Jerry LaCroix [also known as Jerry "Count" Jackson of Boogie Kings fame] agreed to do a concert that night at the unveiling, so the whole thing worked.
>
> Janis's sister Laura and her husband came; her brother Michael came. We had an early dinner and then moved from there to the civic center. I was so anxious because I was fearful that we were going to be embarrassed as a community, that no one would be there. We were in a caravan of cars, and I was leading the way to show Laura and Michael, [and] we headed [out] on Texas Highway 73 where the civic center is located, and I see cars parked on the highway. And we finally get into the parking lot, and there

JANIS JOPLIN MEMORIAL DEDICATION

and SOUTHEAST TEXAS
MUSICAL HERITAGE CELEBRATION

THE GREATER PORT ARTHUR CHAMBER OF COMMERCE
proudly presents

JERRY ⚬ COUNT JACKSON ⚬ LACROIX
HOSTING AN ALL STAR TRIBUTE TO THE WORLD FAMOUS
MUSIC OF THE GOLDEN TRIANGLE

TUESDAY ~ JANUARY 19, 1988 ~ 7:00 P.M.
(JANIS JOPLIN'S BIRTHDAY)
Free No Admission Charge
PORT ARTHUR CIVIC CENTER

SCULPTOR: DOUG CLARK   ©1988-FIRST EDITION   ILLUSTRATOR: TOM WINDHAM
BENEFACTOR: JOHN PALMER   A HOMER PILLSBURY PRODUCTION

No Admission CHarge

*The 1988 dedication of a memorial statue and tribute concert became
a turning point for Joplin's legacy in Port Arthur.* Promotional poster in
authors' personal collection.

are cars everywhere! There are thousands of people everywhere!
Two television stations from Beaumont, two television stations
from Houston, one from Lake Charles, one from Lafayette . . .
they're all doing live broadcasts in the lobby of the Port Arthur
Civic Center. And when the building over-filled—to what was
estimated to be about five thousand people—the police cor-

doned off the building and refused to admit any additional people. And there were still about two thousand people outside. And so we ran extension cords and speakers out to the parking lot so that people outside could hear what was going on inside.

I never saw anything like that in my life. There hadn't been an event like that, in my experience, in this community, before or since. Just a phenomenon. There was just an outpouring of emotion. I get emotional thinking about it, because it was sort of a catharsis. People that night forgave Janis for all the negative [things] she'd said about the town and all. I think that was the turning point.[24]

For a number of years after the 1988 event, Port Arthur hosted an annual Janis Joplin Birthday Bash. Guest concert artists included the remaining members of Big Brother and the Holding Company as well as Kris Kristofferson. That event evolved into the Gulf Coast Music Hall of Fame and the Music Legends Exhibit Hall in the acclaimed Museum of the Gulf Coast, an institution that grew from the small display at Gates Memorial Library. Over the years, the Janis Joplin exhibit, anchored by a replica of her psychedelic-painted Porsche convertible, has remained a major attraction. People still come from around the world to pay homage to the queen of rock and roll who finally gained respect in her hometown. By the turn of the twenty-first century, billboards advertising the museum could be seen along major highways in Southeast Texas, touting the area's history "from Jurassic to Joplin," and a museum brochure offers a map and driving tour of local places associated with her life in Port Arthur, including the house in Griffing Park—across the road from Trinity Baptist Church—where an Official Texas Historical Marker honors the meteoric life of a simple local girl who took every wrong direction on her lonely way back home.[25]

MARKER LOCATION: 4330 32nd St., Port Arthur

RAINBOW BRIDGE

In the summer of 1957, six-year-old Christy McClintock, sitting with her grandfather on a porch swing, had an idea. The local newspaper in her hometown of Port Arthur was sponsoring a contest to come up with a new name for the soaring bridge over the Neches River that connected Jefferson and Orange counties. Asked by her grandfather what she would name the bridge, she immediately said, "Rainbow." He wrote her entry on a postcard and mailed it, and a couple of months later the judges declared her the winner. A photograph in the *Port Arthur News* shows Christy, all dressed up in a fluffy dress, petticoats, and white gloves, standing on a chair to accept the fifty dollars in prize money awarded by the local Lions Club.

In the early twentieth century, the rapid growth of the petrochemical industry in the area led to a population boom in Orange and Jefferson counties, and soon the Dryden Ferry crossing at the Neches River on State Highway 87 (the "Hug-the-Coast-Highway" that ran from Orange to Brownsville) became inadequate to handle local transportation needs. With Port Arthur officials leading the campaign for a new bridge, plans began to take shape, but controversy soon ensued when Beaumont officials, worried about a new bridge's effects on the region's lucrative river navigation, objected to the plan. Both pro- and antibridge forces argued their positions before the state highway commission, and several local bond elections failed when the citizens of the two cities could not come to an agreement. Eventually, however, the opposing factions put their differences aside, and in 1934 the Texas legislature passed a law that enabled a combination of county and federal Public Works Administration funds to help pay for the new state highway bridge.

Designed to allow for passage of what was at the time the tallest ship afloat—US Navy dirigible tender USS *Patoka*—the bridge was built to a clearance height of 176 feet and spanned 7,752 feet across the river and adjacent marshland.

Spanning 7,752 feet across the Neches River and adjacent marshland, the Rainbow Bridge, named by six-year-old Christy McClintock in a local newspaper contest, quickly became a popular regional landmark, with teenagers such as Janis Joplin and her friends climbing it for a thrill. Photograph by Cynthia J. Beeman.

Its official dedication on September 8, 1938, drew a massive crowd and featured speeches by Gov. James Allred and numerous other dignitaries. As part of the festivities, Ogden Smith, a "daredevil high diver" who received three hundred dollars for the stunt, leapt from the top of the bridge, "cut the water cleanly, feet first," and resurfaced to wild applause from the cheering crowd. Prairie View, the small community on the Orange County side of the Neches, became known as Bridge City soon after the dedication. The soaring bridge quickly became a popular local landmark, with teenagers such as Janis Joplin and her friends climbing it for a thrill.

Within fifty years of its construction, the Rainbow Bridge proved inadequate to handle the increased amount of daily traffic across the river. A new parallel span, dubbed the Veterans Memorial Bridge, opened in 1991. It now carries northbound traffic, while the Rainbow Bridge, which underwent renovations in the mid-1990s to bring it up to current highway safety standards, carries southbound traffic.

MARKER LOCATIONS: There are two markers for the Rainbow Bridge on SH 87 as it approaches the Neches River: one in Port Arthur (Jefferson County) on the north side of the bridge and the other in Bridge City (Orange County) at the south end of the bridge.

Sources: Rainbow Bridge, Jefferson and Orange Counties, THC marker files; Mildred S. Wright, "Rainbow Bridge," Handbook of Texas Online, www.tshaonline.org/handbook/online/articles/err03, accessed January 19, 2011.

PART TWO
The Texas Cultural Landscape

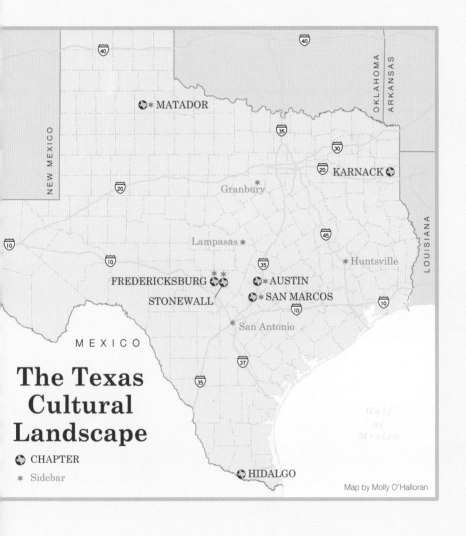

NEW MEXICO

OKLAHOMA
ARKANSAS

40

40

35

30

◐✷ MATADOR

20   KARNACK ◐

Granbury ✷

10

20

10

LOUISIANA

45

Lampasas ✷

FREDERICKSBURG ◐◐

35

✷ Huntsville

10

STONEWALL

◐✷ AUSTIN
◐✷ SAN MARCOS

10

MEXICO

✷ San Antonio

The Texas
Cultural
Landscape

37

35

Gulf
of
Mexico

◐ CHAPTER
✷ Sidebar

◐ HIDALGO

Map by Molly O'Halloran

7 And the Cars Keep Rolling By

In his seminal study of the evolving American roadside landscape, *Main Street to Miracle Mile,* cultural historian and preservationist Chester H. Liebs provides a visual context of what he terms "the movie through the windshield." With the advent of the Automobile Age in the early twentieth century, individuals experienced a newfound freedom of travel that personalized transportation and opened it to myriad new dimensions, so "simply by whirling the crank and opening the throttle," Liebs observed, "the windshield of any car could be transformed into a proscenium arch framing one of the most fascinating movies of all—the landscape played at high speed."[1]

Though now regarded as a defining benchmark event in social structure, the debut of the automobile initially brought little noticeable change. Gasoline-powered automobiles entered the cultural scene largely as anomalies, seen more as luxuries or amusements than necessities. They were for many the toys of the elites. The lack of adequate roads proved a limiting factor in their use, as did the ready supply of fuel, and few early automobile owners rarely ventured far from home. Change came much more dramatically, though, with the opening of the middle class markets, made possible in large part by the success of Henry Ford's modestly priced Model T, which debuted in 1908. Within a year there were over one hundred thousand sales of that model, and with exponential increases in production and sales in the following years, as well as viable competition, prices dropped and related industries struggled to keep up with demand.

Much has been written about the early development of the American road system, which initially served to enhance market accessibility but soon came to provide a means of independent travel for tourists as well. Relatively little, however, has been written about the development of innovative fuel delivery systems, which, as they improved, also contributed to increased demand for travel. In the days before dependable pumps, automobile owners often had to secure fuel at bulk supply depots by means of a tedious and dangerous transfer that involved gravity flow storage tanks, funnels (later, garden hoses), cloth filters, and small, portable metal containers. It was not a speedy process, but it proved adequate for a locally based phenomenon. As automobile operators traveled farther afield, though, consuming more gasoline in the process, the need for more strategic delivery points away from the central supply depots grew.[2]

The first efficient gasoline pumps date to 1905, and soon companies such as Tokheim, Gilbarco, and Bowser began producing them in great numbers, initially for existing establishments such as liveries, general stores, and hardware suppliers. These were largely Main Street businesses that simply converted space in front of their operation for one or two pumps. They were independently owned pumping (or refueling) stations, and in the era before industry standardization and centralized brand marketing, almost anyone could set up their own operation with little concern for zoning or health and safety restrictions. There were no drive-in spaces for off-street fueling, and the resulting lines of motorists often clogged already narrow streets. Of even greater concern, perhaps, was the vulnerability of the curbside pumps and the potential for property damage or personal injury resulting from accidents or misuse.[3]

Public opposition to the curbside pumps resulted in the relocation of such operations to areas outside the central town cores, where larger lots provided greater off-street access. By World War I, so-called filling stations began to appear regularly at the edges of towns, but also in reconfigured downtown lots as well as in rural areas. These were not, however, the iconic, streamlined service stations that would emerge later in the evolutionary process. In the 1920s, filling stations not associated with established businesses were often little more than shacks or sheds, minimally constructed of studs and planks or maybe metal siding to provide enough space for a lone attendant. The emphasis was on quick fuel delivery and little else in order to maximize profits.

Continued increases in fuel production, coupled with improved product lines and a renewed interest in personal travel, drove competition within the marketplace. As a result, the filling station soon began offering other services designed to build a dependable base of satisfied customers. Station attendants over time became car care specialists, and service station owners added work bays for repairs. Customers stopped by for car parts and products, highway maps, and maybe even a cold drink and a conversation. As Michael Karl Witzel observed in his book *The American Gas Station,* by the mid-1920s—the beginning of what he termed the boom years— "selling refined petroleum to the motorist had developed into an art form."[4] In order to be successful in such an environment, a service station operator had to understand general business practices but also be competitive, innovative, and a good neighbor, and maybe even a bit of a showman.

It was during this boom era that Luther Bedford "Bob" Robertson moved to the town of Matador, the seat of Motley County. Born in 1894 at Greenville, in Hunt County, Robertson served with the US Marines in World War I before heading west. Little is known of his life before he arrived in Matador, and there was speculation at the time that there could have been more to his personal story than most people knew. Regardless, Robertson quickly made a name for himself in his adopted hometown through his hard work and obvious business sense. He worked for a time at the Spot Cash Grocery, owned by J. H. Sample, and later ran a service station across from the courthouse on the northwest side of the square. In 1925 he married Olga Cunningham, a native of Oklahoma whose family moved to Motley County by 1910. The couple had one child, Reatha Rayne Robertson, who they called Bobbie.[5]

Matador in the 1920s offered great promise to those seeking to set up businesses in the area. It was a relatively new town, dating from 1891, and had strong ties to the massive Matador Ranch. One of the founders of the Matador Cattle Company, Henry H. "Hank" Campbell, was instrumental in the establishment of the townsite and served as the first county judge when Motley County organized the same year. Not on a rail line until 1913, Matador nonetheless grew early on as a vital commercial center for both cattle and farm production. Local residents soon outgrew the early political influence of the Matador Ranch operation, although significant economic ties remained, and they voted to incorporate the county seat in 1912. Growth remained steady in the ensuing years, with the town's population reaching more than 1,300 by 1940.[6]

By 1932 Bob Robertson was ready to go into business for himself, and he decided to open a new service station on the west side of town, where, interestingly, what would be US Highway 70—running east and west—crossed the north-south corridor designated State Highway 70. An innate businessman, he believed the 70s crossroads afforded an ideal location for not only local customers, but also highway travelers passing through the area. Even though he began his operation at the height of the Great Depression, he most likely placed his hope in the necessity of travel, as did the author of a 1933 *Harper's Magazine* article, who wrote, "There's gold in them shacks [roadside establishments]—as long as the cars keep rolling by. And they are still rolling by."[7]

A transcontinental route across the southern part of the country, US 70 reached from North Carolina to Arizona, with overlapping connections on to Los Angeles. Originally conceived as a southern counterpart to the Lincoln Highway of the North, the new highway system proved to be a viable route for commerce and western migration. From the east it traversed North Carolina, Tennessee, and Arkansas, remaining just north of the Red River in southern Oklahoma before crossing into Texas north of Oklaunion and east of Vernon in Wilbarger County. From Vernon, the route headed west through the Texas towns of Paducah, Floydada, Plainview, and Muleshoe, eventually exiting to the west at Farwell. From there it continued on across New Mexico, eventually ending at Globe, Arizona. Today, the highway merges with various other roads along its historic route, but it remains in service to the modern traveler.

With the construction of new transcontinental highway systems, with their emphasis on speed relative to distance covered, came a new form of commercial architecture designed to open up competition for businesses along the way. As Liebs noted: "Travelers eventually grew hungry, tired, and restless for diversions. Soon gas stations, produce booths, hot dog stands, and tourist camps sprouted up along the nation's roadsides to capitalize on these needs. As competition increased, merchants looked for new ways to snag the new market awheel. Each sign and building had to visually shout: 'Slow down, pull in, and buy.'[8] Designed for another time and a much slower pace, Main Street operations for the most part failed to meet the demands of the new motoring public, which favored fast service and brand recognition over the older establishments. Somehow Bob Robertson must have had a sense of the changing commercial environment, and he was among those pioneers there at the point of transition out along the new highways. As Liebs and others have pointed out, many of the successful new breed of highway merchants were amateurs, unschooled formally in business and marketing practices but nonetheless aware of developing trends. Choosing in effect to break with traditional design idioms by means of new and expansive locations and innovative advertising, they drove trends rather than follow them, and soon the national companies followed suit.[9]

One of the seemingly new forms of advertising the roadside merchants employed in their efforts to get the attention of the traveling public actually had roots that reached back deep in business history. It involved what Liebs termed *mimetic architecture,* a design principle that played on the imitation, or mimicry, of commonplace themes and objects and sometimes accentuated "the lure of the bizarre." Such structures might, for example, include architectural references to windmills, haciendas, boats, or lighthouses but could also whimsically represent anything from coffee pots and seashells to oil cans and even animals. By also building on comfortable design stereotypes, both regional and national, business owners hoped to present visual images that were evocative, compelling, and worthy of further inspection. With regard to service stations, the general trend farther to the east was the welcoming cottage by the side of the road, complete with gabled roofs and chimneys that seemed to offer road-weary travelers a place of rest and comfort, at least visually. Out West, merchants also built on historical stereotypes, with architectural references to cowboys, Indians, and even Spanish influences.[10]

At his new place in Matador, Bob Richardson made the decision to tap into the same general trend by incorporating an oil derrick into the design of his new service station. Utilizing iconic imagery, he chose not only an easily recognizable symbol of Texas business and pride, one that had a strong technological association with the Automobile Age, but also one that would literally tower above anything else on the nearby landscape. As if building a sixty-four-foot replica wooden derrick atop his two-story station were not enough, Robertson also chose to add lighting so the structure could be easily seen from miles away even at night. So unique was his station design that he registered it with the US Patent Office in 1934, noting in his application that he had "invented a new, original, and ornamental Design for a Building." Accompanying drawings show the office part of the derrick with its splayed walls that grounded the structure and followed the gradual sloping lines of the upper derrick. Small pent roofs or canopies above the window openings helped shed rainwater and provided a minimal amount of shade.[11]

Through Bob's Oil Well, as Robertson dubbed his business, he met a fundamental criterion of advertising by first getting the public's attention. The owner achieved this not only through architecture, but also by means of innovative methods that reached far beyond Motley County. Working in partnership with long-haul truckers, he provided them with signs and posthole diggers, and they then placed the advertising at prescribed distances from Matador. As a result, signs promoting Bob's Oil Well soon showed up in various states and even in Mexico. So seemingly omnipresent was the advertising that it even showed up in Europe and the South Pacific during World War II, no doubt carried to those sites by Robertson's friends and fellow veterans.[12]

With the newfound and widespread attention came the added pressure to bring customers into the establishment, and to that end Robertson employed a number of interesting techniques, some conventional and many otherwise. For his product line he

A recent photograph of Bob's Oil Well, an iconic cultural landmark of the Automobile Age on the West Texas landscape. Photograph by and courtesy of Terence A. "Tiger" Russell.

connected with Conoco, which had strong territorial recognition. Founded by Isaac E. Blake at Ogden, Utah, in 1875 as the Continental Oil and Transportation Company, it began initially for the distribution of kerosene and related products. Later it merged with other petroleum companies and expanded its product line, eventually moving its headquarters to Ponca City, Oklahoma. While Conoco was not one of the top-tier petroleum companies nationally, it retained a strong market share territorially throughout the West and Midwest in the years before World War II.[13]

In addition to his association with a stable supplier, Robertson decided to grow his business by offering other services for the motoring public, especially tourists passing through the area. Not long after he opened his station, he drew on another regional stereotype by displaying live rattlesnakes. They proved so popular in attracting customers that he soon added other animals, creating a menagerie that grew to include a bobcat, a raccoon, coyotes, monkeys, and even a buffalo. At one point he constructed a special cage to hold two lions he received from the City Park Zoo in Denver, Colorado. The couple, named Trader and Kit, eventually gave birth to two litters of cubs.[14]

With continued success, Robertson added other structures to his business complex to house Bob's Cook Shack, Bob's Foodway Grocery, and Bob's Garage. He also altered the original design of the oil well, replacing the wooden superstructure in 1939 with one of steel that reportedly reached more than eighty feet in height and sported even more lights. In 1946 he constructed a new structure on the site to house an updated Bob's Cook Shack, which the local newspaper described as "one of the most modern and elaborate restaurants between Albuquerque and Wichita Falls." Cladding the structure in petrified wood and colored stone he had stockpiled for years, Robertson created another landmark of vernacular architecture that complemented his oil well. As the newspaper noted, "No detail was overlooked. His plans were changed frequently but only to include more beauty or more customers or more modern equipment."[15]

Robertson used his standing as a leading businessman in the community to help others. He was an avid promoter of Matador

A photograph from the heyday of operations in Matador, ca. 1940s. In the background are Bob's Oil Well on the right and Bob's Cook Shack on the left. Courtesy Texas Historical Commission, Official Texas Historical Marker files.

and contributed to a number of worthy local causes, including the construction of an elaborate stone archway—using rocks similar in color to those used on his restaurant—at the city's East Mound Cemetery. Of particular interest to him, as a veteran of World War I, was the plight of returning servicemen and the recognition of those who had given their lives in military service. He served as commander of the Fleming Post of the American Legion and worked to establish adequate meeting space for that organization. He was also active in the Lions Club and the Matador Masonic Lodge.[16]

Bob Robertson was arguably the most respected businessman of Motley County in the 1930s and 1940s, admired widely for his hard work, his unselfish commitment to others, and his dedication to the quality of life for his fellow veterans. At home, though, he and Olga had grown apart, and by 1947 they had started the process of divorce. As a result, he moved to the Matador Hotel temporarily. There, in the early evening of Monday, January 13, he visited with Olga and his lawyer, former district attorney John Hamilton, to discuss property settlement. When the meeting ended, his wife and lawyer departed, but as they reached the lobby they were startled by the sound of a gunshot. Olga immediately rushed back to the room, and upon hearing her scream, Hamilton quickly followed. There, he found Robertson lying on the floor with a bullet wound to his temple. Nearby lay a German-made Luger pistol. Hamilton quickly summoned Sheriff John Stotts and local physician Dr. J. S. Stanley, who pronounced Robertson dead. An inquest subsequently conducted by Motley County Judge William R. Commack concluded the death was the result of suicide.[17]

News of Robertson's death spread quickly through the small community, and three days later the weekly newspaper bore the banner headline, "Bob Robertson Takes Own Life in Hotel Here; Colorful Career Ends in Tragedy." The article led off with the following: "Bob Robertson is dead. A gun in his own hand wrote the final chapter in the history of Matador's most colorful character. Spirit of the amiable, 56-year-old, red-faced Irishman who rose from a filling station operator to one of this West Texas town's leading business men, is released from mortal duty." Robertson was, in fact, only 52 years of age at his death, as the article later correctly noted. It also recognized him as "dramatic and dynamic" and a "natural leader." Describing his graveside services, conducted by the Matador Masonic Lodge with a rifle salute from the American Legion, the writer observed, "It was his leadership and work which made Matador East Mound cemetery one of the most beautiful plots in this area. The ornate rock gateway under which his body passed yesterday as it entered the cemetery is one of his many visions which became a reality." And, the article continued, "He was generous to a fault. Bob Robertson lived a full and open life."[18]

For several days following Robertson's death, Bob's Oil Well remained closed, with the derrick lights darkened at night. Olga and her daughter reopened the business within a week, although Reatha Rayne left soon after to return to college studies in Canyon. Within another week, the new proprietress had to face a new setback: on January 28, just fifteen days after Bob Robertson's death, a high wind associated with a sandstorm toppled the superstructure, crashing it onto the roof of Bob's Cook Shack. She and her employees anticipated the collapse, as the derrick, badly deteriorated over time, began quaking dangerously in the wind, and a local machinery company summoned to the scene was attempting to stabilize it with a winch truck when the massive steel structure finally gave way. Although Olga Robertson vowed to reopen as soon as possible—and she did—it took considerably longer to rebuild the derrick. It was not until October 1949 that the completed superstructure once again lit up the Matador skies, and this time with even more lights.[19]

By the late 1940s, though, business at the roadside landmark was not the same. The buildings began to show their age, and without the entrepreneurial spirit of its colorful founder, the operation declined. Working against it, too, were changing trends in roadside commercialization, as the motoring public came to expect more modern facilities, as emphasized by the standard designs of national companies. As a result of these and other factors, Bob's Oil Well closed in the 1950s. Although there were several efforts to reopen it over the ensuing years, none proved successful, and by the 1990s the site was in ruins. Olga Robertson died in 1993, and ownership of the property passed on within her family.[20]

In 2002, preliminary plans for the adaptive reuse of the former service station complex garnered considerable local attention, and in 2004, Preservation Texas, an advocacy group for historic preservation, named it to an inaugural list of Texas' Most Endangered Places, where it joined Houston's Prudential Building, the Old Dallas High School, the Sabine Farms Community Center in Harrison County, and similar properties in need of preservation and reuse.[21] The recognition brought additional promises of support for restoring Bob's Oil Well, and as a result the Motley County Historical Commission applied for an Official Texas Historical Marker, which the Texas Historical Commission awarded in 2005. As of this writing in 2010, much has been done, although some structural repairs are still needed. The necessary preservation work is well within reach, and the site awaits a new era in its history, perhaps as office space, a visitor center, or some other creative purpose. Regardless of that outcome, there is still unified local support to preserve the iconic roadside landmark for future generations as an important symbol of American roadside architecture and early automobile tourism. Meanwhile, the cars keep rolling by, just as Bob Robertson knew they always would.

MARKER LOCATION: southeast corner of US 70 and SH 70, Matador

EAST MOUND CEMETERY

About a mile east of the Motley County Courthouse in Matador and just north of US 70 is the East Mound Cemetery where Bob and Olga Robertson are buried, although not side by side. The graveyard dates to 1903, when the Matador Land and Cattle Company deeded ten acres to Matador Masonic Lodge No. 824. In the conveyance, company officials included a reversion clause and also stated there should be no charge for the gravesites. Three earlier graves in the county, then located on land a mile north of the present site, were later reinterred at East Mound. One of those, that of a cowboy named J. E. Varnier, who was killed on the Matador Ranch, is marked by a stone slab bearing the date 1891.

In 1940, under the direction of Bob Robertson, the Fleming American Legion Post undertook the construction of an impressive native rock entryway with flanking walls on the southeast side of the cemetery. In the 1950s, concern that blowing sand might threaten to cover some of the lower graves led the cemetery association to fund the construction of barrier walls as well as a shelter belt of Arizona spruces.

Although East Mound Cemetery does not bear a state marker at this time, it has been duly designated a Historic Texas Cemetery by the Texas Historical Commission and is therefore eligible. The special state designation means the site is properly recorded in local land records and that its history has been written and preserved as well. The site is well maintained through the efforts of families and a cemetery association, and it continues in service to the people of Motley County well over a century after its founding. Grave markers chronicle the history of the area, from the historical association with the Matador Ranch through the growth and development of the county seat to the military service of local residents dating back to the time of the Spanish-American War and the Civil War. As is typical of cemeteries throughout the state, but especially in rural areas where fieldstones or wooden grave markers may have been used extensively in the early days, there

Bob Robertson oversaw the funding and construction of the elaborate rock entryway to the East Mound Cemetery, where he is buried. Courtesy Texas Historical Commission, Historic Texas Cemetery files.

are a sizeable number of unmarked graves or known gravesites marked only by illegible stones. To lessen such impact to the historical record in the future, volunteers have worked to inventory the various tombstones in the cemetery.

MARKER LOCATION: 0.9 mi. east of Motley County Courthouse on US 70, then north on local road 0.2 mi.

Source: Historic Texas Cemetery designation file, Texas Historical Commission. Application includes a narrative entitled "Tombstones Tell the Tale," by Marisue Potts Powell, chair of the Motley County Historical Commission.

GRANBURY'S TOWN SQUARE SERVICE STATION

The streamlined box service stations of the middle of the twentieth century, with their visual emphasis on clean lines, modernity, and brand identification, are iconic images of the Automobile Age, and even though new designs have since passed them by, they can still be found in all regions of the state. Some serve their original purpose, while countless others have been rehabilitated for other purposes or stand vacant as reminders of a vibrant past. On the southeast corner of the historic courthouse square in Granbury, Hood County, though, is a unique building that represents an even earlier era, one representative of the commercial transition from curbside pumps to filling stations. Now used for other purposes, the unique structure is still one of the state's best extant early examples of how the delivery of gasoline to consumers changed over time.

In 1892, Daniel Oscar Baker and Jefferson Davis Rylee purchased a town lot that included two small commercial structures. Three years later, the frame structures gave way to a new building of ashlar-cut native limestone that housed the Baker-Rylee Hardware Company. Described as a handsome structure in a *Granbury News* article about the opening, it included a windmill and water storage tank on top to provide a measure of fire security. Not long after the store opened, Rylee divested his interest to brothers D. O. and Jess Baker, and the business name changed to Baker Hardware Company. A successful operation, it grew over the years to include a tin shop and plumbing store as well as the sale of implements. The brothers prospered and ventured into other enterprises, and Jess Baker even entered politics, serving in the Texas State House of Representatives. D. O. Baker eventually became sole owner of the longtime business, but in 1929 the Transcontinental Oil Company of Tulsa, Oklahoma, purchased the Baker-Rylee Building.

By the 1920s automobiles and trucks were becoming more common in Hood County, and new paved sections of roads opened as well. Responding to an increased demand for gasoline, the oil company transformed the former hardware building into a service station. Removal of the south and west walls, except for a corner column, allowed for a drive-through area for off-street fueling, and a new stone outbuilding provided space for auto repairs. A Chevrolet dealership opened next door, and a door between the two buildings meant new cars could be displayed in the service station. There was also space for a café. Ownership of the business changed hands many times over the years, but it remained a vital operation into the 1980s, when the owners adapted the space to new commercial purposes. The visual lines of the historic building remained, however, and in 1986 the Texas Historical Commission designated the Baker-Rylee Building and Town Square Service Station a Recorded Texas Historic Landmark for its associations with architectural and commercial history in Granbury.

MARKER LOCATION: 210 E. Pearl Street, Granbury

Source: Baker-Rylee Building and Town Square Service Station, Hood County, THC marker files.

8   "To Have What We Must"

In the late afternoon of Sunday, April 11, 1965, at an informal ceremony just down the road from his Texas Hill Country ranch, Pres. Lyndon B. Johnson signed the Elementary and Secondary Education Act, a sweeping reform measure that marked a new progressive era for the nation's schools. Not one averse to symbolism, the president elected to sign the bill and make his remarks against the backdrop of the one-room Junction Schoolhouse, where he had briefly attended classes as a young child. For added historical effect, he asked his former schoolteacher, Kate Deadrich Loney, to sit by his side at the rustic table as he signed the monumental legislation. He did so with one pen, which he then presented to her. As Johnson's wife Lady Bird later wrote, "It was an accurate, corny, warm setting for the signing of a great education bill, one of the landmarks, one of the victories, one of the real triumphs to be cherished by the Johnson Administration."[1]

While the setting was replete with rural charm, iconic imagery, and undeniable nostalgia, it was also one strangely paradoxical in nature. The former schoolhouse, then owned by an Oklahoma couple who used it as a summer home, had ended its academic service almost two decades earlier as the result of statewide educational reforms that led to unprecedented numbers of consolidations. Such state and local reforms, in effect, mirrored national trends that by the 1960s led to the extensive modernization of programs under the direction of the federal government. With his signing of the bill at the historic Junction Schoolhouse, the president not only ushered in a new era of education but also signaled that such sites, and the rudimentary three Rs curriculum of "reading, 'riting, and 'rithmetic" they represented, were squarely in the past. It was a point of no return, although in reality that point had been passed years before in Texas.

Rural common schools underpinned the state's agrarian economy from the late nineteenth century into the middle of the twentieth century. While they were technically the outgrowth of the antebellum Common School Movement led by Massachusetts reformer Horace Mann, they were in reality in Texas, by virtue of the Civil War and Reconstruction, much later adaptations. In 1884 a new state school law promoted the growth of common schools (locally controlled with limited state assistance), and their numbers flourished as a result. In 1904–5, there were more than 10,000 rural common districts in Texas but only 868 independent districts. The peak came in 1909–10, when there were 11,682 common districts and 1,001 independents. The decline began immediately afterward, with increased pressure for centralized control and school consolidations. In 1914 the Texas superintendent for public instruction, F. M. Bailey, left no doubt about his reform objectives when, referencing the dawn of a modern era, he noted, "Our small, short-termed, poorly-housed, inadequately equipped, and ineffectively taught schools must give place to larger schools."[2]

Despite similar attacks throughout the Progressive Era of the early twentieth century and beyond, rural common schools managed to survive, especially in areas of the state largely unaffected by urban growth. Such was the case in Gillespie County in the Texas Hill Country. There, distinct rural communities prospered, easily identified by such determinants as crossroads, stores, churches, cotton gins, and schoolhouses. While farms there were largely dispersed, the agricultural communities retained recognized cores of commercial, social, and religious activities.

When fundamental change finally came to the rural communities, it came relatively quickly—within a matter of only a couple of decades. The economic depression of the 1930s, followed immediately by sweeping societal and commercial changes related to World War II, clearly marked the beginning of the decline. Within that context, the contributing factors were diverse: urban growth fueled by migration from rural areas, declining crop prices, improved transportation systems, new agricultural technologies and more productive practices, and the implosion of an irrelevant and outmoded tenancy system. As young people left the farms, the number of children in the rural areas understandably declined as well. While the final blow against the rural school system is attributed to legislative action in Texas, marginal population numbers in some common schools presaged the inevitable. As one rural schoolteacher noted, "The trouble was, they was running out of kids."[3]

Renewed calls for reform intensified in the years following World War II, and in 1947 Gov. Beauford Jester supported a proposal by Rocksprings representative Claud Gilmer to establish a special investigative committee that would review a broad range of ideas. Senate support came with the active participation of state senator A. M. Aikin Jr., of Paris. With a diverse membership of educators, state leaders, and concerned citizens, the Gilmer-Aikin Committee and its advisory groups remained focused on the long-range objectives, and in 1948, in anticipation of the looming legislative session, it produced a report entitled, "To Have What We Must." The report proposed thirty-three separate reforms that, once rolled into three separate bills, became known collectively as the Gilmer-Aikin Laws. Despite some stiff opposition, primarily from individuals opposed to government control of education, the reform measures passed with considerable margins, and Gov. Allan Shivers signed them into law in 1949. Central to the new legislation were a series of incentives and compliance measures that led almost immediately to the wholesale consolidation of small rural districts in all parts of the state.[4]

As a direct result of the district mergers, countless rural schoolhouses became obsolete in short order, and without a systematic plan for their continued use, many of them disappeared from the cultural landscape. Given the prevailing concept of local control, most school boards simply sold the structures. While some remained *in situ,* others were dismantled for the materials or moved for other purposes, including residences, tool sheds, community centers, and barns. Other schoolhouses burned or fell victim over time to deterioration, neglect, and vandalism. Years after the schoolhouses disappeared, their sites were rarely remembered beyond those who had attended or taught classes there. In some communities, with time, only the school name remained, perhaps on a road sign or a new academic complex. In many others, though, the loss of the schoolhouse meant a significant loss of identity and sense of place that could not be overcome. In Gillespie County, however, there is a different ending to the story of the former schoolhouses, thanks to the concerted efforts of local residents who serve collectively as historians, preservationists, promoters, fundraisers, and custodians. It is a story unprecedented in the state, which is why their work has resulted in both Official Texas Historical Markers and National Register recognition for an impressive number of historic schoolhouses there.

Several factors—some tangible and others intangible—following the implementation of the Gilmer-Aikin laws made it possible for Gillespie County residents to save historic schoolhouses. First, because many of the school communities there were not as dispersed as those in other rural settlements in the state, they maintained a strong sense of place. As a result, there were no clear-cut spheres of influence that immediately led to a particular pattern of consolidation. That began to change with the development of new roads into the rural areas, which in turn opened up market options and job opportunities in nearby towns such as Fredericksburg and Stonewall or even cities farther distant, including San Antonio and Austin, but for a time the rural communities remained somewhat intact and self-sufficient. As long as there were sufficient numbers of school-age children in a community, the schools remained at least marginally viable, especially in the elementary grades, where the focus remained on basic education. None of the rural schools, however, offered sufficient curriculum for high school students and so could not offer the accreditation necessary for any higher education opportunities.

Perhaps more important, in terms of preserving the rural schoolhouses, was that the independent school districts in Gillespie County often retained ownership of the land. While that failed to ensure preservation, per se, it allowed districts to work with local residents for use of the properties, several of which became community centers that played additional roles as precinct polling places. Over time, the districts often had to revisit such arrangements, particularly when rising land values, liability concerns, and escalating costs associated with the maintenance of older buildings no longer used for school purposes became critical issues with taxpayers. Regardless, many of the remaining historic schoolhouses are in place simply because the school districts made no strong effort to purge the inventory.[5]

The most important factor in the broader story of preservation, though, is the human element. As with all such community-based efforts, preservation either works or not, and the reasons for either side of the equation are as diverse and complex as the people involved. With regard to the rural schools of Gillespie County, it was a matter of having the right people at the right place and with clear, common objectives to make it happen. What happened to save some of the remaining historic schools is the classic example of a successful grassroots effort led by individuals who were not intimidated by—or perhaps not fully aware of—potential limitations. To bring that part of the story up to date, it is important to reflect on the value of a good rumor.

In April 1999 the president of the Stonewall Heritage Society and a former Lower South Grape Creek School student, Bernice Weinheimer, received a call from a concerned county resident, who said, "Did you know they were going to sell the county schools?" The schoolhouses in question were twelve still owned by the Fredericksburg Independent School District. Weinheimer enlisted assistance from a number of friends, including her cousin and best friend, Judy Starks; local attorney and heritage society board member Robert Vander Lyn; and a concerned resident named Ronni Pue, who Weinheimer knew to be a good leader and organizer. The core group put out a call to folks they knew who had attended the twelve schools, and they soon met in the Lower South Grape Creek School to discuss the matter. Responses varied greatly, with some expressing interest in purchasing particular school sites for their own use and others hoping to avoid any action that would upset the district trustees. In the end, though, the group agreed to make a formal inquiry about any plans for the rural schools. Meanwhile, representatives of each school began gathering historical information on their respective sites. At subsequent meetings a new organization dubbed the Friends of Gillespie County Country Schools (Friends) began to take shape with Pue as the chair.

On May 11, less than a month after the initial gathering, the Friends met with school and government officials, local preservationists, concerned residents, and others. More than eighty people crowded into the small Lower South Grape Creek School for an open discussion. The school superintendent explained that while there were no immediate plans to sell the rural schools, such sales would be subject to surplus property options under existing state law. That is, they could be sold at appraised value to a government entity or sold to the general public through sealed bids. No provision in the law allowed the district to convey the properties without due compensation to a nonprofit organization.[6]

With that information, the Friends realized they needed political direction and so began working closely with the staffs of their state legislators, Sen. Jeff Wentworth and Rep. Harvey Hilderbran, to draft the necessary legislation. At the same time, members of the organization cast the net farther, contacting other counties to provide information and to solicit their support. It was not an easy process, as Weinheimer recalled: "A lot of times we felt pretty discouraged, because there was a lot of work involved." But, she added, the work gave her and others a new appreciation for their history. "It was just a point in my life," she reflected, "when I was really wanting to preserve all history. And since the schools are very special to a lot of people, I thought that was just the thing to do. And our parents and grandparents had worked hard to get them established, and I couldn't see them just being gone. . . . It's just family history."[7]

The actions of the Friends, while localized and focused, nevertheless tapped into a broader preservation effort in the country, and the members began to network with similar groups in other states, as well as state and national preservation organizations, including the National Country School Association. As historian and photographer Andrew Gulliford observed in his important overview study, *America's Country Schools,* the three basic Rs most commonly associated with historic schools have evolved over the years, thanks to the work of countless preservationists and friends orga-

nizations in every state, into a new paradigm of restoration, rehabilitation, and reuse. "The same populist spirit that sustained the
pioneers in building these schools," he wrote, "now sustains their
descendants as they seek to preserve them."[8]

Buoyed by the steady progress of their collaborative efforts and
the support and encouragement of others, members of the Friends
maintained a broad-based approach of promotion, fundraising, research, and public education. Their hard work paid off with passage
of the enabling legislation followed by the bill signing by Gov. Rick
Perry. Because the bill technically provided for a legislatively approved constitutional amendment, the matter had to go before the
voters in a general election in November 2001. The bill received an
impressive 80.44 percent of the vote, and it went into effect January 1, 2002. As approved, the new amendment provided a means
for school districts to donate historically significant, but otherwise
nonessential, "real property and improvements" to nonprofit organizations in order to enhance opportunities for preservation.[9]

In addressing concerns about perceived threats to twelve locally
revered historic sites, the Friends of Gillespie County Country
Schools ended up securing an important piece of legislation that
will no doubt aid similar efforts throughout the state. To ensure
that likelihood, the group continues its efforts to set an example
of what can be accomplished through a grassroots movement by
raising money to restore the schools and to keep them active landmarks within their early communities. The following case studies
illustrate the historical value of the resources under their charge:

- CRABAPPLE SCHOOL: The cultural setting of Crabapple School
  north of Fredericksburg provides a strong visual example of the
  significant roles education and religion played in such early German settlements. It includes an 1877 schoolhouse, later used as a
  teacherage (teacher housing), and an 1882 schoolhouse. Nearby
  on separate property is a Lutheran church complex dating to
  the late nineteenth century. According to local lore, Mathias
  Schmidt won a footrace with Crockett Riley for the honor of
  donating the school tract. Community residents provided the
  labor for the original schoolhouse and its furnishings. Built with

The teacherage at Crabapple School. Photograph by Dan K. Utley.

locally gathered stone, the rectilinear structure consisted of one large room and a smaller one with a fireplace. The school opened in service to forty students on January 5, 1878, and land donor Schmidt died four days later.

Henry Grote served as the first teacher and lived in the larger of the two rooms with his family, while the smaller room served as the schoolroom. As the area's scholastic population increased, residents added the other schoolhouse, converting the earlier one for use as a teacherage. For a time the two buildings saw dual service, with the former one used as a post office and the latter sharing space for Lutheran church services before parishioners constructed a separate building. Crabapple School remained in operation until declining enrollment led residents to approve consolidation with the Fredericksburg district in 1957. Afterward, the Crabapple Community Club maintained the site, and the presence of barbecue pits, a concession building, and a baseball backstop are current indications the property remains in active use. The Texas Historical Commission (THC) approved an Official Texas Historical Marker for the site in 1994 and certified it for listing in the National Register of Historic Places in 2005.[10]

- CHERRY SPRING SCHOOLHOUSE: School-age children in the German community of Cherry Spring attended classes in local homes until residents built a limestone schoolhouse on property donated by H. Bratherich in 1885. When it opened after only a month of construction, students and their parents marched to the new building from the Christian Strackbein home, which until then had held the school classes. Rectangular in form, the one-room Cherry Spring Schoolhouse featured a gabled roof, masonry gable ends, arched window openings on each of the longer sides, and an offset primary door opening with transom on the west end that served as the original entry. During the Great Depression, residents added a large enclosed pavilion to the site. Cleverly constructed with movable walls and a stage, it served as a second classroom and also as a gathering place for school ceremonies and other community activities. Cherry Spring School remained in operation until 1962 (well after the implementation of the Gilmer-Aikin laws), when it merged with the Fredericksburg district. The schoolhouse became a Recorded Texas Historic Landmark in 1988 and was listed in the National Register in 2005.[11]

- LOWER SOUTH GRAPE CREEK SCHOOL: The site of early meetings associated with the Friends of the Gillespie County Country Schools, the Lower South Grape Creek Schoolhouse dates to 1901, although the institution itself was established much earlier. In 1871 residents of Luckenbach Precinct No. 3 built a log schoolhouse one and one-half miles south of the present school site. There, local students attended classes at the South Grape Creek School until 1899, when trustees designated it a separate district and renamed it Lower South Grape Creek School. Plans

Window detail, Crabapple teacherage. Photograph by Dan K. Utley.

The evolutionary nature often found in rural schoolhouse architecture is reflected in the two distinct sections of the Lower South Grape Creek School. Photograph by Dan K. Utley.

for a new schoolhouse farther north began soon after, and in 1901 the trustees purchased land along the Austin Road from Charles F. and Martha Ahrens. Workers constructed a rectilinear cut limestone building with a metal roof. Changes over the years included the addition of a large porch and the plastering of both interior and exterior walls. The porch was completely enclosed in the 1950s and sheathed in pressed metal in a stone block motif. The resulting asymmetry, which visually placed the bell tower at the juncture of the two rooms, makes the structure a unique example of an evolutionary building type. The available student population at Lower South Grape Creek reached a peak of eighty-two just before World War I, but despite lower numbers in later years there were enough students to keep the building in use until consolidation with Fredericksburg in 1960. Listed in the National Register in 2005, the schoolhouse is also a Recorded Texas Historic Landmark, approved in 1994.[12]

The preservation of landmark rural schoolhouses in Gillespie County is a tribute to the commitment of former students and teachers as well as many interested citizens who never attended the schools but have nevertheless been motivated to join the effort. Among the latter is Dr. James Lindley, who grew up in Houston and retired to the Stonewall area in 2003 following a lengthy medical career. A past leader of the Friends, he has worked to raise money for a master plan to guide restoration and utilization considerations in the years ahead. He is also interested in developing a comprehensive oral history project that will complement the preservation and public education efforts. While providing background information on the current work of the organization, he observed, "The key element to this story is that when the community of people who used these schools perceived the threat, they banded together, used the legal system to overcome the threat, and preserved these schools for the future."[13] In the process they have also, in a sense, provided an important reinterpretation of the phrase, "To Have What We Must," the title of the benchmark report that presaged the changing face of rural education in Texas.

MARKER LOCATIONS

Crabapple School: 14 mi. north of Fredericksburg on FM 965 at the intersection with Crabapple Road

Cherry Spring Schoolhouse: approximately 12 mi. north of Fredericksburg on RR 2323

Lower Grape Creek School: 10 mi. east of Fredericksburg on US 290

Cave Creek School. Photograph by Dan K. Utley.

LANDMARK SCHOOLHOUSES OF GILLESPIE COUNTY

Friends of Gillespie County Country Schools

The following twelve historic schools are associated with the Friends of Gillespie County Country Schools. All are listed in the National Register of Historic Places; see notes below for those with historical markers. Key: RTHL=Recorded Texas Historic Landmark (building marker); OTHM=Official Texas Historical Marker (subject marker)

Cave Creek School

Established 1870; consolidated with Fredericksburg 1950.

LOCATION: north-northeast of Fredericksburg via US 290 and RM 1631 to 470 Cave Creek Road

Cherry Spring School

Established 1859, consolidated with Fredericksburg 1962; OTHM 1985; RTHL 1998.

LOCATION: RR 2323, Cherry Spring Community

Crabapple School

Established 1877, consolidated with Fredericksburg 1950; OTHM 1994.

LOCATION: 14 mi. north of Fredericksburg on RM 965 at Crabapple Road

Lower South Grape Creek School

Established 1871, consolidated with Fredericksburg 1957; RTHL 1994.

LOCATION: 10 mi. east of Fredericksburg on US 290

Luckenbach School

Established 1855, consolidated with Fredericksburg 1964; RTHL 1982.

LOCATION: 3566 Luckenbach Road, Luckenbach

Meusebach Creek School

Established 1858, consolidated with Fredericksburg 1951.

LOCATION: 515 Kuhlmann Road, via US 87 south of Fredericksburg

Nebgen School

Established 1881, consolidated with Stonewall 1949.

LOCATION: 1718 North Grape Creek Road via RM 2721 east of Fredericksburg

Pecan Creek School

Established 1889, consolidated with Fredericksburg 1955.

LOCATION: northwest of Fredericksburg via US 87 to 3410 Pecan Creek Road

Interior of the Rheingold Schoolhouse showing a wood-burning stove of the kind often used to heat such early buildings. Photograph by Dan K. Utley.

Williams Creek (Albert) Schoolhouse. Note the metal replica of the structure in the fence. Photograph by Dan K. Utley.

Rheingold School
Established 1873, consolidated with Fredericksburg 1949.

LOCATION: northeast of Fredericksburg via US 290 and RM 1631 to 334 Rheingold School Road

Williams Creek (Albert) School
Established 1890, consolidated with Stonewall 1950; OTHM, 2002.

LOCATION: 5501 S. RM 1623, Stonewall

Willow City School
Established 1876, consolidated with Fredericksburg 1962.

LOCATION: 2501 RM 1323, Willow City

Wrede School
Established 1871, consolidated with Fredericksburg 1960.

LOCATION: 3929 S. SH 16, Fredericksburg

Not Associated with the Friends of Gillespie County Country Schools
The schools listed below are not associated with the Friends of Gillespie County Country Schools but have been awarded state markers or the National Register designation.

Morris Ranch School
Established 1890, consolidated with Fredericksburg 1962; RTHL 1980; National Register 1983.

LOCATION: Morris Ranch Road, west of SH 16, 13 mi. southwest of Fredericksburg

Cherry Mountain School
Established 1883, consolidated with Fredericksburg 1949; RTHL 1992.

LOCATION: 7.4 mi. northwest of Fredericksburg on US 87 to Cherry Mountain Road, then right 1.8 mi.

Doss School

Established 1884; still in operation for grades K–8; OTHM 1985.

LOCATION: Doss Community, northwest of Fredericksburg via
US 87 and RM 648

Grapetown School

Established 1859, consolidated with Rocky Hill 1949; RTHL 1984.

LOCATION: 3 mi. east of Fredericksburg on US 290, then south
on Old San Antonio Road 7.2 mi. to Grapetown

Pedernales Rural School

Established 1867, closed 1945; OTHM 1993.

LOCATION: 7.5 mi. south of Fredericksburg on SH 16

For information on the Friends of Gillespie County Country Schools, check the
website www.historicschools.org. For information on all schools in Texas that have
historical markers or are listed in the National Register, go to the Texas Historical
Commission website, www.thc.state.tx.us, and click on Atlas.

9 A Journey back to Nature

On September 25, 2010, as part of its Texas in World War II initiative, the Texas Historical Commission dedicated an Official Texas Historical Marker at the site of the former Longhorn Army Ammunition Plant near Caddo Lake in the East Texas hamlet of Karnack. With a cast of characters ranging from scientists and US Army officials to Russian generals and rock-and-roll stars, the full story of the 8,000-acre Longhorn site is one of both international significance and local determination. For more than half a century the site housed a manufacturing facility for war materiel and weapons of mass destruction. But following more than a decade of work by state and federal agencies, local organizations, and many tenacious individuals, it ultimately became a quiet place of refuge for endangered wildlife and an outdoor classroom dedicated to environmental education and tourism. The journey from natural setting to industrialization and back to nature included many twists and turns along the way.

Anglo settlement of the area around Karnack—previously occupied by generations of Native Americans, principally the Caddos—began in the late nineteenth century. One early settler, Thomas Jefferson Taylor, opened a general store in the village in the 1890s and soon afterwards began amassing large real estate holdings in the region. Reportedly the largest landowner in Harrison County by 1930, he donated land to the State of Texas in 1934 for the creation of Caddo Lake State Park. Taylor's daughter Claudia Alta—better known as Lady Bird—married Lyndon Baines Johnson that same year.[1]

In late 1941, as the US government began preparations for entry into the Second World War, plans for construction of a major

Aerial view of the plant at Longhorn Ordnance Works shortly after construction. Courtesy US Fish and Wildlife Service.

ordnance facility in East Texas began to take shape. On December 15, 1941—eight days after the Japanese bombing of Pearl Harbor, Hawaii, precipitated a declaration of war—the US War Department announced that the new munitions plant would be built in Karnack. As historian Gail Beil wrote, "This was not a random choice. At the time, Lyndon Baines Johnson was a US Representative from Texas and a favorite of President Franklin Delano Roosevelt. Johnson's wealthy, influential father-in-law . . . happened to own a great deal of the land involved and assisted in the purchase of much of the rest."[2]

Originally named Longhorn Ordnance Works, the facility was one of sixty government-owned, contractor-operated plants built in the United States just before and during World War II. Construction began in the spring of 1942 and was completed by July 1943. More than three hundred structures stood on the site, including administration buildings, production facilities, shops, heating and cooling plants, and magazines.

The Monsanto Chemical Company of St. Louis signed on as contractor in charge of operations and brought in more than fifteen hundred employees. Inevitably, a housing shortage arose in the area, and the neighborhood of hastily built homes that sprang up in nearby Marshall for the Monsanto workers became known locally as Yankee Stadium. With the plant quickly operating at full capacity, production of the explosive trinitrotoluene (TNT) quickly reached 360,000 pounds per day. By the end of the war in August 1945, TNT production at the Longhorn plant totaled more than 400 million pounds. Designated a standby facility by the US Army in early 1946, the plant maintained a small contingent of Monsanto staff engaged in cleanup work until the army took over operations that summer and assigned three officers and some eighty-five civilian workers to the facility.[3]

In 1952, with the US involvement in the Korean War, the government ordered the facility, then known as Longhorn Army Ammunition Plant (LAAP), back into production with a new operations contract awarded to the Universal Match Corporation of St. Louis. The company, which had supplied aircraft signal flares to US forces during World War II, assembled a new production plant at the Karnack site by renovating existing structures and building forty new ones to manufacture propellant fuel and to assemble pyrotechnic ammunition, including "photoflash bombs, ground signals, simulators, and shell tracer elements."[4] With the plant once again relegated to standby status following the end of the Korean War, the ammunition manufacturing activities ceased, but soon a new use of the facility would figure prominently in the Cold War and take the LAAP to a top secret government classification level.

Building construction at the LAAP site developed in three phases, with each production facility built to meet specific manufacturing needs. The Monsanto Company operated the TNT facilities in the area known as Plant One and also began the construction of Plant Two, which housed the pyrotechnic operations overseen by Universal Match during the Korean War.

Concurrently, in 1953, work began on a third plant to manufacture solid fuel rocket motors. Constructed at a cost of ten million dollars, Plant Three, operated by the Thiokol Chemical Corporation, incorporated some renovated Plant Two buildings as well as some new buildings and a number of infrastructure improvements, including roads, railroad tracks, and water and wastewater treat-

Guardhouse at the entrance to the Universal Match Corporation facility at LAAP, September 1955. Courtesy US Fish and Wildlife Service.

ment operations. Subsequent expansions, all built by the Brown & Root Construction Company, added more structures to the site through 1962.[5]

With new manufacturing facilities in operation, production at LAAP turned to building rocket motors for short- and intermediate-range missiles—including those dubbed Honest John, Falcon, Lacrosse, Nike Hercules, and Pershing I and II—capable of delivering nuclear warheads. A huge Main Rocket Motor Assembly Building and a Static Test Building overshadowed other structures on the site, and although nuclear materials were not assembled at LAAP, the rocket motor manufacturing activity required high levels of security. Pyrotechnic ammunition manufacturing resumed during the Vietnam War, as well, and continued until 1983.

LAAP's mission as a rocket motor production facility also raised its local profile. While the plant had from the start affected the economy of Harrison County, its operations under the Thiokol Corporation brought the largest workforce in its history as thousands of new employees moved to the area. Plant directors and supervisors gradually became involved in local organizations and even local government, serving on the Greater Marshall Chamber of

Commerce board and the Marshall City Council and encouraging their employees to become active in local politics. Journalist and local historian Max Lale accepted the position of public information officer for Thiokol in 1961, and the community profile of the company and plant operations rose significantly during his tenure in that office. The author of a multivolume installation history of LAAP, Lale retired after suffering a heart attack in 1975, but his influence on the facility's public relations continued.[6]

In September 1988, an event at LAAP propelled the plant and its remote East Texas location onto the international stage. After forty years of Cold War nuclear weapons buildup in both the United States and the Soviet Union, and following almost a decade of negotiations, the two superpowers signed the Intermediate-Range Nuclear Forces (INF) Treaty in December 1987. The treaty called for the destruction of "ground-launched ballistic and cruise missiles with ranges of between 500 and 5,500 kilometers, their launchers and associated support structures and support equipment" within three years of its signing.[7]

Under the terms of the treaty, each country would send a delegation to witness the other's operations. The LAAP was chosen to host the first elimination of US weapons with the static firing of two Pershing missiles. Even with a deadly serious mission at hand, the citizens of nearby Marshall, which hosted the Soviet delegation, provided some levity with a headline in the local paper that read "Welcome Y'all" in both English and Russian, and a number of local businesses ran ads to welcome the visitors as well. Vice Pres. George H. W. Bush led the US delegation, while Soviet chief inspector Nikolai Shabalin led the Russian delegation. With scores of government officials and international news reporters looking on, officials loaded two missiles—a Pershing IA and a Pershing II—into enormous steel harnesses and fired them. Each missile burned for about one minute with a deafening roar, and thick clouds of white smoke filled the sky and the nearby woods. Afterwards, forklifts loaded the cooled, spent material into a massive machine that crushed it "like a garbage truck compacting trash," according to an account in the *New York Times*.[8]

Both countries continued destroying missiles as required by the treaty for the next three years. According to Beil, about every six weeks a delegation of "Soviet scientists, military officers, and KGB agents arrived in Marshall, occupied a special 'secure' wing of the Ramada Inn hotel, and remained for a month." While in town, the Russian visitors also shopped in local stores, visited schools and churches, and even attended local high school football games. In May 1991 the United States fired the last Pershing missile under the agreement, also at LAAP. "With a single motion," wrote a *Dallas Morning News* reporter, "Ambassador Ronald F. Lehman II, director of the US Arms Control and Disarmament Agency, threw the switch igniting the Pershing missile's first stage and ending the Pershing program, which began in 1958. 'Today marks the end of the Pershing but not the end of the INF treaty. The INF treaty itself must carry on,' Mr. Lehman said at the Longhorn Army Ammunition Plant ceremony in Karnack." In all, the US and Soviet governments destroyed 2,692 weapons and more than one thousand missile launchers.[9]

With its primary purpose at a standstill following the INF treaty, the LAAP's workforce was reduced to a fraction of its pretreaty number by the early 1990s, and an official deactivation ceremony took place in June 1995. After decades of industrial use, the site was included in the US Environmental Protection Agency's (EPA) list of federal Superfund sites, an ignominious designation reserved for the nation's most toxic areas. The EPA supervised cleanup operations by US Army and Thiokol personnel over the next several years, with various state agencies and other environmental organizations closely monitoring the project. Hoping to reclaim the area around Caddo Lake and institute new environmental protection measures, a coalition of interested organizations and individuals began looking at ways to turn the land into a public space and at the same time promote their conservation agenda. Legally, the army could either retain the land or offer it to another federal agency. Under that regulation, the bulk of the property, excluding the most polluted areas still under the jurisdiction of the EPA, transferred to the US Fish and Wildlife Service for creation of the Caddo Lake National Wildlife Refuge. While public access to the land was still years away, plans for development of the wildlife refuge began to take shape and generated increasing interest from conservation-ists.[10]

In 1993 musician Don Henley, an East Texas native who gained fame as a member of the Eagles folk rock band, founded the Caddo Lake Institute (CLI), a nonprofit organization with the mission to promote the conservation of the lake and its associated wetlands and parkland as well as to provide educational advocacy programs to teachers and students in the region. In 1996 CLI signed a thirty-year contract to lease more than a thousand acres of former LAAP property—an area known as Harrison Bayou—for an environmental education and research center. Henley, who grew up in the small town of Linden in Cass County and spent much of his youth fishing at Caddo Lake, said, "I'm an education advocate and I want to give something back to the area where I came from." Speaking about his hopes for the institute and referencing the nature preserve in Concord, Massachusetts, made famous by the writer Henry David Thoreau (and which Henley himself had helped preserve by founding the Walden Woods Project earlier in the decade), Henley added that he considered Caddo Lake his Walden Pond. The primary goal of the Caddo Lake project, he said, was "to show some local young people that they have a unique and valuable resource in their own back yard." Indeed, soon after the signing of the lease, the CLI established the Caddo Lake Scholars Program, an initiative aimed at providing practical, on-site training in wetlands expertise to science teachers, who then would help spread the knowledge to their students and fellow teachers. With plans for additional programs and training, the CLI continues to be a major player in the wider conservation movement at Caddo Lake.[11]

Concurrent with the Caddo Lake Institute activities, plans for the larger national wildlife refuge developed through the end of the 1990s and continued into the first decade of the twenty-first century. When a group of business people in Harrison County proposed turning part of the former LAAP land into an industrial park, immediate and vocal opposition arose from increasingly organized conservation advocates. After a series of well-attended public meetings, the industrial park idea failed to gain the necessary governmental approval.

The Caddo Lake National Wildlife Refuge officially opened with a grand public ceremony on September 26, 2009, a date planned to coincide with National Public Lands Day, an annual nationwide observance coordinated by the National Environmental Educational Foundation. Former Texas state legislator and Court of Appeals judge Ben Z. Grant, an active preservationist in Harrison County, served as master of ceremonies. Following presentation of the colors by a local Boy Scout troop, the East Texas–based Caddo Culture Club and members of the Caddo Nation, who traveled from Oklahoma for the occasion, offered ceremonial blessings for the new refuge. Local, state, and national political leaders spoke as well, as did army, EPA, and US Fish and Wildlife Service officials and the manager of the new park. Don Henley, who spoke last, told the large crowd—estimated to number almost a thousand—about catching his first fish at Caddo Lake in 1955, adding, "The older I got, the more I realized the importance of the ecosystem here." An editorial in the *Marshall News-Messenger* praised the opening of the refuge and related the sustained efforts that brought it to fruition. Projecting the positive impact the refuge would likely have on the area economy through a boost in tourism, the writer also recognized its larger mission, saying "this refuge is certainly about more than putting money in the pockets of local citizens. It is about offering a safe habitat for hundreds of species of animals and plants."[12]

Almost exactly a year later, with the Caddo Lake National Wildlife Refuge and the Caddo Lake Institute both welcoming visitors in large numbers, it was time to look back to the Longhorn Army Ammunition Plant legacy with the dedication of an Official Texas Historical Marker and a reunion of former US Army and contractor company staff. Oral histories and media interviews with former plant workers helped personalize the story of the operations that brought international attention to the East Texas woods. Former Thiokol employee Johnny Frazier, whose father and grandfather both worked at LAAP, told a reporter that his father, Milton "Mit" Frazier, went to work as a guard for the Universal Match Corporation in 1954. Reflecting on the current use of the property, he said, "Daddy protected that plant down there for 34 years, and now it's going to be a protected wetlands area. I think that is really fitting."[13]

The former LAAP Superfund site now provides renewed habitat for flora and fauna. An American lady (Vanessa virginiensis) butterfly rests on a native yellow thistle. Courtesy Vanessa Adams.

(opposite) *Vestiges of industrial structures remain at the Caddo Lake National Wildlife Refuge. This remnant of a 1943–45 TNT production building can be seen along the wildlife viewing trail.* Courtesy Vanessa Adams.

Jackson Browne, Don Henley's contemporary and occasional musical collaborator, wrote lyrics for a song he recorded in 1974—with Henley singing backup harmony—that seemed to foreshadow the spirit of the conservation efforts of his friend and others surrounding Caddo Lake and the former LAAP lands: "Some of them were dreamers, and some of them were fools, who were making plans and thinking of the future. With the energy of the innocent, they were gathering the tools they would need to make their journey back to nature."[14]

MARKER LOCATION: 15600 SH 134 at intersection with SH 449, Karnack

THE INVASION OF LAMPASAS COUNTY

In early 1952, as an international war intensified in Korea and the uneasy relationship between the United States and the Soviet Union grew more and more strained, gripping many Americans with fears of a communist menace, US armed forces conducted a training exercise in Central Texas to assess the country's readiness for an armed invasion by enemy forces. Dubbed Operation Long Horn, the massive training maneuver—a joint operation of the US Army and Air Force—centered on Lampasas County. Designed to simulate an enemy invasion and an ensuing war involving nuclear weapons, the operation involved virtually every citizen of the county and affected landowners along a wide swath of Texas stretching from Waco to San Angelo who signed agreements to allow use of their land for campgrounds and mock battles.

With the mock war scheduled to take place from late March through mid-April, more than 115,000 troops began arriving in February. Citizens in Lometa, in the northwestern part of the county, remembered watching as groups of 500 trucks and jeeps passed through town in fifteen-minute intervals. Within days, the sleepy town of 900 swelled to more than 22,000, and the surrounding hills became tent cities filled with soldiers ready to defend the country from invading forces. Local newspapers and radio stations announced the "invasion" plans, and pamphlets distributed throughout the area instructed citizens to resist the enemy until US forces came to the rescue. Local residents enthusiastically embraced the simulation, instituting rationing and even opening a mock USO club at the Methodist church in Lometa.

To carry out the maneuvers, paratroopers of the 82nd Airborne Division from Fort Bragg, North Carolina, acted as the invading army, while members of the 31st Infantry, 47th Infantry, and 1st Armored Divisions from Fort Hood formed the US defense. In a highly publicized event, more than 20,000 people gathered east of Lometa to watch an airdrop of 2,500 soldiers with weapons, vehicles, equipment, and supplies. Once all the troops were in place, the maneuvers kicked into high gear and spread out over an 1,800-square mile battle area ranging from Killeen and Gatesville on the east to Regency and Bend on the west, Evant on the north, and Lampasas on the south. The carefully planned war game called for three primary phases: aggressor forces pushing back US troops and capturing the city of Lampasas; US troops fighting back and taking control of the Lampasas River crossings; and finally, US forces liberating Lampasas and the Colorado River crossings and repelling the aggressor forces. With locals playing their part, Lampasas was captured on April 2, city officials went on trial, and the invading military took over the newspaper, radio stations, and utilities and instituted a curfew affecting everyone in the occupied town. The war raged on for another week, with battles and various maneuvers taking place throughout the countryside. Finally, on April 9, victorious US forces liberated Lampasas.

Operation Long Horn unfortunately left many area ranchers with extensively damaged property. As Janie Potts wrote in her application for an Official Texas Historical Marker about the event, "Camp areas were packed hard as city streets, and it was years before grass grew again. Fences were cut and knocked down, cattle guards were shattered, gates were destroyed, frightened livestock ran away, chickens quit laying, and turkey eggs didn't hatch. After one of the biggest combined Air Force–Army maneuvers in United States history, the brass talked over lessons learned, and ranchers vowed never to sign another easement."

Still, many Lampasas County citizens, as well as military veterans of the maneuvers, look back on the exercise fondly and see the value in its lessons regarding military and home front preparedness. Former paratrooper Tom Hershey visited Lampasas and Lometa in October 2010 and recalled his experiences there as a nineteen-year-old soldier in 1952. As one of the aggressor troops, he said he spent most of his time camping in a cattle pasture. Relationships between the military and civilians were cordial, to say the least. As Potts reported, "Even after the actual fighting began, military leaders said it was hard to conduct the war because the farmers and ranchers would ask you in for coffee in the middle of a battle."

MARKER LOCATION: Lometa Regional Park, south of town on US 190

Sources: Operation Long Horn, Lampasas County, THC marker files; David Lowe, "Soldier Recalls 'Invasion' of Lampasas County in Operation Longhorn [*sic*]," *Lampasas Dispatch Record*, Oct. 26, 2010.

10 Lift High the Water

On a clear spring day in April 2010, three men sat around a table in the middle of a museum in Hidalgo, Texas, reminiscing with a writer about their respective roles in preserving the historic building where they met. All were modest, and one even begged off early rather than talk too much about himself. "These other fellows know as much as I do," he said as he left the table. While they all talked and shared stories, museum patrons passed nearby, viewing detailed exhibits and touring the elaborate industrial complex, while tourists outside photographed birds and wildflowers or walked and biked on nearby trails. Few, if any, of the visitors to the Old Hidalgo Pumphouse that day realized that the historic site they enjoyed remained in existence because of the unselfish work of the three men and others like them. Given the vagaries of historic preservation and municipal planning, the story could easily have had a different ending.

This is a story of why some communities like Hidalgo embrace their history in whatever form it takes and then interpret it, celebrate it, and make it accessible, rather than allowing it to disappear. Viewing such a historic site today, it is difficult to believe there was ever any serious consideration to the contrary, but its history is one marked by both progress and setbacks and ultimately tempered by a series of decisions to persevere despite the odds.

The story of the pump station along a cutoff of the Rio Grande goes back a century, but it also in effect represents part of a much broader agricultural and social history that is considerably older. For countless generations, settlers along the lower Rio Grande—an area known simply as the Valley—have worked to exploit the available water resources for their own existence, to sustain their

148

families, to expand agricultural lands, and to develop viable commerce. The result is one of the most productive areas in the nation, recognized worldwide for the quality and abundance of its crops and livestock. It is also an area that thrives on tourism, both cultural and ecological, and that ultimately brings the story back to what is presently happening in Hidalgo. This is a stratified story with many layers.

Colonial settlement of the area along the lower Rio Grande began in the late 1740s with the establishment of several communities, on both sides of the river, by Spanish native José de Escandón in what was then known as Nuevo Santander. The celebrated military leader enjoyed widespread political support for his vision to colonize a vast area of northern Mexico that reached from Tampico north to present-day Corpus Christi, Texas. In all, he established more than twenty villas, many of which remain in existence more than two and a half centuries later. One of those grew up near Mission San Joaquín del Monte, a *visita* or submission serving Reynosa. Known early as La Habitación and Rancho San Luis (San Luisita) and later as Edinburg and eventually Hidalgo, it served as the first seat of government for Hidalgo County, established in the years following Texas statehood. It retained that distinction until the early twentieth century, when political and economic pressures, coupled with periodic flooding, caused officials to move the county seat to Chapin, present Edinburg. Hidalgo failed to materialize as a rival to the rapidly developing railroad towns farther north and instead grew incrementally but steadily. It remained strategically viable in terms of the local economy, however, because of its proximity to the river. Water from the Rio Grande tapped at Hidalgo proved to be a determinant of sustainable growth throughout the county.[1]

Plans for irrigation systems along the Rio Grande date from the colonial era, when Escandón envisioned a network of *acequias* similar to those successfully used by missions along the San Antonio River. Such gravity-flow systems failed to work in the Valley, though, where the shallow riverbed proved impractical for redirecting water to the higher elevations of the surrounding land. Large-scale irrigation there was only feasible if the water could be lifted, and in the early days of settlement in that region the requisite technology for widespread use of such systems did not yet exist. It was not until the advent of practical pumps, steam engines, and lift stations that irrigation on such a scale was even possible. As a result, ranching predominated in the semiarid lands of the area during that era.

A major effort to employ an integrated irrigation system in the Valley began in the 1890s through the direction of John Closner, a key figure in both law enforcement and agricultural development of the area (see sidebar). A Wisconsin native of Swiss descent, Closner came to Texas about 1870, settling first in Bosque County and initially working as a freight hauler. By 1884 he was in Hidalgo. There, he worked in local law enforcement, serving for years as sheriff and then in other county offices as well. He also made shrewd investments in inexpensive farmland, eventually acquiring 45,000 acres. In 1895 he initiated the first large-scale Rio Grande irrigation system with an elaborate system of portable engines and pumps. Additionally, he joined with other local investors, including noted businessman and Harlingen founder Lon Hill, to convince the St. Louis, Brownsville, and Mexico Railway to extend a line westward to the area, opening up important new markets.[2]

Closner's efforts gained widespread attention through development of his San Juan Plantation (at the present town of San Juan), which featured a diverse crop selection that included alfalfa, melons, nuts, bananas, tobacco, sugarcane, and vegetables. Irrigation of the rich alluvial soils of the Valley, coupled with the region's long growing season, allowed him to manage multiple crop yields annually. And establishment of a *colonias* system of self-contained tenant communities directly tied to his operations ensured a steady and inexpensive source of labor that underpinned the plantation structure. Closner understood the formula for success at the time, and his land produced bounteous and noteworthy crops. When his sugarcane won top honors at the 1904 Louisiana Purchase Exposition (St. Louis World's Fair), ironically beating out competition from the sugar stronghold of Louisiana, it was big news.[3]

Stories quickly spread about the remarkable agricultural potential of the Valley, and soon substantial outside investment capital—much of it initially from sugar concerns in the Bayou State—

flowed into South Texas to fund new developments and usher in unprecedented growth. By the close of the first decade of the twentieth century, planning was well under way for the development of permanent water delivery systems substantial enough to lift Rio Grande waters miles beyond the river's banks. This would result in a boom era of farming never before experienced in Texas. At the center of the planning were small riverine communities, such as Hidalgo, which served as the gateways for the irrigation systems.

Investors and industrial engineers quickly formed irrigation companies to take advantage of what was, in effect, a new land rush. Among them was the Louisiana–Rio Grande Canal Company, which began operations at Hidalgo in 1909 and formally incorporated the following year to ensure further capitalization for its aggressive plans. Development at the Hidalgo site escalated at a dizzying pace. It began with placement of a thirty-six-inch steam pump powered by a Twin City engine. At the same time, several thousand workers under the direction of chief engineer E. B. Gore used mule-powered fresnos, or scoops, to excavate miles of canals and feeder lines. The irrigation company also employed more than two hundred workers to cut and haul firewood for the steam boilers that powered the engines. Mesquite was in abundant supply in the area, but it was also a hindrance to the cultivation of agricultural lands, so its removal aided not only the pumping operations but land development as well.[4]

With a flush of new capital, the company continued to grow the operation at Hidalgo in 1911, adding a second pump, powered by an Allis-Chalmers engine, as well as new boilers and a towering, one-hundred-foot smokestack. The following year it expanded the facilities again for a new pump house, additional boilers, and a second smokestack. The earliest structures were clad in sheet metal, but the company invested in greater design detail with the 1912 addition. Built of brick, it reflected elements of the Mission Revival style, including a distinctive arched parapet. The regional style, popular from the 1890s to the 1920s, accurately referenced the area's Spanish colonial heritage while also contributing a sense of permanence to the site.

The 1911–12 improvements to the system significantly expanded

its capacity. Pump stations southeast of the town and farther north effectively lifted water from the Rio Grande and transported it beyond a geologic landform, known as "the ridge," that proved a deterrent to early irrigation efforts in that area. By conquering the ridge, the effective range of the Hidalgo pumps grew from forty thousand acres to more than seventy-two thousand acres, providing a vital water source for agricultural production near the communities of Pharr, San Juan, and Alamo. With increased demand, the station operated twenty-four hours a day, and the distinctive sound of its engines and pumps became a way of life for residents in the surrounding area. It was the sound of progress, as many observed, and few—especially those employed in the process—offered any complaints.[5]

In 1920 the Louisiana–Rio Grande Canal Company transferred its assets to the Hidalgo County Water Improvement District No. 2 (now Hidalgo County Irrigation District No. 2). Work continued unabated in the ensuing years, but in 1933 the district faced what could have been a catastrophic change of events. Late in August of that year a tropical storm formed east of Cuba and intensified steadily as a hurricane when it entered the Gulf of Mexico, taking an arrow-straight course toward the lower Texas coast. It went ashore just north of Brownsville as a category three storm late on September 4 and immediately tracked south-southwest over the Hidalgo County area. Property loss was extensive, with most of the region's citrus crop destroyed. (A hurricane that crossed the region exactly one month earlier had already weakened the crop extensively.) Record rainfall in the river basin led to floods that eventually formed a new channel for the Rio Grande below Hidalgo, effectively cutting off the pumps from their source. District officials wasted little time in charting a new course for their facilities, though, and by 1935 they cut a channel from the new riverbed to supply water to the pump house. The channel required regular dredging, but the

(opposite) *The Hidalgo Pumphouse complex, like many industrial sites, evolved over time as operations expanded to meet the demand of a growing service area.* Photograph by Susan Oglesbee.

system worked, and the Hidalgo plant remained online, even increasing its capacity again in the 1940s and 1950s.[6]

There were other storms and floods over the years, and even extended freezes that proved equally devastating to local farming operations, but still the pump station performed efficiently, continually meeting the agricultural demands of the area. By the 1970s, however, it showed its age, and planning moved forward for a more modern replacement station farther downriver. With work on the new all-electric facility completed by 1983, the district decommissioned the old pump station at the end of Second Street in Hidalgo after almost three-quarters of a century in service.

There were no immediate plans for repurposing the abandoned pump station, and so it declined, subject to weather, vandalism, overgrown vegetation, and occasional floodwaters. This is where the men at the table become a part of the building's history. One of them was a McAllen veterinarian named Dr. Robert Norton, a transplanted Minnesotan who in the 1980s served as chair of the Hidalgo County Historical Commission. Under his leadership the local commission earned a reputation as one of the leading local preservation groups in the state. It actively participated in the state marker program and other activities, in the process helping establish a preservation ethic throughout the county. Residents who valued their heritage knew the local commission supported their interests, and members of the group worked in every community to record and save elements of the past.

In 1984 word reached Norton that workers had started demolishing the pump plant, so he drove to the site to investigate. He was already familiar with the property. "I just came down here [on occasion] because I enjoyed seeing the steam pumps, and so forth and so on, and generally you couldn't get in here. But," he added, "I enjoyed looking through the old doorway." When he drove over to investigate the demolition, though, he discovered workers had already removed the sheet metal from the north wall of the structure. They told him, "In two weeks we're supposed to have this all torn down and bulldoze dirt over everything and get all those old pumps covered up." The district's board of directors, understandably, had serious concerns about public health and safety liability issues associated with the abandoned building.[7]

Norton followed up his site visit with a trip to nearby San Juan, where he met with a district official and confirmed the plans for the old pump house. He then opened a discussion with the Hidalgo County Chamber of Commerce, and there he found a kindred soul in manager Joe Vera III. The chamber and the city had long worked to preserve local history through the promotion of heritage tourism programs, so the chamber board was willing to consider a partnership effort to preserve the structure if it could be proven to be financially feasible. Almost immediately, though, the chamber, city, and Heritage Foundation of Hidalgo County faced a major setback to their plans when inspectors discovered asbestos throughout the structure. Planning remained on hold for several years while both city officials and local preservationists sought funding for the asbestos removal. In a Catch-22 situation, though, no one would fund a restoration until the asbestos could be removed, and no one would fund that part of the work. Ultimately, over time, the cost of abatement dropped, allowing the city and chamber to provide funding through local and federal community development block grants. That proved to be the key to additional support, with the Meadows Foundation of Dallas offering seed money for replacement of the roof over the pumps to seal off the interior and allow other work to proceed. In 1991, following a working retreat of city and chamber leaders, the city, under the direction of the council and Mayor John David Franz, launched a capital campaign and obtained the largest source of funding through federal enhancement grant support from the US Department of Transportation. Additionally, the Texas Historical Commission provided important technical advice for the project.

While outside sources paid for structural repairs and the development of interior exhibit space, volunteers worked to restore the pumps and other hardware. Enter another of the men at the table, a man named Spurgeon "Spud" Brown, a McAllen native and also a relatively new member of the Heritage Foundation of Hidalgo County at the time of the restoration. When asked what motivated

The massive centrifugal pump, sometimes referred to as a snail, is an integral component of the Hidalgo Pumphouse. Photograph by Susan Oglesbee.

him to join Dr. Norton, he said simply, "Well, he needed help. We had roofs that were down. We had water in the pump pits. It was a mess in here." But, Brown added, "He had more energy than I did, so I pitched in there and was working right with him." The two men—the right men at the right time, it seemed—were soon joined by others, and over the years countless volunteers contributed sweat equity to the cause.[8]

While the volunteers had energy and a shared vision, they lacked the technical expertise about what they were preserving, so they grew to rely on the third man at the table, Walter Wisdom. Born in Hidalgo, Wisdom had three generations of family ties to the old pump station: both his grandfather and his father—Rufus Lee Wisdom Sr. and Rufus Lee Wisdom II, respectively—worked there. His father began as a laborer working to keep the giant engines running, and so his title became engineer. As a teenager in 1975, Walter Wisdom started by assisting his father during the summer months, and then he too signed on full-time, working on the pumps, boilers, and engines until 1983. Among his projects during that time was assisting with the dismantling of one smokestack, which had rapidly deteriorated, thus posing a safety hazard, and the removal

Part of the inner workings of the pumping operations. Preservation of such complex sites involves the continual and systematic efforts of a vast network of volunteers. Photograph by Susan Oglesbee.

of boilers. Ironically, the site of the smokestack was at the same location as that of the table around which the three men gathered in April 2010. Each would be quick to note that their efforts were neither singular nor exemplary. Rather, they represented a much larger effort that drew on resources from within the community and city government, as well as the Hidalgo County Historical Commission, the Hidalgo County Historical Society, and the Heritage Foundation of Hidalgo County. And there was also support and recognition from the Smithsonian Institution and from the Texas Historical Commission, through its historic designations and a nascent heritage tourism project called Los Caminos del Rio.[9]

Once there was a shared vision for the site from all the stakeholders, the various aspects of the seemingly overwhelming preservation and interpretation project began to coalesce. Along the way, those involved in the work enjoyed the recognition that came with having an Official Texas Historical Marker placed at the site and having the property listed in the National Register of Historic Places. Federal officials even designated it a National Historic Landmark, the most prestigious recognition for a historic site in the United States. The State Capitol, the Alamo, the Fair Park Centennial Buildings in Dallas, and NASA's Apollo Mission Control are among the other select properties in Texas that share that unique distinction.

After countless meetings and untold hours of planning, fundraising, and restoration by a wide spectrum of individuals over many years, the Old Hidalgo Pumphouse officially opened to the public as a museum and education center in 1999 under the direction of the City of Hidalgo. Now part of the World Birding Center as well, the historic site serves not only as a focal point for community activities and an important reminder of local heritage, but also as the centerpiece of a lavishly landscaped park. On April 4, 2009, during the centennial year for the Rio Grande pumping operation, scores of visitors and friends gathered in the adjacent amphitheatre to celebrate history along the river. They came to experience a special presentation that featured an original musical piece *Tapping the River,* commissioned by the city and composed by Carl Seale of McAllen. As they listened to the McAllen Symphonic Band perform Seale's stirring musical interpretation of the river and its natural and cultural history, they watched as a visual display of compelling historic images and striking contemporary photos put together by the father-son team of Vernon and Paul Denman lit up a screen set against the backdrop of the pump plant edifice. Appropriately, Mayor Franz provided the narration.

Now more than a century after the first boilers slowly built up the steam to power the engines that lifted the water of the Rio Grande through miles of canals to farms across the region, giving new life to the Valley, the Old Hidalgo Pumphouse remains in silent service to the people. Once one of maybe a dozen such plants that marked a formative era of development for the area, it is now the last intact reminder of the role steam power played in irrigation. But why is it the only such site that remains? What motivates a small town such as Hidalgo to preserve its past when others let it slip away? The answer is complex and ongoing, as each generation has to renew the effort, but it certainly involves a preservation ethic, a progressive municipal government that realizes the connection between the past and the future, a dedicated group of volunteers who work as a team despite the odds, committed funding sources based on mutual trust and proven accomplishments—and maybe even a well-placed table or two for planning and later reminiscing. Dr. Robert Norton, who most agree was responsible for the original vision of what is now the Old Hidalgo Pumphouse (and who, sadly, passed away in December 2010), summed it all up in his usual modest way when he observed, "It's still here. That's my feeling toward it; it's still here."[10]

MARKER LOCATION: S Second St. at the river levee, Hidalgo

DAM, DITCH, AND AQUEDUCT

Throughout Texas history and prehistory, the acquisition, containment, and exploitation of water have influenced the development of civilization, as reflected in settlement patterns, land use, and community determination. The significance of water is also clearly evident in the number and diversity of Official Texas Historical Markers that deal with the resource. There are, for example, markers commemorating reservoirs, water towers, ditches, windmills, irrigation systems, swimming holes, artesian wells, springs, municipal water systems, floods, cisterns, healing baths, streams, and even rainmakers. One marker with the particularly alliterative title of "Dam, Ditch, and Aqueduct" interprets the value of water to the existence of Mission San Francisco de la Espada, established in 1731 as the southernmost Spanish mission in the immediate vicinity of San Antonio.

Using long-standing technology and Native American labor, Franciscan missionaries at Espada established a complex of interrelated structures in the early 1740s centering on a dam that backed up the San Antonio River and channeled water into *acequias,* or irrigation ditches, for the mission proper and its vast cultivated fields nearby. The extensive alluvial acreage watered by the gravity-flow ditches produced, as the marker text noted, "maize, beans, melons, calabashes, sweet potatoes, and cotton." A large rock and mortar aqueduct—essentially an arched water bridge evocative of similar works by the Romans, Greeks, and other ancient cultures—carried water over Piedras Creek (Six Mile Creek), ensuring a steady flow of water.

Repaired and restored over the years to ensure its viability, and maintained in the late twentieth century by the Espada Ditch Company, the mission's water system holds a unique place in the history of successful riparian exploitation in the United States. As a result, it is not only a Recorded Texas Historic Landmark and listed in the National Register of Historic Places, but also a National Historic Landmark, the highest level of recognition for a historic site.

Espada aqueduct, San Antonio. Courtesy Texas Department of Transportation.

It is now part of the San Antonio Missions National Historical Park and open to the public.

MARKER LOCATION: Espada Road, San Antonio

Sources: Mission San Francisco de la Espada Dam, Ditch, and Aqueduct, Bexar County, THC marker files; Clint E. Davis, "San Francisco de la Espada Mission," *New Handbook of Texas,* vol. 5, pp. 845–46.

11 The Normal on Chautauqua Hill

A prominent ridgeline, part of the vast Balcones Escarpment system that defines the eastern edges of the Texas Hill Country, provides a dramatic backdrop for the cultural landscape of San Marcos, the seat of Hays County. At the eastern end of the ridgeline is a stately castlelike edifice that visually dominates smaller buildings dotting the nearby hillside. Constructed of buff-colored brick and topped with a red roof, the structure is evocative of an earlier time, conveying a strong sense of the past to the present cityscape. Known as Old Main, it is the iconic symbol of Texas State University.

The high promontory on which Old Main rests was known in the early days of San Marcos as Wood's Hill, so named because of its ownership by Judge W. D. Wood. In the 1880s, the Reverend Horace M. Dubose, a Houston minister, visited Wood's Hill and proclaimed it an ideal location for a Texas Chautauqua. Dubose proposed a summertime educational gathering for the general public, modeled on a program established at Chautauqua, New York, in the 1870s, that would feature a broad range of topics from religion, science, and philosophy to the arts and history. Judge Wood agreed to sell the land, and in June 1885 the San Marcos Sunday School Assembly and Summer Institute, better known as the Texas Chautauqua, formed. One of the first directors was Edward S. Northcraft, who would later figure prominently in another and more lasting phase of history associated with the hill. Meetings got underway late that summer beneath a large tent, and by the following year there was an immense (sixty-foot by ninety-foot) wooden tabernacle in place that could accommodate more than a thousand participants on what was by then called Chautauqua Hill. Additionally, the educational center included a restaurant tent, campsites, and water fountains, with access provided by horse-drawn vehicles.[1]

While early accounts of the Texas Chautauqua indicated its potential, citing overflowing crowds in attendance at the summer events, the social experiment fell on hard times in only a few short years, and the organization found itself in considerable debt to both the city and a number of individuals, including Edward Northcraft and his daughter, Lucy Northcraft Burleson. In an effort to readjust its liabilities, the organization deeded twenty-five acres back to Judge Wood in the early 1890s, and he in turn provided clear title to eleven acres at the crest of the hill. The last summer event evidently occurred in 1895, although the organization remained in effect several years longer, hoping to escape from under the mounting debt. Eventually the Texas Chautauqua defaulted on several obligations, including a loan from the City of San Marcos. City minutes detail what happened next: "Whereupon, on June 7, 1899, Judge Wood presented a resolution to the City Council of the City of San Marcos requesting the City to instruct W. O. Hutchison, trustee, to foreclose the deeds and sell the Chautauqua property as specified in the deeds of trust."[2]

The property thus went up for public sale at the courthouse in August, and the city registered the high bid of $2,375 for the eleven acres.[3] The following day, city officials offered to convey the land to the State of Texas for development of what was then known as a normal school, an institution designed specifically for the training of teachers. Based on a European idea and promoted widely in the United States through the innovative work and advocacy of Massachusetts educational reformer Horace Mann, the "Father of the Common School Movement," the so-called normals established standards, or norms, for educating teachers, thereby driving the development of high-quality education programs throughout the nation.

Although Mann began his reform efforts in the antebellum period, the experiment failed to take hold in the South until after the Civil War. Texas established its first teacher school, the Sam Houston Normal Institute (now Sam Houston State University), at Huntsville in 1879 and followed it in 1881 with one for African American students at Prairie View (now Prairie View A&M University) near Hempstead. Politicians soon began to consider two other normals to serve the growing areas of North Texas and Southwest Texas. The one for the northern part of the state opened in 1890 at Denton and is now the University of North Texas, but development of a normal for the last region remained problematic because of the lack of adequate sponsors or land donations. As a result, the state approved a stopgap measure that would allow the existing Coronal Institute in San Marcos to offer teacher certification classes. A respected private school founded in 1868 by Orlando Newton Hollingsworth and later operated by the Methodist Episcopal Church, South, Coronal was located on a hillside southwest of the Hays County Courthouse square. The association between the state and the private school proved to be short-lived, however, and the legislature soon moved to consider other options.[4]

After an initial bill for a San Marcos normal filed by Rep. Fred Cocke received committee approval but eventually failed in 1899, Sen. J. B. Dibrell filed a similar bill the same year that received approval, thanks in large part to the support of Rep. Fergus Kyle. The bill made the establishment of a normal contingent on the conveyance of Chautauqua Hill, an action the city had already set in motion. In the following legislative session, Dibrell and Kyle again teamed up, this time for the successful passage of a bill to fund the new school. Gov. Joseph D. Sayers signed the bill in 1901, and planning began for the new Southwest Texas Normal School, which would be placed administratively under the State Board of Education with oversight by three local trustees.[5]

Initially, all classes were to be held in one central building, so it had to be adequate in size and layout to accommodate a wide range of activities. Equally important was the dramatic hilltop setting, which seemed to call for a strong architectural statement that would convey a sense of permanence and a commitment to lofty public values. To provide such a design, the trustees turned to local architect Edward Northcraft, who had extensive experience with public buildings as well as the building trades.

Born in Fulton, Indiana, in 1833, Northcraft spent his late teen

Early photograph of Old Main shows its dramatic setting on Chautauqua Hill.
Courtesy Texas State University, San Marcos, Texas.

years and early adulthood in Missouri, where he met and wed Mary Elizabeth Donalson. Following the end of the Civil War and the birth of their first child, Lucy, in June 1865, the couple moved to San Marcos. In the 1870 census Northcraft listed his occupation as farmer, but by 1880 he is shown as a jail contractor. In the ensuing years, though, he gained considerable experience in designing and overseeing the construction of numerous public buildings, including courthouses and schools. He even patented a fire extinguishing system for cotton gins. As state superintendent of public buildings from 1887 to 1891, he worked on the State Orphan Asylum in Corsicana, the House of Correction and Reformatory in Gatesville, and the State Capitol in Austin. Significantly, he also served as supervising architect of the main building at Sam Houston Normal Institute designed by Arthur Muller. The massing, detailing, and setting of that structure in particular would figure prominently in Northcraft's later design of Old Main at San Marcos.[6]

Using the Victorian Gothic style popular at the turn of the twentieth century, Northcraft used the hilltop setting to his advantage. As architectural historian Willard Robinson noted, the design provided "a condition dramatizing the vertical aspects of the perpen-

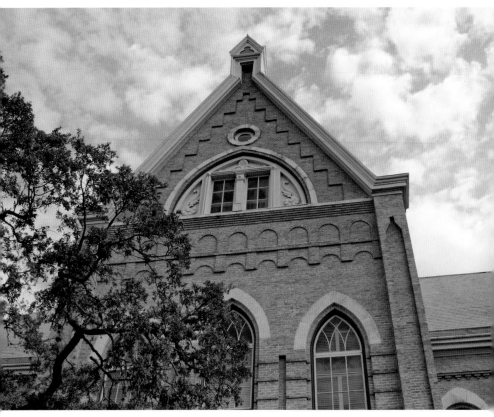

This photograph of a gable treatment on Old Main shows architect Edward Northcraft's attention to ornamentation. Photograph by Cynthia J. Beeman.

dicular style." Appearing from a distance to rise from the solid rock of the ridgeline in organic fashion, the walls of the structure continue upward to a massive roof structure accented by corner towers with pyramidal roofs. Further accenting the soaring verticality, Northcraft deftly incorporated steep-sided gables, roof dormers, intricate finials, and high arched windows with contrasting hood moulds, all with the purpose of moving the eyes heavenward. While his design was less exuberant than Muller's work, it nonetheless made a powerful architectural statement.[7]

On the inside, the Main Building followed a floor plan similar to that of Old Main at Huntsville. Originally, there were eight classrooms on the ground floor, with transecting hallways. On the second floor, four classrooms flanked a central chapel. According to

Robinson, such chapel spaces were common in main buildings of the Victorian era, reflecting "the focus upon morality, religion, and ethics that typified the values of the period." Students attended the required weekly services there, as well as concerts, public speaking engagements, and a variety of school activities.[8]

Work on the Main Building at Southwest Texas began in earnest in 1902, with Francis Fischer and R. C. Lambie as general contractors, but it soon met with some unexpected delays, most significantly the sealing of a cave on the northeast corner of the proposed foundation. Following that, the foundation and first-floor walls rose steadily, and that same year Governor Sayers assisted in the laying of the cornerstone and predicted the new structure would be a monument to his administration and to the work of the Texas legislature. A subsequent election resulted in a new governor, S. W. T. Lanham, who made a trip to Chautauqua Hill early in 1903 for a personal inspection of the Main Building with architect Northcraft. The construction ended later that year, just in time for the arrival of the first class, which consisted of 303 students. Principal Thomas G. Harris and sixteen faculty members provided instruction and direction, and among them was Northcraft's daughter, Lucy Burleson, who served as secretary, English assistant, and the school's first librarian. There were no dormitories for the students, and many of them lived in boarding houses scattered near the base of the steep hill. Then, as now, it took considerable stamina to attend classes in Old Main.[9]

With teacher education as the core of the curriculum, students agreed to teach school one year for each year they attended the normal, and the course of instruction generally took up to three years. In keeping with the scholastic social structure of the time, there were a number of early literary societies, including the Shakespeare, Harris Blair, and Idyllic. Later groups included the United Order of Fiery Tops, the Elberta Peaches Club, the Comenians, and the Pierians. There were few interscholastic sports activities in the early days, but debate proved particularly competitive and popular. Contests involving other normals, most notably the rival North Texas group, drew large crowds as school teams debated current social issues. In 1916, for example, the Southwest Texas club bested the North Texas team by arguing the affirmative on the resolution "That immigration into the United States should be further restricted by the imposition of a literary test."[10]

In its early years, the regulations and policies set by the normal were an accurate reflection of the times and the surrounding community. They covered both campus time and personal time. A 1905 set of rules by Principal Harris, for example, set tight limits for scholastic studies: "School will be in session from 8:45 a.m. till 2 p.m. on each Tuesday, Wednesday, Thursday, Friday, and Saturday. Home study periods will be from 3:30 p.m. till 5:30 p.m. and from 7 p.m. till 10 p.m. each Monday, Tuesday, Wednesday, Thursday, and Friday. From 2 p.m. on Saturday till noon Monday students may devote their time to rest, appropriate exercise and recreation, attendance on Sunday School and Church services and other duties." And just to emphasize the importance of study, Harris added: "The purpose which justifies the existence of the Normal is the preparation of young men and women to teach, not to afford opportunity to marry. Any marked indications that students are spending their time in courting, or in being courted, or in trifling about such matters, will be deemed sufficient for the prompt removal of such students from the Normal." To aid in the enforcement of his regulations, the principal let it be known he expected full cooperation from the keepers of local boarding houses as well.[11]

Through the formative years, Harris managed to keep the school program focused, as did his successor, C. E. Evans, who took over in 1911. As a result, the school grew in both numbers of students and programs offered. One particularly important change came in 1914 with the establishment of an on-site training school that allowed the would-be teachers to hone their skills in a real classroom setting with their own students. As noted in the 1915 course catalog, "The practice school bears the same relation to the profession of teaching as the laboratory does to science, or the work shop does to Manual Training." While much of the training school centered on expectations in larger schools, the type more commonly found in towns, there was also a one-room schoolhouse setting "in the Westover section" for those who might pursue careers in rural areas of the state. In the days before mandated consolidations, one-room schools remained viable options for many of the students.[12]

By the second decade of the twentieth century, Southwest Texas State Normal showed steady signs of permanence and continued progress. There were new ancillary structures on the campus, including a library and classroom buildings for education, science, and manual arts. There were also new programs that gradually, under the leadership of Evans, began moving the institution on a course that would expand it from a normal to a full college in the future. Planning for that eventuality, the trustees acquired additional land, and the campus soon grew from eleven acres to more than twenty. Also, along the San Marcos River, just below the hill, the trustees initially leased several acres of land for what became Riverside Park, later named for mathematics instructor S. M. "Froggy" Sewell, who proposed its development. Sewell Park became an important recreational area for the students, albeit within the realm of acceptable mores of the time, as well as the site of an annual water pageant that began in 1920.[13]

The formal transition from normal to college came in 1916 with approval by the board of regents (which had earlier superseded the local trustee system). As a result, the institution developed a curriculum that would guide students toward degrees and not simply educational certification. Progress on that front continued even through the years of the Great War, and in 1919 Southwest Texas State Teachers College conferred its first bachelor's degree on Mamie E. Brown, daughter of mathematics teacher J. S. Brown. A longtime student of the school, Miss Brown, in effect, held three separate teaching certifications, which no doubt helped her secure a position with Texas A&I College in Kingsville.[14]

The year 1919 also marked the death of Old Main architect Edward S. Northcraft. Following a long and distinguished career, he had once again turned his attention to farming, although he continued to live in San Marcos. His obituary in the *San Marcos Record* spoke fondly of his many contributions, both to his profession and to his hometown. "It was said of him," the article noted, "that he was a man who believed in giving a 'square deal.' Many carpenters throughout Texas cherish his memory because of his kindness of heart which prompted him to find a job for them when they were out of work." And, it continued, "What must have been his experience. How great his influence. Only eternity itself can gather up the influence of a life full of 'length of days' as his was." Lamenting the loss of Northcraft and several other prominent civic leaders that year, the obituary writer added, "One of the great assets San Marcos has is its citizens who have been here for a long period of years. It is their influence that has made the town what it is. It is deplorable that we have lost so many of them in the last few weeks. There have recently gone from us those who have been here from twenty to fifty years. Their going has impoverished San Marcos. Let us cherish those who remain with us."[15]

Following a simple funeral service at the family home, the body of Edward Northcraft was laid to rest at San Marcos Cemetery. A landmark there is the cemetery chapel—actually an open-sided pavilion or tabernacle—he designed in 1886. Listed in the National Register of Historic Places and designated a Recorded Texas Historic Landmark, the small chapel features elements of Carpenter Gothic design with board-and-batten siding, a cruciform plan, and distinctive pointed archways.[16]

While Northcraft's cemetery chapel and other structures remain as legacies of his work, his masterpiece is Old Main, which continues in use more than a century after its construction. One of the state's few remaining "temples of knowledge" from a golden era of collegiate design that reached from the antebellum era to the early twentieth century, it still provides a dramatic architectural statement. School officials have systematically worked to maintain the historic structure over the years, providing funds for restoration and rehabilitation. In 1963 the Texas State Historical Survey Committee (now Texas Historical Commission) recognized it as a Recorded Texas Historic Landmark, and a sizeable crowd later gathered at the site for a special dedication ceremony. Among the special guests was Helen Hornsby Crawford, the last surviving member of the original faculty.[17]

Less than a decade later, another crowd gathered on the hill, this time to dedicate a newly restored Old Main. Guests at that event included the school's most famous alumnus, Pres. Lyndon B. Johnson. In his remarks on that occasion, he observed, "One that is not proud of his ancestry cannot have great hopes for his prosperity, and by coming back to the scenes of our childhood, back on this old quadrangle in front of Old Main is rather concrete evidence of our pride in our ancestry."[18]

In 1983 Old Main was formally listed in the National Register and thereby recognized for its historical statewide significance in the fields of education and architecture. Completed in 1903 on eleven acres atop Chautauqua Hill to accommodate 303 students seeking certification as teachers, it is now the historic centerpiece of a sprawling campus that serves more than thirty thousand students working toward myriad degrees in a wide range of disciplines. Although the name, scope, mission, and cultural landscape of the school have changed over the years, the hope and promise so strongly reflected in the design of its first building remain viable objectives of the institution.

MARKER LOCATIONS

Old Main: Old Main Drive on the campus of Texas State University–San Marcos. Access by vehicle is limited by university parking regulations.

San Marcos City Cemetery, site of Northcraft's chapel: on RR 12, just over 1 mile north of the Hays County Courthouse. There is a Recorded Texas Historic Landmark marker on the chapel and also an Official Texas Historical Marker commemorating the history of the cemetery.

NORTHCRAFT'S SAN MARCOS CHURCHES

While Edward S. Northcraft's name is most often associated with public buildings, such as Old Main at Texas State University, he also designed a number of other structures, including churches. Two examples of his ecclesiastical work that survive in his hometown of San Marcos have been commemorated with state markers.

The Reverend Henry Thomas, a circuit preacher, established the First Christian Church in 1853 with what he described as "two zealous members." The congregation grew steadily from that inauspicious beginning, though, and had fifty members within three years. The first church building was on Guadalupe Street, but following a split over doctrinal matters, several progressive members who withdrew asked Northcraft to design a new sanctuary on San Antonio Street in 1893. Using simple classical detailing that featured pediments and columns and emphasized the templelike massing of the rectilinear building, the architect provided a design theme reflected in later structures on the site as the congregation continued to grow. The church has since moved to new facilities, but the heritage of the early buildings remains an important part of its cherished past.

The First United Methodist Church dates to 1847 and the organizational work of a circuit rider, the Reverend Alfred B. F. Kerr. The congregation met in homes, a log house, and two earlier buildings at the present site on Hutchison Street, the latter building dating to 1872. Apparently the second building did not hold up well, for a December 1892 newspaper article noted, "A plan has been adopted for the new Methodist church and E. Northcroft [sic], architect, has been employed to superintend the work. The old building is now being torn down. . . . Everybody rejoices that the old eyesore is to disappear and that a sightly church is to take its place." For the design of the new sanctuary, Northcraft chose elements of the Gothic Revival style, which featured steeply pitched rooflines,

(opposite) *Another San Marcos landmark designed by Northcraft is the sanctuary of the First United Methodist Church.* Photograph by Dan K. Utley.

lancet windows and door openings, squared towers, gable barge-board detailing, and a central tripartite window treatment on the primary façade.

Together, the stately sanctuaries of the First Christian Church and the First United Methodist Church in San Marcos provide a strong visual record of Northcraft's design capabilities. They also demonstrate, as does Old Main, that he understood fundamental details of the popular architectural styles of his era and that he was skilled in adapting them to local sites and uses.

MARKER LOCATIONS: The sanctuary of the First United Methodist Church, designated a Recorded Texas Historic Landmark, is located at 129 Hutchison Street. An Official Texas Historical Subject Marker for the First Christian Church is at 216 W. San Antonio Street.

Sources: First Christian Church and First United Methodist Church, Hays County, THC marker files and NR files; websites www.fumcsm.org and www.fcc-sm.org, accessed December 18, 2010; *Dallas Morning News,* December 10, 1892, n.p.

ORLANDO NEWTON HOLLINGSWORTH

Given the brevity and focus of historical marker inscriptions, some layers of stories often go unexplored in lieu of other relevant information. Such is the case with the opening line of the state marker for the site of Coronal Institute, the San Marcos school that pre-dated Southwest Texas Normal Institute. The text reads simply: "Established 1868 by educator O. N. Hollingsworth." Since the inscription offers no further information on the founder, his personal history, or his accomplishments, and since he is not himself the subject of a state marker, the reader is left with little to evaluate his historical significance. But one of the stories beyond the marker in this case is that Hollingsworth was an interesting and complex historical character who, it turns out, was also a pivotal player in the history of Texas education.

Orlando Newton Hollingsworth was born in 1836 in Alabama. Following his father's death, his mother moved the family to Rusk

ROSA KENDRICK
MEMORIAL HALL
—1896—

THE INFLUENCE OF
CORONAL
WILL LIVE IN OUR
HEARTS FOREVER
CORONAL CLUB
1940

A plaque commemorating Coronal Institute is located on the grounds of the First United Methodist Church, San Marcos. Photograph by Dan K. Utley.

County, in East Texas. He attended the University of Virginia, and when the Civil War broke out, he joined the Third Texas Cavalry of the Confederate Army and served under Capt. Robert H. Cumby, a Rusk legislator and planter. Severely wounded in the 1862 Battle of Corinth, Mississippi, Hollingsworth eventually returned home, where he married Ruth Grace Katherine "Kate" Platner in 1864. The couple soon moved to San Antonio, where O. N. taught in a private school, and in 1866 they moved north to San Marcos when he took over a school started by Charlton Yellowley. Two years later, Hollingsworth formally established the Coronal Institute, so named, it is said, because it was like a crown resting on a hill.

Relying on his personal integrity and a strong vision for high-quality educational programming, Hollingsworth invested heavily in the construction of a two-story stone schoolhouse at the corner of Moore and Hutchison Streets, and in the first years of its existence Coronal Institute showed great promise. In recruiting students from throughout the state, Hollingsworth touted the school's broad curriculum as well as the healthy environment of San Marcos, an important factor in an era when yellow fever resulted in student deaths at other institutions. Within a few years, though, facing mounting debts and a personal desire to study law, he sold his school to the Reverend Robert Hixon Belvin.

Successfully admitted to the bar, Hollingsworth became a state legislator in the early 1870s and then was selected the state superintendent of public instruction, later becoming secretary of the Board of Education. He assumed the leadership of the Texas education program at a crucial point in its development, as the state emerged from Reconstruction and moved forward under a new constitution. The gravity of the office he assumed is clearly evident in his first formal report to Governor Richard Coke, when he wrote, "Less than twelve months ago I entered without sympathy, without encouragement, upon the arduous and responsible duties of this department, surrounded on every hand by embarrassments, disorder, distrust, and worst of all, unsupported by adequate legislation." Regardless, Hollingsworth persevered, laying the foundation for state education reforms to follow and even starting the *Texas Journal of Education*. Although short-lived, the publication nevertheless served as an important early venue for identifying and discussing critical issues in public education.

Leaving the state education program in 1883, Hollingsworth embarked on other endeavors, working for a time as a receiving clerk in the General Land Office in Austin and establishing a real estate and livestock agency on Congress Avenue. By 1900, though, for reasons unclear in available records, he had moved his business to Decatur, Georgia. Later, he evidently moved to California, where some of his family lived, and it is believed he died there in 1919.

Like its founder, the Coronal Institute had a varied history. The San Marcos District of the Methodist Episcopal Church, South, took over the operation in 1875 and formally chartered it four years later. The original building burned in 1890, but the church soon built a larger, three-story schoolhouse on the property and eventually added dormitories. In 1917, when the United States entered the Great War and the number of available teachers declined, the federal government leased the site for military training. Briefly the site of the Coronal Military Academy after the war, the main building later housed apartments, and the men's dorm became a hospital. In the mid-1920s ownership conveyed to the San Marcos Independent School District. By the following decade the main building had outlived its original purpose and was in need of extensive repairs, so in 1932 the city demolished the structure in preparation for the construction of a new school plant. Efforts to have the facility named Coronal High School rather than San Marcos High School, though, failed to succeed.

Hollingsworth's early school continued to be a source of nostalgic pride in the lives of its former students and teachers, resulting in various reunions and the formation of a Coronal Club that, in 1940, placed a special commemorative plaque on the schoolhouse cornerstone, which had been salvaged and moved to the grounds of the San Marcos Methodist Church (see sidebar "Northcraft's

San Marcos Churches"). The inscription reads: "The Influence of Coronal Will Live Forever in Our Hearts."

MARKER LOCATION: 500 W. Hutchison, San Marcos

Sources: Roland Miller, "A History of Coronal Institute," MA thesis, Southwest Texas State Teachers College, 1940; Mary Doyle, "Orlando Newton Hollingsworth," in *Biographical Dictionary of American Educators,* vol. 2, ed. John F. Ohles (Westport, CT: Greenwood Press, 1978).

REMEMBERING OLD MAIN ON CAPITOL HILL

Shortly after midnight in the early morning of February 12, 1982, several people noticed smoke emanating from historic Old Main on the campus of Sam Houston State University but assumed, incorrectly, that the fire department had already been summoned. After the first call reached the department around 1:15 a.m., firefighters responding to the scene faced an overwhelming inferno. High flames already engulfed the upper floors of the massive structure and poured from window openings that had held ornate stained glass tributes to Texas history. Fueled by dried timbers and oiled floors, the fire quickly spread virtually unchecked throughout the late-nineteenth-century structure, resulting in additional calls for assistance from fire departments in neighboring towns. The unprecedented effort proved to be too late, however, and within a couple of hours the outcome was inevitable. Crews thus transitioned to a strategy of tight containment, as flames had already reached the nearby Austin College Building, an even earlier landmark on the campus. Morning light revealed the true extent of the damage, which some described as the aftermath of a battle, and news of the devastation spread quickly outside Walker County. Even as smoke still billowed from the site, people from across the state and nation mourned the tragic loss of a major historic site in a town known for its strong historical ties.

Huntsville's Capitol Hill, so named because early town residents aspired to have the state capital located there, had a long and distinguished association with higher education. The Presbyte-

Fire destroyed the historic Old Main at Sam Houston State University in February 1982. Courtesy University Archives, Newton Gresham Library, Sam Houston State University.

rian school, Austin College, opened at Huntsville in 1850, and work on a main building atop the hill began soon after. Designed in the Greek Revival style and featuring a pronounced portico supported by Tuscan columns, the structure reflected a dramatic sense of permanence and community cultural values at its elevated setting a half mile south of the town square. The school showed great promise in its early years, but declining enrollment and financial backing through the Civil War and Reconstruction led the Texas

Synod of the Presbyterian Church (USA) to move the institution to Sherman, in North Texas, in the 1870s. Shortly after, the Texas legislature approved establishment of the Sam Houston Normal Institute at Huntsville as the first public institution for teacher training in the state. It opened in 1879 on the Capitol Hill site.

Later, in preparation for a larger Main Building, school officials chose Galveston architect Alfred Muller to draw up the plans.* Muller was a native of Krefeld, Prussia (now Germany), who studied at the prestigious Royal Academy of Architecture in Berlin before emigrating to the United States. Working first at New York City and then Washington, DC, he made his way to the Texas port city of Galveston about 1886 and worked for Nathaniel W. Tobey Jr. His first large public commission came through an 1887 competition for the design of City Hall (no longer extant). Although he was a rival to the more widely known Galveston architect Nicholas Clayton, Muller generally worked on more modest projects, but ones that included commercial structures (E. S. Levy Building and Southwestern Telegraph and Telephone Company Building), public buildings (Galveston Orphan's Home and Letitia Rosenberg Home for Women), and residential properties (J. C. Trube House and H. Marwitz Residence). The Sam Houston Normal Institute Main Building, though, is considered his masterpiece.

In his design of Old Main, Muller reached back to the roots of his European schooling, drawing on the High Victorian Gothic style then popular in institutional architecture. The style, detailing, and massing of the structure he proposed were in marked contrast to the more sedate, classical lines of the Austin College Building, which would remain in place only a few steps immediately to the south of the new main building, although it would thus be hidden from the main hillside view corridor from town. Architectural historian Willard B. Robinson wrote that the new building was notable for its "irregular skyline" and "its extraordinary pinnacles, steep-pitched roofs, and pointed arches." Other significant features included decorative brickwork, most notably through extensive use of banding and corbels, and the dominance of a tripartite gabled design on the primary façade. It was a grand edifice, and it set a standard for other elaborate public buildings to follow.

During construction of the Main Building at Sam Houston Normal Institute, Muller often found himself at odds with both the supervising architect, Edward S. Northcraft, and the builders, brothers George Henry Wilson and A. J. Wilson. The most serious differences appeared to be about the integrity of the foundation, which Northcraft and the Wilsons held was not substantial enough to withstand the pressures of such an enormous structure, especially on the slope of a hill. In the end, the supervising architect prevailed, and it is believed Muller eventually acquiesced and left the project before its completion in 1891. Regardless, he continued to have a prosperous business in Galveston until his death in 1896 of typhoid fever. As his obituary in the *Galveston Daily News* conveyed, "Mr. Muller rapidly attained prominence in his chosen profession and leaves behind him enduring monuments to his memory in some of the finest buildings in the south." In his honor, flags at various Galveston buildings he designed or supervised flew at half-mast.

Not long after Muller's death, Northcraft received the commission for the Main Building at Southwest Texas Normal College. Borrowing heavily on the principal plans for the Huntsville structure—work he had closely reviewed and supervised for years—the San Marcos architect employed a somewhat similar design, although his lacked the exuberant exterior ornamentation of the earlier structure. Sharing similar features, functions, and hillside locations, the two sister structures served as important symbols of their respective institutions, where they were revered by generations of students. By the 1980s, though, both buildings were in need of extensive repairs to keep them updated and viable. Funds were not readily available, however, through either the legislature or the governing board. As various interested parties, including the Texas Historical Commission and the Walker County Historical Commission, searched for means to address the dilemma, tragedy struck.

The 1982 fire at Huntsville served as a wake-up call that galvanized preservation efforts on both campuses. At Sam Houston it led school officials to fund restoration of the Austin College Building, heavily damaged by collateral fire. At Southwest Texas, it ensured full consideration of adequate fire protection systems in restoration plans for the Old Main there. While there was talk of rebuilding Muller's Old Main, the estimated cost of the project — sixteen million dollars — ultimately proved too steep for the university or legislature. As a compromise, though, funding came through for a unique memorial that incorporated salvageable elements of the ruins so visitors to the site can get a sense of the building's immense size, dramatic setting, and possibly its historical significance. For those seeking a stronger visual reference to the past, there is still the sister structure on Chautauqua Hill in San Marcos.

MARKER LOCATION: on the campus of Sam Houston State University at 17th and University Streets in Huntsville

Sources: Willard B. Robinson, "Temples of Knowledge: Historic Mains of Texas Colleges and Universities," *Southwestern Historical Quarterly* 77, no. 4 (April 1974), pp. 445–80; "The Late Alfred Muller: The Well-Known Architect Crosses the Dark River after an Illness of Only Five Weeks," *Galveston Daily News*, June 30, 1896, n.p.; Helen D. Mooty, "Alfred Muller and Galveston's Late Nineteenth-Century Architectural Style." MA thesis, University of Houston at Clear Lake, 2005; Fred Afflerbach, "Born from Bricks: The Story of Old Main, Its Sister and Tragedy," *University Star*, December 1, 2005; Lisa Trow, "Old Main Building Burns Down," *Huntsville Item*, February 12, 1982, p. 1.

*Although the last name is spelled in some accounts (including the historical marker for Old Main) as Mueller, a possible phonetic Anglicization of the Germanic Müller, the architect used Muller in his signature, personal records, and business advertising.

12

History on
the Grounds

Texans love to remember, commemorate, and celebrate their history. In numerous studies conducted by travel and tourism organizations, historic sites and museums consistently rank in the top ten on lists of places Texans, as well as out-of-state visitors, travel to see. The Texas Historical Commission's website proclaims, "Welcome to Texas. Everything is bigger and better here, even the history!" Indeed, if the number of historical markers is any indication, that boast can be substantiated by the energy and enthusiasm Texans put into interpreting their history. With an estimated fifteen thousand markers currently dotting the landscape, and hundreds more added to the inventory each year, Texas has more historical markers than any other state in the union.

While some proud Texans would argue the reason there are so many markers is that Texas has more history to celebrate than other states, a more modest explanation can be traced to the fact that the Texas marker program, unlike those in most other states, commemorates not only topics of statewide and national importance, but also topics of local significance. Believing the history of Texas is the collective story of its people, places, and events, the founders of the marker program designed a system in which local citizens, through participation in or interaction with county historical commissions, play an integral part in recounting that history. Taken together, the thousands of markers tell the sweeping story of Texas from the perspective of its people.

In an essay entitled "Sense of Place," the celebrated Western historian, writer, and environmentalist Wallace Stegner wrote, "No place is a place until the things that have happened in it are remembered in history, ballads, yarns, legends, or monuments." Similarly, another writer observed, "A sense of history and sense of place are inextricably intertwined; we attach histories to places, and the environmental value we attach to a place comes largely through the historical associations we have with it." If, as yet another historian has said, "The challenge of history is to recover the past and introduce it to the present," Texans have taken such philosophies to heart with their participation in the state marker program, as well as through placement of monuments and other commemorative objects. One historic site where these concepts are exhibited to a high degree is the Texas State Capitol in Austin. While the building itself stands as a monument to the state's pride and history, over the years the cultural landscape of the Capitol grounds has also provided a venue for varied approaches to historical interpretation.[1]

In 1839, shortly after the Republic of Texas Congress designated the village of Waterloo as the new Texas capital and renamed it in honor of Stephen F. Austin, surveyors laid out a town grid and designated an area on a hillside north of the Colorado River at the end of Congress Avenue as Capitol Square. For the next five years the Republic of Texas Congress met in temporary buildings in downtown Austin, and following annexation to the United States as the twenty-eighth state in 1845, the first permanent state capitol building opened in 1853 on Capitol Square. In 1881, the same year the state legislature began making plans and seeking bids for the design of a grand new capitol, the 1853 building burned to the ground. Architect Elijah E. Myers of Detroit, who had previously designed the Michigan capitol, won the contract to design the new building, and in May 1888, after six years of construction, the current Texas State Capitol was dedicated in a festive ceremony at which Texas senator Temple Houston, son of legendary Texas hero Sam Houston, was the featured speaker.[2]

Immediately following completion of the new building, it seems, people started making plans to use its parklike grounds as a place of public memory and commemoration. It perhaps came as no surprise to Texans that the first monument installed, in 1891, was one dedicated to heroes of the Alamo. Five years later, a statue honoring volunteer firemen went up nearby, and by the end of the first decade of the twentieth century, three Civil War memorials appeared on the grounds: the Confederate Soldiers monument (1903) and the Terry's Texas Rangers statue (1907) on the south lawn, and the Hood's Texas Brigade monument (1910) on the southeast side. Following installation of the Texas Cowboy statue on the southwest lawn in 1925, no additional monuments were installed until the addition of a Spanish-American War memorial and a replica of the Statue of Liberty in 1951, and a tribute to the 36th Infantry Division of the Texas National Guard in 1959. A memorial to soldiers of World War I and a granite tablet inscribed with the Ten Commandments were additions to the grounds in 1961, and installation of memorials honoring disabled veterans (1980), Pearl Harbor veterans (1989), Texas children (1998), Texas pioneer women (1998), Korean War veterans (1999), and Texas peace officers (1999) completed the inventory of monuments through the end of the twentieth century.[3] A Tejano monument was installed in March 2012, and the final design for a Juneteenth/African American monument is now pending.

While the statues and monuments at the Capitol provide one type of commemoration, interpretive markers also enhance the visitor experience by offering narrative explanations regarding the historic appearance of the grounds as well as stories of associated events, organizations, and people. The markers themselves have an interesting history, though, one that reflects changing ideas of interpreting historic landscapes.

The earliest Official Texas Historical Markers placed on the Capitol grounds date to the 1960s. The Texas State Historical Survey Committee (TSHSC, now Texas Historical Commission) designated the 1856–57 General Land Office (now the Capitol Visitors Center) a Recorded Texas Historic Landmark and awarded it a building medallion in 1962. At that time, the agency allowed the distinctive circular medallions to be placed on designated buildings without interpretive plaques, so there was no accompanying background information. Three years later, in conjunction with widespread efforts to commemorate the Civil War centennial through a special series of Texas in the Civil War markers, the TSHSC placed large interpretive markers for the Texas Secession Convention, the Civil War Committee on Public Safety, and Confederate Texas

The historical marker for Confederate Texas Legislatures, located just north of the Capitol, refers to a campsite where some of the members stayed while the legislature was in session. Photograph by Cynthia J. Beeman.

Legislatures on the Capitol grounds. The topic of each marker had clear historical connections to the Capitol, since the governmental bodies referred to had gathered there for meetings and deliberations. The text of the marker for the Confederate Texas Legislatures, for example, described an unusual aspect of the wartime lawmakers' situation that relates the marker to its site: "Legislatures were in almost continuous sessions. Poor pay and inflated Confederate money caused many members to live in tents and covered wagons on the Capitol grounds and cook over campfires."[4]

As incongruous as it seems, an agricultural industry based hundreds of miles away from Austin in East Texas was the basis for a marker placed on the north side of the Capitol grounds in 1969. State representative Billy Williamson of Smith County introduced House Concurrent Resolution 105 in the regular session of the Sixty-first Texas Legislature to authorize the planting of a Tyler Rose Garden along with the installation of an Official Texas Historical Marker for the Tyler Rose. Calling his hometown crop "one of the best loved flowers in America" and "a silent ambassador of beauty from the Great State of Texas," Williamson also paid homage to the Tyler Rose Festival, an annual event that dates to 1933. Following legislative approval of the resolution, TSHSC staff began working with Representative Williamson and the Smith County Historical Survey Committee to write a suitable text for the marker that would be placed next to the rose garden.

The first text proposed by Williamson consisted entirely of a quote from national radio personality Paul Harvey, who had attended the Tyler Rose Festival in 1962: "Tyler, Texas, is famous because of a scrawny little East Texas rose that grew wild thereabout. No flower ever had to fight harder for its life than that wild rose in the white sand. So what did it do? It sank a network of roots, hungry roots, so deep that the thorny East Texas rose developed such a stubborn, hearty, virile root system that today it is exported all over the world. Nurserymen have grafted beautiful varieties, hybrids that show what happens when God and man work together."[5] Faced with an official request from a member of the legislature to approve a text she found to be unacceptable, Deolece Parmelee, the TSHSC director of research, fired off a memo to her boss, executive

*A mockingbird—the state bird of Texas—perches on the historical marker
for the Tyler Rose in the rose garden on the north side of the Capitol.*
Photograph by Cynthia J. Beeman.

director Truett Latimer. "The comments of Mr. Paul Harvey on 'Tyler
Rose' are beautiful," she wrote. "However, these remarks are editorializing about an historical subject, and it has been established
that on markers bearing the well-known emblem of the State of
Texas, editorializing is not permissible." THC records do not reveal
the details of negotiations between Latimer and Williamson, but
the final text appears to be a compromise, with the first section
dealing with the history of the rose industry and the final sentence

reflective of Williamson's request to include Harvey's quote: "The beauty of the Tyler Rose is an example of what happens when God and man work together."[6]

Much as the centennial of the Civil War engendered renewed interest in commemorating that era's history in the 1960s, the US bicentennial in 1976 spurred countless individuals, organizations, and communities to plan special events and projects to mark the two hundredth anniversary of American independence. The members of Austin's Kiwanis Club of the University Area decided the Capitol itself should have an Official Texas Historical Marker, so they sponsored the marker application as their bicentennial project. State representative Wilhemina Delco, who happened to be the wife of one of the club members, introduced the legislation that authorized placement of the marker "in a suitable permanent position on the capitol grounds."[7]

Elora B. Alderman, chair of the Travis County Historical Commission, shepherded the application through the county and state approval processes and coordinated plans for a dedication program she hoped would feature current and former governors as speakers. Unfortunately, for various reasons, none of the governors were able to attend. Undaunted, Alderman then turned her attention to the current and former first ladies. In a letter addressed to "Mrs. Dolph Briscoe, Mrs. John Connally, Mrs. Price Daniel, Mrs. Allan Shivers, and Mrs. Preston Smith," she invited the women to attend the dedication ceremony and unveil the marker. "Bring your grandchildren to help you if you wish," she wrote, and then added, "Oh, yes! Bring your husbands too."[8]

The marker was completed and ready for dedication in August 1976. John Ben Shepperd, former THC chairman and one of the architects of the state marker program, gave the dedicatory address at the ceremony in the Capitol rotunda. Shepperd, who had also served on the Texas Civil War Centennial Commission, alluded to the conflict between the North and the South in his remarks. In relating the history of the Capitol, he said:

> When the dreaming and planning started in 1875, Texas had just broken the yoke of unjust reconstruction . . . the state was broke

and couldn't have borrowed enough to build another Capitol building out of logs. But it did have a lot of public land that nobody lived on, or nobody knew if anybody could live on it. It was being offered at 50¢ an acre, on credit, with few takers.

The courageous leaders in the Constitutional Convention set aside 3,000,000 acres in the Panhandle to erect a new Capitol. 1876, one hundred years ago, the voters of Texas approved. The surveyors sent to locate the land were guarded by Texas Rangers against Indian attacks.

Designs and bids were advertised for in several out-of-state papers. A Yankee from Detroit won the contest for the best design. Another one from Illinois got the contract in 1882, then he sold three-fourths of it to four more Yankees to get the money to build it.

The Civil War was Over![9]

Following Shepperd's speech, Ima Smith, wife of former governor Preston Smith, unveiled the marker. It remained on display in the rotunda until early 1977, when, after receiving final authorization from the legislature, it was placed at the south entrance to the Capitol grounds at 11th Street and Congress Avenue. During the Capitol and grounds restoration project of the late 1980s, workers relocated the marker from the west side of the main entrance to the east side, but some years later—no one knows exactly when—the marker disappeared and only the post remained in place. Texas State Preservation Board officials surmised it was likely the victim of vandalism.[10]

Two more markers that began as bicentennial projects now mark sites of churches that once stood on streets that have since disappeared with the expansion of the Capitol grounds. In a coordinated effort to gain approval for both markers, the Travis County Historical Commission appealed to one of the county's legislators, State representative Sarah Weddington, to sponsor a bill to authorize their placement. The churches, each founded in the nineteenth century, not only represented Austin's religious history but also had strong ties to the city's European immigrant population. In addition, the markers help relate to the public a sense of the resi-

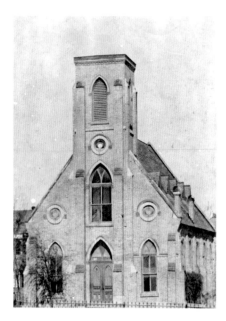

Built in 1884–85, St. Martin's German Evangelical Lutheran Church stood on 13th Street northwest of the Capitol. Courtesy Texas Historical Commission, Official Texas Historical Marker files.

dential neighborhood that thrived just north of the Capitol until the middle of the twentieth century.

The Reverend Carl Charnquist and eleven lay people organized Austin's Swedish Methodist Church in 1873. The congregation's first sanctuary stood at the corner of Red River and 15th Streets, but by 1898 the church had moved to the corner of Colorado and 13th (Peach) Streets—on what is now the northwest corner of the Capitol grounds—to a building formerly occupied by Central Methodist Church. After its relocation, the congregation became known as the Swedish Central Methodist Church. The church parsonage stood next door at 106 West 13th Street. In August 1956, as plans to enlarge the Capitol complex with the addition of several new office buildings developed, the church sold all of its property to the State of Texas for $130,000. Renamed Memorial Methodist Church, the congregation then moved to a site on Berkman Drive in northeast Austin.[11]

Twenty German families joined with the Reverend Henry Merz to organize St. Martin's German Evangelical Lutheran Church in 1883. They held worship services in members' homes or in facilities borrowed from other churches until December 1884, when they

After Texas historian Walter Prescott Webb bought the former St. Martin's German Evangelical Lutheran Church building in 1937, he leased it to the State of Texas, which used it for Texas State Parks Board offices. The Reverend F. G. Roesener is shown here later visiting the site. Courtesy Texas Historical Commission, Official Texas Historical Marker files.

laid the cornerstone for a new church building at 106 East Peach (later 13th) Street immediately north of Capitol Square.

Completed in April 1885, the Gothic-style brick building featured a truncated bell tower and numerous stained glass windows, and a parsonage sat just north of the church at 105 East 14th Street. According to the history prepared for the marker application, the church building developed structural problems by the 1920s: "As time passed, the building started leaking which caused walls to be water stained. The Rev. [F. G.] Roesener would permit no renovation as he wanted the congregation to realize how badly a new structure was needed." The pastor's plan evidently worked, because by 1929 the congregation completed a new building one block north at 1400 Congress.[12]

In 1937 noted Texas historian Walter P. Webb bought the original St. Martin's church building, evidently as a real estate investment, for he immediately leased it to the State of Texas to house offices of the Texas State Parks Board.

As the Capitol complex expansion project progressed in the late 1950s, the state brought a condemnation suit against Webb to acquire the former church property. Although the state razed both of the St. Martin buildings to make way for new state offices, the legal case between the state and Webb regarding the 1885 church site did not reach its ultimate settlement (in favor of the state) until December 1963, more than nine months after Webb's death. St. Martin's Evangelical Lutheran Church, meanwhile, had built a much larger facility on the corner of 15th and Rio Grande Streets, five blocks west of the Capitol.[13]

Located directly east of the Capitol, the Lorenzo de Zavala State Archives and Library Building houses the state's most treasured documents, including the Texas Declaration of Independence, the Texas Constitution, and Col. William B. Travis's famed letter from the Alamo. The most colorful episode in the history of the Texas archives is commemorated on an Official Texas Historical Marker in front of the building. Approved in 1978, the marker tells the story of the Archive War, a casualty-free skirmish that occurred in late December 1842 when Republic of Texas president Sam Houston, who wanted to relocate the republic's seat of government to his namesake city, ordered the removal of the official government records. Austin innkeeper Angelina Eberly, upon seeing Houston's men loading the records into a wagon in the middle of the night, fired off the city cannon—located at the corner of Congress Avenue and Pecan (now Sixth) Street—in their direction as they fled toward the east. Alerted by the ruckus raised by Eberly, according to the marker text, "About 68 citizens rode after them, hauling along the city cannon. Some 20 miles from Austin they retrieved the archives without bloodshed."[14]

From pioneer settlers such as Angelina Eberly and her compatriots to educators, preservationists, and everyday citizens of the twenty-first century, Texans love their history. Hosting thousands of visitors each year, the Texas State Capitol remains one of the most popular tourist sites in the state, and the monuments and

The marker for the Archive War stands in front of the Lorenzo de Zavala State Archives and Library Building on the east side of the Capitol grounds. Photograph by Cynthia J. Beeman.

markers located on the grounds help convey the multilayered story of the Lone Star State.

MARKER LOCATIONS

General Land Office: Although the medallion is not currently displayed, the 1857 General Land Office Building, located on the southeast corner of the Capitol grounds, now houses the Capitol Visitor Center, which includes historical exhibits about the Capitol as well as a gift shop.

Texas Secession Convention: in front of the Lorenzo de Zavala

State Archives and Library Building, directly east of the Capitol on Brazos St.

Confederate Texas Legislatures: northeast Capitol grounds, adjacent to Texas Peace Officers memorial

Tyler Rose: northwest Capitol grounds in Tyler Rose Garden, east of Texas Supreme Court Building

Swedish Central Methodist Church: corner of Colorado St. and 13th St., adjacent to underground Capitol parking garage entrance

St. Martin's Evangelical Lutheran Church: northeast Capitol grounds near entrance pavilion to underground Capitol Extension

The Archive War: in front of the Lorenzo de Zavala State Archives and Library Building, directly east of the Capitol on Brazos St.

CAPITOL MARKERS—THE REST OF THE STORY

While a number of Official Texas Historical Markers remain in their original positions at the Capitol, others have been relocated or are missing. Some were moved from one location on the grounds to another during the Capitol restoration project; one went to a new site away from the Capitol, but nearby; one ended up in storage; and another left Austin altogether.

A marker previously mounted on a wall on the third floor of the Capitol told the story of the historic Supreme Court Courtroom. Dedicated in 1968 in conjunction with an earlier Capitol renovation project, the marker read, "In this room, the Texas Supreme Court, highest civil appellate court of the state, sat for 70 years, until removal in 1959 to the new Supreme Court Building." The courtroom underwent a careful restoration in the 1990s that returned it to its historic appearance. Because the marker was not a historic feature of the room, the Texas State Preservation Board— the agency that oversees the Capitol and its grounds—elected to remove it and place it in storage. Both the Supreme Court Courtroom and the Court of Criminal Appeals Courtroom across the hall now feature museum-quality furnishings and exhibits.

The Capitol restoration project included a plan to recreate the historic appearance of the Great Walk on the south side of the grounds, and implementation of that plan required the removal of three historical markers. The 1965 marker for Confederate Texas Legislatures now stands on the northeast grounds, and the Secession Convention marker—also from 1965—is now in front of the Lorenzo de Zavala Texas State Archives and Library Building directly east of the Capitol.

The third marker that previously stood along the Great Walk told the story of Moses Austin, "initiator of Anglo-American settlement in Texas." Although Moses Austin died in the summer of 1821 before he could fulfill his colonization contract (carried out by his son, Stephen F. Austin, "the Father of Texas"), he certainly met the significance requirement for approval of an Official Texas

Historical Marker, and the State Capitol seemed to be the most appropriate placement. Unlike the other two markers relocated from the Great Walk, however, it ended up completely removed from the Capitol grounds and now stands a few blocks north on Congress Avenue in front of the modern Stephen F. Austin State Office Building.

A marker for Civil War Confederate Veterans, initially erected in 1965 in front of the Texas Confederate Veterans Home on a hill overlooking West Sixth Street in Austin, made several journeys. After the home closed in 1968, a security fence erected around the property made the marker inaccessible to the public. Texas Historical Commission executive director Truett Latimer wrote to William Burke, his counterpart at the State Board of Control, to request that the marker be relocated to the Texas State Cemetery, where a number of former residents of the Confederate Veterans Home were interred in what is known as the Confederate Section. Burke approved the request, and workers moved the marker to the cemetery in August 1968.

Two years later, following the razing of the veterans home building and its replacement by an apartment complex for married students attending the University of Texas, Mrs. L. J. Gittinger, chairwoman of the Texas Confederate Museum Committee of the Texas Division of the United Daughters of the Confederacy (UDC), wrote to Latimer to request that the marker be moved once again, to the museum that was then in operation in the Old General Land Office Building on the Capitol grounds. In her letter she indicated that the UDC would include the marker in an exhibit along with "the old bell that hung in the tower above the Mess Hall at the Confederate Veterans Home." Latimer approved the request, saying, "Permission is hereby given to the Board of Control to saw the marker off at the ground, clean it up and take it to the Museum." Two decades later, however, the marker was on the move once again.

In 1988, plans began to take shape for the major Capitol restoration project, which included renovating the Old General Land

Office Building into a Capitol Visitors Center. As a result, both the UDC and the Daughters of the Republic of Texas (DRT), which also operated a museum in the building, moved their operations. The DRT museum remained in Austin, but the UDC moved its collection first to Waco, where it was part of a temporary exhibit from 1990 to 1992. The collection went into storage until 1994, after which many of the items were on display at the History Complex of Hill College in Hillsboro until 2000 and others were loaned to a number of Texas museums. In 2006 the Texas Confederate Museum Collection became part of the permanent collection at the new privately funded Texas Civil War Museum in Fort Worth. According to THC files, the Confederate Veterans marker remains part of the collection and is now at the new facility.

Sources: Supreme Court Courtroom, Confederate Texas Legislatures, Secession Convention, Moses Austin, and Texas in the Civil War Confederate Veterans, all Travis County, THC marker files.

THE LITTLEST DREADNOUGHT

Perhaps one of the more unusual markers formerly located in the Capitol complex is one approved in 1970 for a model of the USS *Texas* battleship. The 1:48 (1 inch to 48 inches) scale model arrived in Austin on January 22, 1965, on loan from the US Navy. Encased in a wood and glass display case, weighing an estimated one thousand pounds, and measuring more than thirteen feet long, three feet wide, and seven and a half feet tall, the model required a crew of about a dozen men to unload it from the moving van and position it in the lobby of the Sam Houston State Office Building on the northeast Capitol grounds. A small crowd gathered to watch the installation as photographers recorded the event.

The model's long-term loan to Texas came at the request of Adm. Hugh R. Nieman Jr. (1906–89), a World War II veteran who at the time served as executive director of the State Building Commission located in the Sam Houston Building. Although an accompanying interpretive plaque offered statistical information about the ship, Nieman also wanted an Official Texas Historical Marker

A scale model of the USS Texas battleship was displayed in the lobby of the Sam Houston State Office Building from 1965 to the 1980s, when it was moved to Texas Parks and Wildlife Department headquarters. After a brief stay at the Bob Bullock Texas State History Museum in 2001, it is now on display at the Great Lakes Naval Training Center near Chicago, Illinois. Courtesy US Naval Sea Systems Command.

for the display, so he wrote to Texas State Historical Survey Committee executive director Truett Latimer to request one. Latimer, in turn, assigned the job of researching and writing the marker text to Deoloce Parmelee, the agency's director of research. Parmelee visited the display, took notes from the navy's interpretive plaque, and began the task of crafting an inscription for the marker. She telephoned the former skipper of the USS *Texas* (which by that time was in a berth in the Houston Ship Channel adjacent to the San Jacinto Battlefield and operated as a museum by the State of Texas) to ask for assistance. Parmelee, explaining a delay in the project in a September 1970 memo to Latimer, wrote: "Not until yesterday did we receive the data from the skipper of the *Texas*. He told me the second time I called that he lost the request for data when somebody used the paper napkin he had written [the] memo on."

In 1910 the US Congress authorized funding for the USS *Texas*, a new battleship to be built to emulate the mighty British ship HMS *Dreadnought*. Commissioned in 1914 upon its completion at Newport News, Virginia, the *Texas* would see action in World War I and World War II. During the latter it sailed in the Pacific Fleet under the command of a native Texan, Adm. Chester W. Nimitz of Fredericksburg.

The model, like the ship it commemorates, has an interesting history. Beginning in 1883, as the US Navy began construction of each new class of ship, workers built a model to use for public relations and educational purposes. Eventually, more than twenty-five hundred models would be displayed around the country. Built at the New York Navy Yard in 1910—four years before commissioning of the USS *Texas*—the model originally replicated the USS *New York* (for which the New York class of battleships is named). First installed at the US Naval Academy in Annapolis, Maryland, the model later went on display at New Rochelle, New York; Ogden, Utah; and Bremerton, Washington. By 1965, when Nieman requested that it be moved to Austin, navy personnel renamed it the USS *Texas* and provided updated markings.

The interpretive plaque provided by the navy conveyed little in the way of history, and instead concentrated on statistics regarding the ship's engines, size, and armaments. The state historical marker, then, offered Parmelee the opportunity to tell more of the ship's impressive story. The model and the state marker remained on display in the Sam Houston Building lobby until the late 1980s, when the Texas Parks and Wildlife Department—which by then had authority over the battleship—assumed responsibility and moved the model to its headquarters in southeast Austin. The Bob Bullock Texas State History Museum borrowed the model for a special exhibit, "It Ain't Bragging If It's True," in 2001, and Texas state officials returned the model to the US Navy in January 2002. After undergoing repair and conservation treatment at the Office of the Curator of Ship Models at the US Naval Surface Warfare Center in Bethesda, Maryland, it went on display at the Great Lakes Naval Training Center near Chicago, Illinois, in 2008. The ultimate disposition of the Official Texas Historical Marker is unknown.

Sources: Scale Model of the USS Texas, Travis County, THC marker files; Dana Wegner, Curator of Ship Models, US Naval Surface Warfare Center, Bethesda, MD, email correspondence with Cynthia J. Beeman, February 2011, copies of correspondence in authors' files.

PART THREE
Texans Reaching Out

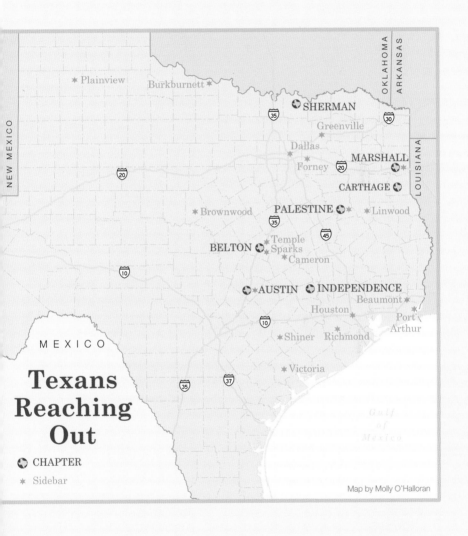

Plainview *

Burkburnett *

OKLAHOMA

ARKANSAS

⦿ SHERMAN

🛣35

🛣30

Greenville *

Dallas *

MARSHALL ⦿

Forney * 🛣20

CARTHAGE ⦿

LOUISIANA

* Brownwood   PALESTINE ⦿   * Linwood

🛣35

🛣20

🛣45

BELTON ⦿ Temple *
Sparks *

🛣10

* Cameron

⦿ * AUSTIN   ⦿ INDEPENDENCE

Beaumont *

Houston *

Port
Arthur *

🛣10

* Shiner   Richmond *

MEXICO

* Victoria

Texans
Reaching
Out

⦿ CHAPTER

* Sidebar

🛣35

🛣37

Gulf
of
Mexico

Map by Molly O'Halloran

13

Justice Is the Corporate Face of Love

World events in the early and middle years of the twentieth century, including the difficult era of the Great Depression and the monumental effects of two world wars, engendered social, religious, and political changes to the American landscape that combined to inspire countless people to become involved in civil rights and social justice movements. John E. Hines, through his leadership as bishop coadjutor and bishop of the Episcopal Diocese of Texas, and later as presiding bishop of the Episcopal Church in the United States, promoted widespread social and religious outreach in accordance with his support for the Social Gospel movement—a Christian response to social ills such as poverty, racial prejudice, urban blight, labor issues, and legal discrimination against the poor and dispossessed. His activist efforts left a legacy of educational, religious, and social change not only in Texas, but also throughout the United States and beyond.

Born October 3, 1910, in Seneca, South Carolina, John Elbridge Hines was the eighth and youngest child of Dr. Edgar A. Hines and Mary Woodbury Moore Hines. Edgar Hines, a respected medical doctor, served on the local school board and community health board and, as an officer of the South Carolina Medical Association, helped found the South Carolina Public Health Association. Mary Hines, a prominent civic leader in her own right, was a founder of the South Carolina Federation of Women's Clubs and served in various capacities in numerous civic and educational organizations. Her primary passion, however, was Seneca's Ascension Episcopal Church, and she is credited with keeping its doors open at a time when the diocese considered closing it.[1]

His mother's influence led to young John E. Hines's confirmation in the church at the early age of nine in May 1920. Active in his local parish as well as diocesan-level camp activities throughout his youth, Hines also excelled academically and in athletics in the public schools of Seneca. Although he grew up in a racially segregated Southern community, Hines's sense of social justice manifested itself early as he witnessed his father's often unpopular struggles for adequate healthcare and equal rights for African American and poor citizens of Seneca and Oconee County. Skipping a grade because of his stellar academic performance, John Hines graduated from Seneca High School at age fifteen in June 1926. The following fall he enrolled at The University of the South at Sewanee, Tennessee, where he was the youngest student in the freshman class. He quickly became a leader at the university, serving as head of student government and editor of the school newspaper. As he had in high school, he excelled in sports as well as academics.[2]

By the time of his graduation from Sewanee in 1930, Hines had abandoned his initial plan to become a doctor and instead enrolled at Virginia Theological Seminary for graduate work in preparation for ordained ministry in the Episcopal Church. With a sterling academic record, he again became a leader of the student body and began to look beyond the walls of academia to observe firsthand the social ills brought into focus by the growing Great Depression. In a passage presaging his subject's later civil rights activism, Hines biographer Kenneth Kesselus wrote: "Living near the nation's capital, besieged by destitute protesters and the famed 'Bonus Army,' enhanced Hines's understanding of the growing economic calamity. Washington also provided a social education for many Southern seminarians who had never witnessed racial integration. Hines later insisted that he, unlike some others, had no bigotry to overcome because of the positive attitude of his family. Influenced by his father's views about racial equality, he said, 'I never succumbed' to racial prejudice."[3] Graduating from seminary in 1933, Hines moved to Missouri, where after his ordination to the priesthood he worked as assistant rector at the Church of St. Michael and St. George in suburban St. Louis. The Right Reverend William Scarlett, bishop of Missouri, soon proved to be an important and lasting influence on the young clergyman. An early and vocal proponent of the Social Gospel movement, Scarlett encouraged Hines to embrace the tenets of the movement as well, and his mentorship shaped Hines's ministry. While serving in St. Louis, Hines met Helen Orwig (1910–96), to whom he became engaged in 1934. As the couple made plans for their wedding, they also visited Grace Episcopal Church in Jefferson City and Trinity Church in Hannibal, both of which were considering calling Hines as rector. He accepted the call from Trinity, and they moved to Hannibal just a week after their marriage in April 1935.[4] The couple eventually had five children, and three of their four sons became Episcopal priests.

In early 1937, Hines accepted a call to become rector of St. Paul's Episcopal Church in Augusta, Georgia. As he settled into his first position as rector in charge of a parish, he also became more active in the national Episcopal Church, particularly in liberal interest groups and committees involved with social justice issues. Employing the outstanding oratorical and preaching skills for which he was known throughout his ministry, he used his pulpit as well as his church bulletin to address social injustice and racial discrimination. He became known throughout the region for his progressive leadership both within the church and in the wider community.[5]

Hines began a twenty-four-year ministry in Texas when he became rector of Christ Church (later Christ Church Cathedral) in Houston in January 1941. Just thirty years old at the time, he nevertheless brought with him a reputation as a progressive leader, caring pastor, and inspiring and challenging preacher. As rector of a dynamic downtown urban church, he continued to advocate social action as a clergyman and as an active member of the community. His work with young people resulted in increased membership for the parish, and he inspired a number of people to study for the priesthood. Within the diocese he served on a committee to evaluate the church's work among African Americans, and through that work he continued to advocate for equal rights. As a priest in the Diocese of Texas, Hines worked under the supervision of Bishop Clinton S. Quin. In 1945, when Quin called for an election for a bishop coadjutor (an assistant bishop who would succeed him upon his retirement), clergy and lay delegates to the diocesan council elected John E. Hines to that office. He was consecrated

Christ Episcopal Church (now Christ Church Cathedral), Houston, as it looked during John Hines's rectorship in the 1940s. Courtesy Texas Historical Commission, National Register of Historic Places files.

bishop on October 18, 1945, in a festive service at which his mentor, Bishop William Scarlett of Missouri, preached.[6]

To better serve the geographically large and diverse diocese, which included fifty-seven counties that covered large swaths of East Texas, Central Texas, and the upper Gulf Coast, diocesan officials decided that Hines and his family would move to Austin and open a second diocesan office. The new bishop and his family settled into a house on Bowman Road in the Tarrytown neighborhood, and Hines began what would be a highly productive ten-year term as bishop coadjutor. Exhibiting the leadership skills for which he had been known since his youth, Bishop Hines shepherded a vast array of improvements and growth initiatives in the diocese, including increasing the number of mission congregations in the diocese by more than forty and helping another twenty-one to achieve self-sustaining parish status; strengthening or establishing chaplaincy programs at many colleges and universities, including the University of Texas, Texas A&M University, Rice University, the University of Houston, Stephen F. Austin State University, Sam Houston State University, Lamar State College of Technology (later Lamar University), Baylor University, Huston-Tillotson College (now Huston-Tillotson University), and Prairie View A&M University; and founding St. Stephen's Episcopal School in Austin in 1948, the Episcopal Theological Seminary of the Southwest (now Seminary of the Southwest) in Austin in 1951, and St. Luke's Episcopal Hospital in Houston in 1954.[7]

In recognition of Hines's guidance and concern for all people, regardless of their status or condition in life, Gov. Allan Shivers appointed him to a position on the newly created Board for Texas State Hospitals and Special Schools in 1949. Years later, at a testimonial dinner for Bishop Hines, Gov. John Connally said, "He entered that service in a time of disgrace for the mental hospitals of this state. Bishop Hines lent his wisdom, his compassion and his depth of understanding to one of the most formidable problems in our history." In addition to his duties as a bishop in the Diocese of Texas, Hines remained active in national church activities as well, serving on a number of committees and fulfilling his responsibilities as a member of the House of Bishops. He spoke often in favor of equal opportunities and representation by women and minorities in the church, never wavering in his views despite opposition from conservative groups and individuals in the diocese or the uphill struggle he faced.[8]

In December 1955, upon Bishop Quin's retirement, John E. Hines became the fourth bishop of Texas, and the Hines family moved back to Houston. Exhibiting the same energy and passion as diocesan bishop as he had as bishop coadjutor, Hines oversaw even more growth in new mission churches; established St. James House, a church-affiliated nursing home in Baytown; and continued to press the church and its members to become involved with social justice ministries, particularly in the movement to end racial segregation. Through his leadership, racial integration was achieved at St. Stephen's School, the Seminary of the Southwest, and diocesan youth camps, despite some strong opposition within the church and in the communities in which the schools and camp were located. Although many people in the diocese supported Hines's progressive programs, others held stubbornly to more conservative views and expressed their displeasure with their pocketbooks by withholding donations to church programs. As a result, several of his major fundraising efforts fell short of their goals.[9]

Decades later, in an interview with television journalist Hugh Downs, Hines remembered the controversy surrounding the integration of St. Stephen's School and praised those who were willing to take an unpopular stand:

> The week after we successfully integrated St. Stephen's Episcopal School, I had three telephone calls from three different people. And in that week St. Stephen's School lost seven hundred and fifty thousand dollars from these three people, who never again contributed a dollar to St. Stephen's School. When the chips are down, and the issues have to do with human life, and with justice and love, somebody's got to pay the cost, and if you're going to be this kind of person, you've got to be prepared to pay. And there were people who really did an about-face, and paid the cost, and stood up for what counted when the time came.[10]

Never wavering from his belief in the responsibility of Christians to address society's ills head-on, Hines stood fast in the face of opposition and criticism, challenging his flock to join him in fighting racial and social injustice. Speaking to the 109th Annual Council of the Diocese of Texas in Houston in 1958, he eloquently stated his case for supporting civil rights within the church while at the same time acknowledging the difficulties inherent in advocating such significant social change. "It would be foolish to pretend that all this is going to be easy," he said, "for it will mean that—in the foreseeable future—the chances are that we shall have to struggle against the prevailing opinions of much of our land. But even this should not deter our Christian witness, for it has ever been creditable to oppose erroneous ideas, however powerful they may be."[11]

Hines's dynamic leadership of the Diocese of Texas gained him a national profile not only within the denomination, but also in the press. In November 1958 he introduced a resolution at a meeting of the church's bishops in Miami, Florida, "calling on all Christians and civic leaders to join in bringing an end to racial discrimination and separation." According to an Associated Press story that ran in the *Dallas Morning News,* the resolution passed unanimously. "It urged parents to guide their children into attitudes free of prejudice. It also urged work toward a 'society in which every race will have the freedom to enjoy without discrimination and without separation, all opportunities in education, housing, employment, public accommodations and all other aspects of church and civil life.'"[12]

In October 1964, at the national church's Sixty-First General Convention in St. Louis—the city where he began his ministry three decades earlier—Hines was as surprised as many others when he was elected presiding bishop of the Episcopal Church, the denomination's highest office in the United States.

Reflecting on the monumental task ahead of him, he told a writer for the *Houston Chronicle*—who described the bishop as "a blue-eyed man with the build of a half-back and the compassion of a poet"—"The numbness is still there. But it is being replaced by fear." But, as the reporter noted, Hines was "no stranger to trying times and no stranger to awesome responsibility."[13] Officially installed at a service at the National Cathedral in Washington, DC, on January 27, 1965, he was poised to lead the church through one of the most exciting yet difficult and controversial periods in its history.

Based at the National Church Center in New York City, Hines took office at the height of the civil rights era and soon instituted pro-

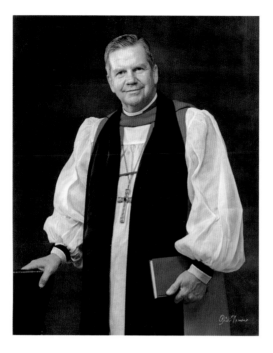

*The Right Reverend
John Elbridge Hines,
presiding bishop of
the Episcopal Church.*
Courtesy Hines family.

grams that brought major changes to the denomination, the lasting results of which are still debated within the church today. Believing that "the church must speak out for justice and equality or
risk becoming irrelevant in the modern world," he called for delib-
erate action to address what he saw as society's ills. In early March
1965, following the pivotal civil rights march at the Edmund Pettus
Bridge in Selma, Alabama, and the beating two days later of volunteer James Reeb, a Unitarian minister who died of his injuries,
Bishop Hines went to Selma to participate in Reeb's memorial service along with Greek Orthodox Archbishop Demetrios Iokovos and
the Reverend Martin Luther King Jr. and to take part in a march
to the Selma courthouse afterwards. Referring to the event some
years later, he said,

> I saw it as the responsibility of the symbolic head of the Epis-
> copal Church, the Presiding Bishop, to indicate that at least
> through the Presiding Bishop's office the church has a concern
> about the black man, and also the white man, in a situation in
> which there are conflicting points of view and opinions about

their status and about dealing with liberty and freedom and the dignity of the human race. So I went primarily to say that as far as *this* (referring to himself) symbolic head of the Episcopal Church was concerned, the church has got to be concerned here, and has got to do its best to make its witness. It was a frightening experience, but it was one about which I had no regrets.[14]

In October 1965, after an all-white jury acquitted Lowndes County, Alabama, deputy sheriff Thomas Coleman of fatally shooting civil rights workers Jonathan Daniels, an Episcopal seminary student from New Hampshire, and the Reverend Richard F. Morrisroe, a Roman Catholic priest, Hines released a statement assailing the verdict, declaring, "What it said about the likelihood of minorities securing even-handed justice in some parts of this country should jar the conscience of all men who still believe in the concept of justice in this land of hope."[15]

Deeply disturbed by urban riots throughout the country in 1967 in the wake of civil rights struggles, opposition to the war in Vietnam, and the effects of poverty, Bishop Hines personally walked the ghettoes of several large US cities to see firsthand the situation inflaming American society. Believing the church had a responsibility to address the issues, he boldly called for the Episcopal Church's General Convention to change its priorities—both programmatic and budgetary—to come up with ways to offer help to those most in need, whether they were Episcopalians or not. The result was the General Convention Special Program (GCSP), a far-reaching plan to offer no-strings-attached financial assistance and services to community organizations, neighborhoods, and inner-city programs, with the aim of encouraging self-determination. The program reached out to all minority groups, regardless of faith tradition, but also empowered African Americans, Hispanics, and other minorities within the church, including members of the Episcopal Society for Cultural and Racial Unity, and led many parishes around the country to initiate social outreach ministries.[16]

Hines's influence reached beyond the Episcopal Church as well. He was an active participant in national and international religious organizations, including the National Council of Churches and the

World Council of Churches. In 1971, in response to the ongoing racist system of apartheid in South Africa, he led the movement for corporate divestment in that country. At a meeting of General Motors stockholders, armed with the church's twelve thousand shares of stock, he eloquently and passionately spoke against the company's continuing operations in South Africa. Although the change he sought was not immediate, his actions inspired other churches and institutions to take the same position with regard to investments in numerous international corporations. In a February 1972 statement on behalf of the Church Project on US Investments in Southern Africa—an alliance which included participation from the United Church of Christ, the United Presbyterian Church (USA), the Episcopal Church, the American Baptist Convention, and the United Methodist Church—Hines wrote, "It is because we advocate self-determination, justice and human development for all Africans and oppose colonialism, racism and repression that we must give special attention to the international operations in southern Africa of companies in which we invest.... We come to this concern with the conviction that there is no moral defense for a philosophy and policy of racism or colonialism." According to Archbishop Desmond Tutu, leader of the Anglican Church in South Africa and eventual winner of the Nobel Peace Prize, Hines's initiative led to widespread financial pressures to end investments in South Africa and played a major role in bringing about the end of apartheid. As Hines later said:

> The church can only exercise an authority . . . if it has itself been crucified in the marketplace, and unless it is as just as it proclaims its gospel to be. Justice is the corporate face of love. To seek justice in corporate society is about as close as Christian love can get in society. What the church can do—and must do—in order to exhibit as best it can the kind of love reflected in that declaration, "God so loved the world," is see that justice is enacted in society for all men and women, whoever they are.[17]

Back in the United States, the GCSP was making waves within the denomination. In a 1973 article about changes the program brought to the church, a writer for *Time* magazine said, "The once conservative Episcopal Church has flowered into one of the most progressive of mainstream Protestant denominations in the US." By the time of that article's publication, however, dissatisfaction among many of the church's conservative and more traditional parishes had begun to manifest itself in a backlash that moved the church away from many of Hines's reforms, as well as from what many saw as a growing centralization of the church in the office of the presiding bishop. A weary Hines surprised many when he announced his intention to retire from office in 1974. Delegates to the General Convention in Louisville, Kentucky, in October 1973 elected a conservative bishop, John M. Allin of Mississippi, to succeed him.[18]

Bishop Hines retired with his wife, Helen, to a home they owned in the mountains of North Carolina. They continued to live there for the next two decades, until declining health prompted them to move back to Austin in 1993 to be closer to their children. Helen Orwig Hines died in 1996, and Bishop John E. Hines died on July 19, 1997, at age eighty-six. News of his death, which came during the church's general convention, appeared in the national and international media and brought numerous tributes and testimonials of his impact on both the church and society at large. Newly elected presiding bishop Edmund Browning officiated at overflowing memorial services at St. David's Episcopal Church in Austin and at Christ Church Cathedral in Houston. Bishop and Mrs. Hines were buried on the grounds of the Episcopal Church of the Good Shepherd in Cashiers, North Carolina, near their former home. The Seminary of the Southwest in Austin, which hosts an annual John Hines Day each October, established the John Hines Chair of Preaching in 2006 to honor its founder and his legendary oratorical and preaching skills, and Hines's alma mater, Virginia Theological Seminary, established an annual Hines Preaching Award in 1998.[19]

Bishop John E. Hines's leadership, both in Texas and nationally through his ministry as presiding bishop, brought about sweeping changes in the Episcopal Church. His unswerving devotion both to the church and to the Social Gospel movement resulted in vastly changed outreach programs that addressed racial and gender equality and social issues in the United States and beyond. Although not all of his programs survived his administration, and some people credit the backlash resulting from his liberal and progressive programs as a reason for declining church membership in the latter half of the twentieth century, his legacy remains strong in the growing numbers of minority and women clergy, a more racially diverse church membership, and the increased social outreach ministries of Episcopal churches throughout the country. His lasting influence on the church is a mixed one, to be sure, but it also is undeniably significant. As one writer stated, "His ten years as bishop coadjutor of Texas, eleven years as bishop of Texas, and nine years as presiding bishop were characterized by outspoken, courageous, and often costly witness against racism and all forms of social injustice."[20]

MARKER LOCATION: Seminary of the Southwest, 501 E. 32nd St., Austin

CHRIST CHURCH CATHEDRAL

Officially founded on April 1, 1839, downtown Houston's Christ Church Cathedral is the second oldest Episcopal church in Texas. Its early leaders included the Reverend R. M. Chapman and William Fairfax Gray, a soldier and attorney from Virginia who was a pioneer Texas settler, participant in the Convention of 1836 at Washington-on-the-Brazos, and clerk of the Republic of Texas Congress. Gray led a petition drive to recruit supporters for the mission church, and the Right Reverend Leonidas Polk, bishop of Louisiana and missionary bishop from the United States, visited Houston to encourage the new venture. Polk, a native of North Carolina, attended the US Military Academy at West Point, but shortly after graduation in 1827 resigned his commission and entered Virginia Theological Seminary to study for the Episcopal priesthood. At the urging of his old West Point friend, Confederate president Jefferson Davis, Bishop Polk returned to military life at the outbreak of the Civil War and was commissioned a major general. He died in Georgia in June 1864 when he was hit by a cannonball in the Battle of Pine Mountain in the Atlanta Campaign.

Early services for Christ Church took place in what was then the Capitol of the Republic of Texas at the corner of Main Street and Texas Avenue. The first wooden church building was completed in 1844 at the corner of Texas Avenue and Fannin Street. The congregation built a new brick structure to replace it a year later, but it was deemed too small to serve the congregation within a decade. Construction began in 1859 on a new building designed by Edwin Fairfax Gray, son of the congregation's founder. According to church history, a cattleman driving a herd of cattle down Texas Avenue to market happened on the construction site, asked what was being built, and roped a steer out of his herd to donate to the cause. As the story goes, it was because of that event that the official seal of the Episcopal Diocese of Texas includes the image of a steer's head. Construction of the church slowed during the Civil

Interior of Christ Church Cathedral, Houston, showing the elaborately carved wooden rood screen. Courtesy Texas Historical Commission, National Register of Historic Places files.

War years, but the building was finally completed in 1866. It was enlarged ten years later.

The current building dates to 1893 and includes elements from earlier structures, including stained glass windows and the altar cross. Its most prominent interior feature is an elaborately carved wooden rood screen that separates the nave (the congregational area) from the chancel (the altar area).

Designated the cathedral for the Diocese of Texas in 1949, Christ Church officially became Christ Church Cathedral during the term of Bishop Clinton S. Quin. Six of its rectors, including John E. Hines, later became bishops. In addition to its function as the official see of the Bishop of Texas, the cathedral hosts an active congregation that has continued to be a leader in outreach and social justice ministries in Houston, including many programs begun by Hines when he served as rector from 1941 to 1945.

MARKER LOCATION: 1117 Texas Avenue, Houston

Sources: Christ Church Cathedral, Harris County, THC marker files; Marguerite S. Johnston, *A Happy Worldly Abode: Christ Church Cathedral, 1839–1964* (Houston: Cathedral Press, 1964); Andrew Forest Muir, "Gray, William Fairfax," *Handbook of Texas Online,* www.tshaonline.org/handbook/online/articles/fgr27, accessed December 16, 2010; Christ Church Cathedral website, www.christchurchcathedral .org, accessed December 16, 2010; www.historynet.com/leonidas-polk-southern-civil-war-general.htm, accessed December 17, 2010.

14 A Light on the Path of Wisdom

A brief article in a 1937 issue of the *Sherman Daily Democrat* listed the accomplishments of a prominent local citizen: "The mother of three sons has been a leader of girls continuously for 16 years, and her contributions to local, district, state and national projects of the Camp Fire Girls organization has won for her national recognition as a welfare worker. In addition, she has been a commercial secretary, a wife and homemaker, a successful club woman, religious leader, a federal court reporter, a commercial instructor and is the author of a historical volume. She is Mrs. H. E. Hall."[1] Speaking of his mother more than seven decades later, one of her sons remembered, "She just never slowed down. She was always up to something. She was out to save the world."[2]

Born in Fair Dealing, Kentucky, in 1885, Mita Holsapple was five years old when her father, J. W. Holsapple, a minister in the Disciples of Christ denomination, moved his family to Texas. After a few years as a circuit-riding preacher, Holsapple settled his family in Sherman, Grayson County, where he served as pastor of Central Christian Church. Mita Holsapple grew up in Sherman, graduated from the local Mary Nash College, and went to work as a secretary for a nursery company. She married William M. Gordon in 1906, and they were the parents of a son they called Bill. By 1917, though, the Gordons' marriage had ended, and Mita established a separate household with her son and a young orphaned cousin from Kentucky.

Feeling a patriotic call to duty upon the United States' entry into World War I that year, the young mother entrusted the children to the care of close relatives and, accompanied by a girlhood friend, went to work as a secretary at the Department of the Navy in Wash-

Mita Holsapple Hall with son Clyde, 1922. Courtesy Clyde L. Hall.

ington, DC, for the duration of the war. She returned to her family in Sherman in 1918, and the following year she married Hugh Edward Hall, secretary-treasurer at the Texas Nursery Company. The Halls had two sons: Clyde L., born in 1922, and Hugh E. Jr., born in 1925.[3]

As was the case with many young women of her Progressive Era generation who found an outlet for community activism through the woman's club movement, Mita Holsapple Hall volunteered her time and talents to a number of causes. As a leader of youth programs at Central Christian Church, she became aware of the national Camp Fire Girls organization and soon thereafter sought to establish a Camp Fire presence in Sherman.

Camp Fire Girls emerged in the early twentieth century as an organization that encouraged health, education, and community service. According to historian Jennifer Helgren, "In 1911, a group of educators, reformers, and youth workers headed by Luther Gulick and his wife Charlotte Gulick began organizing the Camp Fire Girls to provide American girls with a feminine corollary to the Boy Scouts." The movement spread quickly from its New England roots, and within two years had a presence in all forty-eight states as well as the territories of Alaska and Hawaii. As Helgren explained, "Camp Fire was one of many youth organizations and youth centered enterprises to emerge during the Progressive Era. Educators and reformers of the late nineteenth and early twentieth centuries turned to social programs and government legislation to guard youth and prepare them for the rapid social changes that accompanied the modern industrial era."[4]

Camp Fire's primary mission, as stated by Luther Gulick, was "to promote service to others, team work, and opportunities for a well rounded life—a vivid, intense life of joy and service." The organization officially incorporated in Washington, DC, in 1912, and Gulick chose the name and logo "because campfires were the origin of the first communities and domestic life. Once people learned to make and control fire, they could develop and nurture a sense of community." Gulick's vision also included the promotion of what he termed a "balanced life" for adolescent girls. "Balanced living meant recognizing the need for work, play, and rest; for developing body, mind, and spirit; and for incorporating tradition into modern life. An essential statement of this life view was the action oriented Camp Fire Law: 'Seek beauty, Give service, Pursue knowledge, Be trustworthy, Hold onto health, Glorify work, and Be happy.'"[5]

The Camp Fire Girls motto, WoHeLo, coined by Charlotte Gulick, is drawn from the first two letters of the words Work, Health, and Love. It alludes to elements of the Camp Fire Law, as well as to the Native American imagery adopted by local Camp Fire clubs or councils. Rather than promote competition among the girls, the organization instead encouraged individual achievement to earn positive recognition. Members worked on projects for which they "earned small colored beads for completing modest tasks in the seven categories of home craft, hand craft, health craft, camp craft, nature lore, business, and patriotism."[6]

Mita Hall felt a calling to mentor girls in her community, reportedly as a way to encourage them to pursue education, healthy living, and a spirit of independence. She organized Sherman's Tejas Council of Camp Fire Girls in the spring of 1921. Many members of her church youth group joined with Mrs. H. E., as they fondly called her, to make it an immediate success. Within a short time Hall also became active in the regional and national Camp Fire Girls movement and counted among her friends Edith Kempthorne, a native New Zealander who served as the organization's US national field secretary.[7]

A strong proponent of academic and practical education for both boys and girls, Hall devised a plan to offer a group of young people a unique learning experience in the summer of 1925. Enlisting the help of her younger sister, Merle Holsapple, as a chaperone and her oldest son, Bill Gordon, as a driver, she took four girls from the Tejas Camp Fire club—Dorothy Freeman, Hazel May, Frances Taylor, and Catherine Webb—as well as two young men from her church youth group—Paul Andrews and Greg Taylor—on a month-long automobile tour through the southern and eastern United States and into the Canadian province of Ontario. (Decades later, viewing a photograph of the group posing next to its two Model T touring cars, Hall's son, Hugh E. Hall Jr., pointed out that technically he, too, made the trip, since it occurred in June 1925, and he was born the following November. He also remembered that two of the travelers, Hazel May and Paul Andrews, later married.)[8]

Automobile travel in 1925 presented many challenges. Road conditions often were crude at best, with many unpaved sections becoming treacherous in bad weather, and mechanical breakdowns occurred more often than not. As one writer pointed out, "Long-distance travel by auto required both skill and brawn and was not meant for amateurs or 'Sunday drivers.'" Available accommodations also varied widely, and many auto travelers carried tents and cooking utensils and set up temporary campsites along their routes. Eventually roadside motels, or tourist courts, that sprang up along the roadways provided more comfortable overnight lodging as well as restaurants for travelers' convenience. For those who were adventurous enough to set out on the road in the 1920s, however, "auto touring held out the promise of reclaiming the sense of discovery that earlier generations—the pioneer generations—had enjoyed."[9]

With that pioneer spirit, and undaunted by the myriad challenges of road travel facing them, the intrepid Sherman adventurers set out on an itinerary carefully planned by Hall. They often camped out at night, and in many places they were welcomed and

Mita Holsapple Hall (top right), her sister Merle Holsapple (top center), and her son Bill Gordon (bottom right) with Camp Fire Girls and church youth group members as they began their 1925 automobile trip across the United States. Courtesy Texas Historical Commission, Official Texas Historical Marker files. Photograph provided for application by Clyde L. Hall.

hosted by Camp Fire groups. One highlight of the trip included a stay at the national Camp Fire camp on the banks of the Hudson River in upstate New York. They went to Muscle Shoals, Alabama; Stone Mountain in Georgia; Raleigh, North Carolina, where the Reverend George Cuthrell, a former pastor at Central Christian Church in Sherman, introduced them to the governor; and Norfolk, Virginia, where they toured the USS *Texas* battleship, which was at that time in dry dock undergoing modifications after its World War I service. In addition, they visited Washington, DC; Philadelphia;

New York City; and Niagara Falls, crossing from there into Ontario, Canada. A writer for the local newspaper in Sherman reported on the group's safe return in early July: "According to Mrs. Hall, the trip was ideal in every respect, no accidents of any kind having been sustained and no difficulties having been encountered in all the thousands of miles which they covered between Sherman and Ontario and back again."[10]

The success and popularity of the first Camp Fire Girls club in Sherman led Hall to organize two additional groups—named Minnehaha and Otyokwa—and by 1927 she arranged for a summer camping experience for the girls at a site called Camp Grayson in the northwest part of the county. It proved to be the first of many annual summer camps that generations of girls enjoyed, and Hall's sons remembered it as a fun and adventurous way to begin each summer vacation. Such ventures, however, required financial backing, and Hall tirelessly appealed to her fellow Grayson County citizens for assistance. She also enlisted help from her family. Her sons Clyde and Hugh—both of whom were Boy Scouts in a troop led by their father—not only helped raise money for the Camp Fire Girls camp, but also worked there each summer. "Before the community chest," Hugh Hall remembered, "we were the collectors around town. She knew all these people, and they would donate to the Camp Fire Girls, and guess who got to collect them?" Recalling that his own camp experience included running errands, he added: "She always wanted some boys on that thing. The lifeguard was a boy, and I was one of the boys, and I always went to the camp. And by the time I was twelve, I was driving. I could drive to the city limits of Sherman, walk to wherever I needed to walk, come back and get in the car, and drive back out to the camp. So that was my chore."[11] His brother Clyde also remembered the summer camps and told one story in particular that revealed both playful and resourceful aspects of his mother's character:

As for the annual summer camp, she always arranged for the camp to be at a venue with a small lake. Her activity program featured a water pageant in which all girls would participate. The pageant always had a floating "centerpiece" around which all activity took place. What was the centerpiece? Well, my mother long since had developed the quality of floating and so, in effect, she became a table on which the girls could place whatever they wanted with confidence that it would not fall off and sink in the water. A half century later some of her "girls" frequently referred to their "floating platform."[12]

By 1928, with all three Sherman Camp Fire Girls groups engaged in active programs, many of the girls and their parents began to campaign for another summer road trip, and they persuaded Mrs. H. E. to plan a new excursion. Once again, the itinerary called for a drive through the northeastern United States. This time Hall recruited three adults to join her as chaperones for a group of ten Camp Fire Girls that traveled in four cars. Unlike the group on the 1925 trip, who experienced no accidents or mechanical troubles, the 1928 tour participants encountered a few adventures along the road. Traveling through Massachusetts, they were such objects of curiosity that they ended up in a local police court, although not for any infractions of the law. As the Sherman newspaper later reported it:

> Among the thrills which Mrs. H. E. Hall and a party of Camp Fire girls experienced in their 7,000 mile educational tour from which they have just returned, was being mistaken for Texas ranchers. Wherever the party stopped in the New England section, especially, the girls and their chaperones were little short of wonders, Mrs. Hall states.
>
> In Salem, Mass., a newspaper reporter unable to locate the crowd, asked a policeman to give them a ticket requiring their appearance at police court, which he did, and when the tourists finally wended their way to the judge, they found there the reporter whom they all agreed was A-1 in gathering news.
>
> After being closely questioned by the Salem journalist, they read next day his story of the interview which follows, in part:
>
> "The statement that 14 Texas ranchers invaded Salem yesterday might be expected to stir things up in the peaceful old Witch City. Just as true as they were in Salem, equally correct is the fact that they were so quiet that few knew they were here.
>
> "Instead of coming in covered wagons or on pintos, they chose

to come here in three Fords and an Erskine. Aside from having one of the cars skid and turn over into a ditch, another having the transmission and rear end go and blowouts and punctures on the four cars, they report nothing exciting happened and no one was injured."

The Sherman reporter concluded the story with, "Mrs. Hall and her party of Camp Fire Girls believe that the South should stage an educational campaign where information about Texas life and customs may be given the New Englanders."[13]

As she became more involved with Camp Fire Girls on a regional and national level, Hall's activities in Sherman gained the attention of the organization's leadership. In 1929 she won the Harriman Medallion, the highest honor bestowed by the organization in recognition of a local leader's successful program of work. Reported through the wire services, the story of Hall's accomplishment ran in the September 7 issue of the *New York Times:* "Mrs. Mita Hall of Sherman, Texas, the mother of three sons and no daughters, has received the Grace Harriman silver medal from the Camp Fire Girls National Council . . . for having accomplished more this year for the organization than any other Camp Fire Girls group leader in the United States."[14]

Tragedy struck the Hall family in 1931 when Hugh Edward Hall died suddenly. One of his sons recalled that his father had spent a cold Sunday afternoon building playground equipment in the backyard. He repeatedly moved from the warm house, where he heated an iron bar in the fireplace, to the frigid outdoors, where he used the iron to burn holes in the wooden beams of an "acting bar," a jungle gym–like apparatus he was constructing next to a playhouse he had built earlier for his sons. He developed a chill from the constantly changing temperature extremes, contracted pneumonia, and died later that week.

Faced with rearing her two young sons alone, Mita Hall returned to work as a secretary and found a position as a court reporter with the US District Court for the Eastern District of Texas. Her job required her to travel extensively with the judge, who held court in cities throughout the district, and she arranged for caretakers to stay with her boys, who did not always appreciate the effort. Years later, Hugh Hall recounted stories of the mischief he and his brother Clyde got into, saying, "She would get various people to come in there, and we'd run 'em off. We thought we were old enough to stay by ourselves." He also remembered, "She brought us up with a work ethic. And boy, if she told us to do something and we didn't do it! I remember one time she was traveling [as a] court reporter, and she said, 'Y'all varnish the floor.' We washed it first, and it was wet, so we claimed it was too wet. She got in that night, and she varnished the floor that night. Man! She did not put up with us not doing what she said to do."[15]

While she may have been a firm disciplinarian, by all accounts Hall also was a loving mother who planned fun summer vacation adventures for her children each year. Son Clyde recalled, "Solely for relaxation she enjoyed fishing. In the mid-1930s, following her annual stressful period associated with full responsibility for scores of young lasses attending Camp Fire Girls camp, she enjoyed going to Branson, Missouri. In those days Branson was totally different from what it is now. But Lake Taneycomo was there, and she procured a lakeside fishing cabin which she enjoyed with her two young sons."[16]

The family also traveled extensively throughout the United States and into Canada and Mexico. They often took advantage of the Camp Fire Girls network, frequently staying in homes of club friends and associates during their travels. In 1936, though, Hall chose to take the family on an educational tour through Texas to commemorate the Texas Centennial. "It was 1936, therefore we had to have the history of Texas," Hugh Hall said, recounting a driving tour that took them to "every historical site in the State of Texas."[17] Also that year, she was named one of twelve outstanding local Camp Fire Girls executives in the United States and received an award at the organization's annual conference in New York City.

The Texas Centennial year was significant for Hall in another way, as well. Along with her friend Mattie Lucas, she had for years traveled extensively throughout Grayson County in an attempt to learn as much as possible about local history. Together, they collected oral interviews and other resources from longtime citi-

Mita Holsapple Hall. Courtesy Clyde L. Hall.

zens and early settlers. She often took her sons with her on visits to people in isolated settlements, taking notes as she listened to stories about the history of each region of the county. As a centennial project, Hall and Lucas coauthored *A History of Grayson County, Texas,* published in 1936. In addition, they researched and coordinated placement of numerous Texas Centennial Commission historical markers in the county. One of Hugh Hall's childhood memories is of riding along with his mother as she determined the placement of the historical markers and driving stakes into the ground to mark each spot.[18]

In addition to her extensive work with Camp Fire Girls on the local, regional, and national levels, Hall also maintained an active schedule of involvement with many other community organizations. She held leadership positions in the Sherman Shakespeare Club, the Business and Professional Women's Club of Sherman, and the Sherman Community Concert Association. During World War II she served on the local United Service Organizations (USO) board of directors and was treasurer of the American Red Cross chapter that served troops stationed at Perrin Field, a US Army Air Forces flight training base in Sherman, and Camp Howze, a US Army infantry training base in nearby Cooke County. She loaned a piano to the USO facility at Perrin Field, and it was returned to her some twenty years later thanks to a note reading "This belongs to Mrs. H. E. Hall" that she had the foresight to attach to the back of the instrument. Her work on behalf of the troops was not limited to those serving on the home front, however. She used connections she had formed in Washington during her service there as a secretary during World War I to assist her son Hugh. As he recalled, "By working there she knew enough to call the secretary of the navy in World War II when I didn't get my mail for nine months, and didn't get paid or anything else, when I was in the South Pacific. She rattled a few cages up there, and I got my mail, too."[19]

By the end of World War II, Hall's active involvement with Camp Fire Girls began drawing to a close, but her legacy within the organization continued. A half-dozen former Sherman Camp Fire Girls followed in her footsteps and went on to work for the organization on both regional and national levels, and at least one girl she mentored became a high-ranking national Camp Fire Girls, Inc. official. Indeed, National Field Secretary Kempthorne later stated, "She produced more executives for Camp Fire through her leadership than any other person in Camp Fire."[20] In her later years, Hall also remained active in numerous church and community organizations, including the Grayson County Historical Society and the Grayson County Historical Survey Committee (later Grayson County Historical Commission).

When she died in February 1965, tributes poured in from a wide array of friends and colleagues. Camp Fire Girls national director Martha F. Allen sent a telegram saying, "Her life was one of service and beauty and Camp Fire Girls was fortunate in having had a generous share of them both in the many capacities in which she served this organization for many years. Her true memorial is a living one in the hearts and lives of the people who bear the marks of her influence."[21] The Sherman Council of Camp Fire Girls passed a resolution in her honor which read in part, "We have lost our guiding star and inspiration. During the twenty-four years of active Camp Fire Girl leadership, from 1921 to 1945, she was a monument of strength and inspiration, instilling the highest standards of character, integrity, and comradeship into the thousands of young ladies privileged to be inspired by her in the Camp Fire Girl movement."[22] The Sherman chapter of the USO also passed a resolution extolling her service and commitment to the military and the community, and on Sunday, February 7, 1965, an editorial in the *Sherman Democrat*, entitled "The Flame Burns," summed up Mita Holsapple Hall's life's work in a heartfelt epitaph:

> She left a long and varied list of achievement in private life, church and community, but probably the service for which she is known best was her immeasurable contribution to Camp Fire Girls. Mrs. Hall had no daughters. But literally thousands of girls in North Texas, and indeed the entire nation, grew into richer womanhood through her understanding, interest and influence. . . . Through the greater part of her life, Mrs. Hall earned her own living. She brought up and educated her sons. But always she reached beyond the family and gave her time and talent without stint to the community, the poor and privileged. . . . She followed the path of wisdom. She invested her life in youth. She passed on to the future her love of God's earth and the beauty in it, her vision of the heavens, her joy in home and family, her respect for achievement, and her pleasure of companionship in work and fun. These are the works that praise Mrs. Hall. In them she has bequeathed the force of her purpose and the light of her spirit.[23]

Thirty-seven years later, the Texas Historical Commission, in response to a request from the Grayson County Historical Commission, placed an Official Texas Historical Marker in Sherman to honor the accomplishments and contributions of this remarkable Texas woman.

MARKER LOCATION: West Hill Cemetery, 1304 W. Lamar St., Sherman

FAIRLY FLYING FROM TERRELL TO DALLAS

An unusual sight greeted the citizens of Dallas on the evening of October 5, 1899. Edward H. R. Green—who, six feet, four inches tall, weighing an estimated three hundred pounds, sporting an artificial leg, and widely known as one of the wealthiest men in Texas, was something of a curiosity himself—rode into town in a "horseless carriage" automobile. Accompanied by the vehicle's designer and builder, George Preston Dorris of St. Louis, Green left Terrell in Kaufman County at 2:20 that afternoon and arrived in Dallas at 7:30 p.m. The following day the *Dallas Morning News,* reporting on the thirty-mile trip, said "the automobile vehicle created a sensation along country roads yesterday, and Dallasites were startled."

A railroad capitalist and chairman of the state Republican Party executive committee, Green was a flamboyant character who maintained homes in both Terrell and Dallas. The son of exceedingly wealthy parents, he moved to Texas from New York in 1892 at the behest of his mother, Hetty Robinson Green, a colorful character in her own right. Known as "the Witch of Wall Street" for her miserly ways, Hetty Green reportedly was responsible for her son's leg amputation when, after he was injured in a skating accident while still a teenager, she refused to pay for quality medical care. She invested widely in railroads in the 1880s and 1890s and sent her son to Texas to take charge of the Texas Midland Railroad, a subsidiary of the Texas & Houston Central Railway. Establishing his headquarters in Terrell, Edward Green lived in an apartment over the town's downtown opera house but also made frequent trips to Dallas, where he maintained a second home that housed his paramour, a former prostitute named Mabel Harlow. (He married Harlow in 1917 after the death of his mother, who disapproved of the relationship.)

Green's historic automobile trip—supposedly the first in Texas, although that claim could not be documented and thus does not appear on the historical marker text—brought him the public attention that he craved. He purchased one of the first two St. Louis horseless carriages manufactured by the St. Louis Motor Carriage Company, a firm Dorris co-owned with John L. French. Dorris accompanied the car during shipment via rail from St. Louis to Terrell, gave Green a few driving lessons upon arrival, and rode along with him to Dallas on his first road trip.

A crowd gathered to watch the two men embark on their journey. "When we left Terrell we struck a very sandy stretch of road," Green told the *Dallas Morning News* reporter, "and because of the dust thrown up by the vehicle, we had to go very slowly. After this bad stretch was passed we turned on more power and fairly flew." Their route followed an old wagon road that paralleled the Texas and Pacific Railway line west from Terrell, through the town of Forney, along a rural dirt road into Dallas County at the crossing of the East Fork of the Trinity River, through Mesquite, and on into Dallas. "It was amusing to note the sensation our appearance caused along the road," Green said. "Cotton pickers dropped their sacks and ran wildly to the fences to see the strange sight. And the interest was shared by the farm animals, too. One razor-back sow that caught sight of us is running yet, I know. At least a dozen horses executed fancy waltz steps on their hind legs as we sped silently by, and but for the fact that we went so soon out of sight, there would have been several first-class runaways."

As the travelers approached Forney, however, they encountered a farm wagon that forced them off the road and into a ditch. They quickly enlisted the help of a local blacksmith to repair the car's broken water tank. Although the historical record is not precise on this detail, the blacksmith reportedly was Reeve Henry, an African American businessman and inventor who applied for several patents and whose descendants consider him the first automobile repairman in Texas. After an hour's delay caused by the collision and subsequent repairs, the car and its passengers continued toward Dallas, where, according to the newspaper account, they rode up and down Main Street at a rate of fifteen miles an hour and caused a sensation among a crowd of observers. "I enjoyed my trip immensely and intend to make many more like it in the near future," Green said. He later had a special railroad car built to ferry the automobile—and a chauffeur—around the country as he traveled in his private coach.

Green returned to New York about 1910 to help run his mother's varied financial interests, although he continued as president of the Texas Midland Railroad until 1928. He and his wife maintained homes in Florida, New York, and Massachusetts. He died of heart disease in 1936, leaving an estate worth an estimated forty million dollars. Mabel Green, following the wishes of her husband, had his amputated leg exhumed and reburied with his body at the family estate in Bellows Falls, Vermont. The car he drove from Terrell to Dallas in 1899 resurfaced in the news in 1910. Nicknamed "Old Hurricane" in the *Dallas Morning News* story, it reportedly was put to use as a pace car for horse races at Fair Park.

MARKER LOCATION: Bell Park, Trinity and Bois D'Arc Streets, Forney

Sources: 1899 Automobile Trip, Kaufman County, THC marker files; Debbie Mauldin Cottrell, "Green, Edward Howland Robinson," *Handbook of Texas Online*, www .tshaonline.org/handbook/online/articles/fgr33, and "Green, Hetty Howland Robinson," Handbook of Texas Online, www.tshaonline.org/handbook/online/articles/ fgrrw, accessed February 27, 2011.

15

Two Generations Striving for Civil Rights

Life in Texas and the South shaped the characters of two men whose spiritual, intellectual, and organizational leadership had enormous impact on the modern civil rights movement. The Reverend James Leonard Farmer Sr. and his son, James Leonard Farmer Jr., differed in their approaches toward achieving racial equality in America, but each advanced the cause in concrete ways. Both were influenced by their time in Texas, and both are subjects of Official Texas Historical Markers.

James Leonard Farmer Sr., a son of former slaves, was born in South Carolina on June 12, 1886. As a poor African American child of the rural South, he faced the challenges and injustices of poverty, racism, and a segregated society. His superior intellect and thirst for knowledge, however, propelled him beyond the backwaters of the South onto a path that would earn him the distinction of being recognized as the first African American PhD in Texas. Farmer attended Cookman Institute, a Methodist school for African Americans in Jacksonville, Florida, and his work there qualified him for scholarships to study at Boston University. According to a family story, there were no funds with which to pay travel costs, so he walked from Florida to Boston to begin his studies in 1909. Living in a boardinghouse in nearby Wellesley and working as a valet for a wealthy white family, he traveled daily by train to the university, using his commuting time to read and study. He completed a bachelor's degree in 1913, a master's in 1916, and his doctorate in 1918, all in the field of sacred theology. In 1917 he married Pearl Houston, a schoolteacher he had met in Florida. The couple soon moved to Texas, where the Texas Conference of the Methodist Episcopal Church ordained Farmer an elder and assigned him to churches in

Texarkana, Galveston, and Marshall. Pearl Houston Farmer gave birth to the couple's first child, a daughter named Helen, in Texarkana in 1918, and by January 1920, when their second child, James Leonard Farmer Jr., was born, Farmer served as professor of philosophy, religion, economics, Hebrew, and Greek at Wiley College, a Methodist-sponsored school for African Americans in the East Texas town of Marshall. Later in 1920, Farmer accepted a position at Rust College, so the family moved to Holly Springs in northwestern Mississippi when their son was six months old.[1]

In his autobiography, *Lay Bare the Heart*, James Farmer Jr. recalled a rarefied existence as the son of a professor living on a college campus, mostly shielded from the ugliness of segregation in his early years. The senior Farmer's academic credentials earned him a grudging respect among the white residents of the small Southern town. In addition to his status as a minister, "he had another mystique, equally definitive in Holly Springs, Mississippi, in the early 1920s," his son wrote. "He was an authentic scholar at a time and place in which scholarship was mysterious and a PhD degree magical—among both blacks and whites."[2]

However sheltered his life on campus, it was also as a small child in Holly Springs that Jim Farmer—as he became known to his friends—had his first personal encounter with racism in an incident that would lay the groundwork for his life's work in civil rights. Walking home with his mother one hot day, he asked to stop in a local store for a cold drink. His mother said there were soft drinks at home, and he would have to wait. Seeing another child sitting in the store enjoying a beverage, he failed to understand why he could not have one as well. His mother told him the reason was because the other child was white, and he was black. He remembered seeing his mother crying after they arrived home, and with a sad realization he understood the awful truth of the situation. "Children of a tender age are unaware of much that goes on," he wrote. "One thing I was aware of, though, was the soft drink episode. Every black child in the South has an early experience of racism that shafts his soul. For the lucky, it is sudden, like a bolt of lightning, striking one to his knees. For others, a gradual dying, a sliver of meanness worming its way to the heart."[3]

The historical marker for James Farmer Jr. stands in front of the East Austin house at 1604 New York Ave., where the Farmer family lived when his father served on the faculty and as registrar of Samuel Huston College.
Photograph by Cynthia J. Beeman.

A precocious child, Jim Farmer learned to read early and kept up with his sister's schoolwork before he was old enough to attend school himself. When he was five years old the family moved to Austin, Texas, where his father joined the faculty of Samuel Huston College. Established by the Methodist Church in 1900, Huston College would merge with another black institution, Tillotson College, in 1952 to form Huston-Tillotson College (now University).[4] Living in a rented house in the East Austin neighborhood that bordered the college, the Farmer family quickly settled into their new surroundings.

Jim Farmer described his childhood in Austin as one of adventures with his friends and his beloved dog, but also one in which his awareness of racism and segregation continued to grow. His father, meanwhile, took on administrative duties as registrar at the college and was credited with improving the operation to such an extent that his efforts were praised by state inspectors and led to the school's official recognition as a senior college.[5]

Despite a full schedule of teaching and administrative duties, the elder Farmer frequently contributed articles to scholarly journals and wrote Sunday school lessons for Methodist publications, advancing his belief that education was the key to improving the lives of African Americans. At the same time, young Jim Farmer encountered conflicts between white and black workers at a golf course where he briefly worked as a caddy and noted a change in neighborhood dynamics as children who freely played together in their younger years were gradually separated by their families as they approached adolescence. "If the boy is father of the man," he said, "and if, as they say, one's character and direction are formed in the first ten years, then my course was set in Holly Springs and Austin."[6]

The Farmers' third child, a son named Nathaniel, was born in Austin in December 1927, completing the family. The following spring, driving his family back to town from the countryside where they had visited friends on a Sunday afternoon, James Farmer Sr. accidentally struck and killed a pig that ran into the path of his new car. Stopping down the road for a picnic, the family was accosted by two white farmers demanding payment for the pig. The men threatened Farmer with a shotgun and verbally abused him with racial epithets. Having no cash, and fearing for the safety of his family, the professor offered to endorse his fifty-seven-dollar paycheck from the college. Continuing their threats, the men finally accepted the check, but not without first further humiliating Farmer by dropping it to the ground and forcing him to pick it up. Helplessly observing the exchange between his educated, cultured father and the two crude white men, Jim Farmer was filled with anger, indignation, and rebellion. Later recalling this and other demeaning incidents he witnessed in his youth, he wrote, "I was deeply troubled by my father's accommodation to a system that made him less than a man. I despised that within him that would not fight, perhaps because I saw the same survival instinct in myself. But I swore that when I grew up, scared or not, I'd never kowtow to meanness. Even as a child, I hated the lying, the dissembling, the subterfuge, the pretense—the squeezing of one's soul into a room too small."[7]

After six years in Austin, the family moved to Atlanta, Georgia, where James Farmer Sr. served on the faculty of Gammon Theological Seminary. Soon, however, they were back in Texas, returning to Wiley College in Marshall. Farmer taught religion and philosophy and served as dean of the college chapel, where he regularly preached at Sunday afternoon services. His oratorical skills were well known in the region, and both white and black citizens of Marshall regularly flocked to hear him.[8] Jim Farmer, an advanced student at age fourteen, began his college career as a Wiley freshman in the fall of 1934. Among his teachers was literature professor and poet Melvin B. Tolson, whose leadership of the Wiley College debate team would be immortalized in 2007 in a major motion picture, *The Great Debaters*. Jim Farmer was the youngest member of the Wiley debate team that made history in 1934 by famously taking on—and defeating—the leading white college debate team at the University of Southern California (not Harvard University, as portrayed in the film). Of that time Farmer wrote, "The banquet of my Wiley years was the tutelage of Tolson."

Jim Farmer and some of his fellow team members met in a dorm room one night, discussing the topic of racial segregation and carefully constructing their argument condemning the practice. Relating the discussion to Tolson a few days later, he was taken aback when his mentor calmly pointed out Farmer's own acquiescence to the segregated practices at the local movie theater which he and his friends frequented often. By accessing the theater through a separate entrance and sitting in the "colored only" section in the balcony, Tolson told him, he was helping perpetuate the evil system. "The message struck me like a two-by-four," Farmer remembered. "I had no reply. He referred me to Henry David Thoreau, the essay on civil disobedience. He took it down from a shelf and tossed it to me. I caught it in midair and was riveted to a passage where the book fell open: 'What I have to do is see, at any rate, that I do not lend myself to the evil which I condemn.'" From that discussion with Melvin Tolson, Jim Farmer began in earnest the journey that would take him away from his father's philosophy of gradual change and empowerment through education to his own path seeking swifter justice through civil disobedience and non-violent direct action. Walking home that night, he realized, "Education merely made it harder for the brain to adapt to the demeaning things the system told it to do." He became determined to move beyond adaptation—his father's world—to his own world of action.[9]

Graduating from Wiley College at eighteen, Jim Farmer accompanied his family to Washington, DC, in 1939 and enrolled at Howard University's School of Religion, taking advantage of the free tuition offered by virtue of his father's new faculty position at that institution. He intended to become a doctor or a Methodist minister like his father, but ultimately he turned away from both—from medicine after realizing he didn't have the stomach for it, and from the ordained ministry after deeming the segregationist policies of the Methodist Episcopal Church in the South inconsistent with his beliefs. At Howard University he became acquainted with the teachings of Mohandas Gandhi. He wholeheartedly embraced the Hindu leader's philosophy of nonviolent direct action to effect change, which he believed, combined with Thoreau's call to civil disobedience, was the way to challenge segregation in America.

After earning a degree in theology, Jim Farmer moved away from his parents for the first time in 1941, striking out to pursue his own quest for civil rights, diverging from his father's shadow and, he believed, his father's old-fashioned sensibilities. He went to work for the Fellowship of Reconciliation (FOR), a Quaker-affiliated pacifist organization headquartered in New York City. From his home base in Chicago, he worked with a multiracial group of colleagues, traveling on behalf of the organization and speaking in cities throughout the Midwest. Following the entry of the United States into World War II, he sought conscientious objector status, but a draft board official granted him a ministerial deferment after learning of his theology degree. Although he wanted to make a point of becoming a conscientious objector, he accepted the deferment in order to continue his work with FOR. Among his closest friends were Bernice Fisher, a white University of Chicago theology student, and Ben Segal, a Jewish youth working for the Keep America Out of War Committee. With several other colleagues, they hatched a plan to quietly integrate housing in the Chicago area by sharing rent and setting up co-ops in two houses, one for men and one for women. In May 1942, after Farmer was refused service when he and Segal entered a local coffee shop, the friends staged what Farmer later said was the first organized sit-in for civil rights, an orderly protest that led to a change in the restaurant's policies.

A few months earlier, Farmer had sent a memo entitled "Provisional Plans for Brotherhood Mobilization" to his FOR supervisor in New York. Combining the philosophies of Thoreau and Gandhi, the memo "asked for a nonviolent confrontation with American racism. This movement should be comprised of a pacifist nucleus: black, white, Jewish and Gentile, all mobilized into a Gandhian approach to integration." The coffee shop sit-in showed it could work. FOR leadership accepted and encouraged the principles outlined in the memo and appointed Farmer to chair the new initiative under the FOR umbrella. Named CORE (Committee of Racial Equality, later Congress of Racial Equality) by its Chicago organizers in 1942, the organization ultimately became independent of FOR. Organized through local chapters, CORE quickly gained a nationwide membership, and by the 1960s it had grown to include more than eighty-two thousand members in 114 chapters. Among its activities were campaigns to end segregation in public schools and to promote integration of swimming pools, theaters, bowling alleys, restaurants, and other public places. Its Journey of Reconciliation, in which white and black members rode on buses into the upper South in 1947 to test a Supreme Court decision regarding integration of interstate transportation, resulted in numerous arrests and served as a precursor to the effort that would galvanize the civil rights movement and capture the attention of the world—the Freedom Rides of the early 1960s.[10]

With Farmer at its helm as national director, CORE stood poised to lead one of the most effective campaigns for social justice in

American history. Two groups of volunteers—Freedom Riders—boarded Trailways and Greyhound buses in Washington, DC, on May 4, 1961. Their itinerary called for them to travel through Virginia, North Carolina, South Carolina, Georgia, Alabama, Mississippi, and Louisiana on the bus companies' regularly scheduled routes. White and black riders would sit together on the buses and would go into the stations at stops along the way to challenge the segregated facilities peacefully. They planned to mark the end of their journey with a rally in New Orleans on May 17, the seventh anniversary of the landmark *Brown v. Board of Education* school desegregation Supreme Court case. In the days leading up to the start of the perilous expedition, the riders received intensive instruction in the fundamentals of passive resistance and nonviolent action from Farmer and other CORE leaders. If attacked, they would not fight back; if arrested, they would go to jail without accepting bail. Addressing the volunteers the night before the buses were to head south, Farmer spoke frankly of the almost certain danger they would encounter and gave them the opportunity to withdraw, with no questions asked. Determination outweighed fear, and everyone gathered to board the buses the following morning.[11]

Jim Farmer's parents anxiously monitored the news and followed their son's progress. His father had left Howard University in 1946 for another sojourn at Samuel Huston College as registrar, professor of philosophy, and chair of the social sciences department, but after ten years in Austin he returned to Howard University as professor emeritus in 1956. By 1961 he was gravely ill with severe diabetes and cancer. Visiting his father in Freedman's Hospital in Washington a few days before leading the Freedom Riders, Jim Farmer had received words of both blessing and caution. His father believed the riders would be safe traveling in the upper South, but he worried that they would face violence and danger when they reached Alabama. In the wee hours of Sunday, May 14—Mother's Day—the day the buses would drive out of Atlanta and cross from Georgia into Alabama, Jim Farmer received a telephone call from his mother with the news his father had died. According to Pearl Farmer, the professor, whose health had steadily deteriorated, looked at his son's itinerary each day, saying, "Well, let me see where Junior is today." She believed he hung on until just before the buses were scheduled to reach Alabama and then released his grip on life. Given the dramatic events that soon unfolded, she staunchly believed her husband willfully timed his death to save his son's life. Jim Farmer flew home to be with his family and so was not with the Freedom Riders when they reached Alabama.

Leaving Atlanta about an hour apart, the two buses made their way toward Birmingham, the next stop on the itinerary. The Greyhound bus left first, with fourteen people on board, including seven Freedom Riders, two journalists, and five other passengers, among whom were two undercover Alabama Highway Patrol officers. The bus crossed into Alabama about one o'clock in the afternoon and soon reached Anniston. Anticipating the Freedom Riders' arrival, the local station agent had locked the Greyhound terminal, and a mob that included members of the Ku Klux Klan stood waiting and rushed to attack the bus as soon as it stopped. With no local police protection, the two officers on the bus managed to keep the door closed and prevented the attackers from boarding, but the mob smashed the windows and slashed the tires. When the police finally arrived, they did nothing to quell the attack. They ultimately cleared a path and escorted the bus to the city limits, but then abandoned it to the mob that had followed. When the damaged tires could no longer propel the bus forward, it came to a stop in front of a rural grocery store about six miles west of town. Surrounded by the mob, the bus again came under attack, this time with homemade firebombs thrown through the broken windows. With the door still locked, the passengers managed to escape through the windows, but many were attacked as they disembarked, suffering serious beatings. A reporter who followed the crowd from Anniston managed to photograph the scene.[12]

While the Greyhound bus passengers suffered attacks near Anniston, the riders on the Trailways bus were experiencing their own horrors. A group of Klansmen boarded the bus in Atlanta, and soon after it started its journey they began taunting the Freedom Riders. The bus reached the Trailways station in Anniston with the passengers unaware of the fate that had befallen their colleagues at the Greyhound station some three blocks away and soon afterwards west of town. Two of the Trailways Freedom Riders—one black, one white—entered the station together as planned. The station was eerily quiet, and they nervously returned to the bus. At that point word of the violence on the other bus reached the driver, who refused to drive out of the station unless the black passengers moved to the back of the bus. When they refused and were supported by their white compatriots, the driver disembarked and the Klansmen began attacking the Freedom Riders, severely beating most of them and forcibly moving them to the rear of the bus. The driver returned with a police officer, who calmly observed the group of beaten and bloody victims, then walked away. With the Klansmen taking control and continuing their taunts, the bus rolled on toward Birmingham. Upon arrival, the Klansmen swiftly exited the bus, and when the passengers entered the station more attacks ensued. Journalists on the scene, including CBS radio reporter Howard K. Smith, captured much of the violence, and those reports, along with the story and photographs of the Greyhound bus burning outside of Anniston, helped turn the tide in the civil rights struggles in the American South. Broadcast worldwide, the vivid images and Smith's dramatic eyewitness accounts of the mob violence galvanized support for the Freedom Riders and finally brought about the long-sought-after protection of federal authorities.

Determined to continue their journey to its planned culmination in New Orleans, both groups of battered Freedom Riders gathered at Bethel Baptist Church in Birmingham to assess the situation and do what they could to salvage the crusade. They decided to continue on as a unified group on one bus and spent much of the day on Monday in telephone communication with US attorney general Robert F. Kennedy, discussing strategies for police protection. Although Kennedy reached an agreement with Alabama governor John Patterson to provide a state police escort, when the Freedom Riders arrived at the Greyhound station to board the afternoon bus to Montgomery, the growing tension and threats of additional violence spurred the station manager to cancel the trip, and Patterson did not deliver on his promise for police protection. Realizing the futility of trying to continue their bus trip, the group changed plans and decided to fly to Montgomery instead. But when they arrived at the airport, they were met with more protestors, and their flights were canceled because of bomb threats. As the afternoon and evening wore on, John Seigenthaler, an aide to Attorney General Kennedy, arrived in Birmingham and, working with airport and airline officials, helped secure seats for the weary Freedom Riders and accompanied them on a late plane to New Orleans.[13]

Although the Freedom Riders were unable to complete their bus journey to New Orleans, their bravery and dedication to the cause of civil rights propelled the movement forward and inspired additional Freedom Rides by individuals and other organizations through the end of 1961. Despite continued violent attacks, the arrest and imprisonment of hundreds of volunteers, and, sadly, the deaths of both black and white crusaders, the campaign finally gained the attention of federal authorities and the press. As more and more people streamed toward the South to join in the cause, James Farmer Jr. and his colleagues were buoyed by widespread and overwhelming support. Farmer himself spent time in jail in Mississippi and narrowly escaped a mob in Louisiana when a local funeral home director spirited him out of town hidden in the back of a hearse. Initiated by CORE under Farmer's leadership, the Freedom Rides formed a major turning point in the civil rights movement and proved to be an essential cornerstone in the struggle for racial justice that led to voting rights and civil rights legislation of the 1960s.

Today, both James Farmer Sr. and James Farmer Jr. are remembered for their lasting contributions on behalf of civil rights. Each man left a legacy of inspiration, hope, education, determination, and freedom. Following his death on that fateful date in May 1961, James Farmer Sr. was buried in Freedman's Cemetery in Washington, DC.[14] His son continued working for civil rights through the 1960s and ran for Congress in 1968, but lost. He served as assistant secretary of health, education and welfare in the Nixon administration and worked with numerous civil rights and labor organizations.

Jim Farmer eventually followed in his father's academic footsteps, becoming a professor of history and American studies at

Jim Farmer at the time of his service as assistant secretary of health, education, and welfare. Courtesy Institute of Texan Cultures, UTSA #68–1005, US Department of Health, Education, and Welfare.

Mary Washington College (now University of Mary Washington) in Fredericksburg, Virginia, where a multicultural center, a scholarship, and a professorship are named in his honor. President Bill Clinton awarded him the Presidential Medal of Freedom in January 1998. He died July 9, 1999, at age seventy-nine.

In March 1998, on the campus of Wiley College in Marshall, Jim Farmer helped unveil an Official Texas Historical Marker honoring his father. A decade later, the Texas Historical Commission approved a marker for James Farmer Jr. to be placed in front of the family's East Austin home near the campus of Huston-Tillotson University.[15]

Recalling his early civil rights work in Chicago, Jim Farmer recounted a story told by his friend and colleague Bernice Fisher that illustrates in simple terms his view of the righteousness of equality:

A small boy came home from school and enthusiastically told his mother about his new friend who lived in another neighborhood.

"Freddie," the mother asked tentatively, "is this new child colored?"

"I don't know," the boy replied. "I didn't notice. I'll look tomorrow."[16]

MARKER LOCATIONS

James Leonard Farmer Sr.: Wiley College campus, intersection of University Ave. and Wiley Ave., Marshall

James L. Farmer Jr.: 1604 New York Ave., Austin

HUSTON-TILLOTSON UNIVERSITY

Established through a merger of two earlier schools—Tillotson College and Samuel Huston College—Huston-Tillotson University is a respected institution of higher education in Austin. Tillotson College, founded in 1875 by the American Missionary Association, a Protestant organization that traces its roots to abolitionist activities as early as the 1840s, was named for George J. Tillotson of Connecticut, a supporter of the organization who donated funds to purchase land for the school. Designated a junior college in 1925, it briefly operated as a women's college in the late 1920s and early 1930s. Perhaps the most prestigious of its leaders was Mary Elizabeth Branch, who served as president from 1930 to 1943. The daughter of former slaves in Virginia, Branch attended Virginia State College, the University of Pennsylvania, Columbia University, and the University of Chicago, which awarded her a master's degree in English in 1925. A leader in the Austin civil rights movement, Branch served as president of the local chapter of the NAACP, was appointed to the State Interracial Commission, and worked with the federal National Youth Administration during the Great Depression. In addition, she was one of the founders of the United Negro College Fund. During her tenure as college president, she instituted cooperative programs with faculty at Samuel Huston College and the University of Texas and began the plans to merge Tillotson with Samuel Huston.

Samuel Huston College traces its history to Andrews Normal School, a small institution for blacks that began in Dallas in 1876. Moved to Austin two years later, it held classes in a local Methodist church until Samuel Huston, a wealthy supporter from Iowa, donated funds through the Freedmen's Aid Society for a campus in East Austin. Officially named for its benefactor in 1887, it became a senior college in 1926 during the administrative tenure of James L. Farmer Sr. Noted African American folklorist J. Mason Brewer, a graduate of Wiley College in Marshall, served on the faculty of Samuel Huston College at the same time as Farmer.

The historical marker for Tillotson College stands in front of this historic building on the Huston-Tillotson University campus in East Austin.
Photograph by Cynthia J. Beeman.

Samuel Huston College and Tillotson College officially merged in 1952 to form Huston-Tillotson College (now University). Land along the east frontage road of Interstate 35 that originally was the Samuel Huston College campus is no longer a part of the school, but an Official Texas Historical Marker placed near the site at East 12th Street commemorates the early years of the college. Another marker conveying the history of Tillotson College can be found at 900 Chicon Street, the original Tillotson site and current campus of Huston-Tillotson University.

Sources: Tillotson College, Travis County, THC marker files; Evans Industrial Building, Huston-Tillotson College, Travis County, THC files; Site of Samuel Huston College, Travis County, THC marker files; Olive D. Brown and Michael R. Heintze,

"Mary Elizabeth Branch," *New Handbook of Texas*, vol. 1, pp. 700–701, ed. Ron Tyler (Austin: Texas State Historical Association, 1996); "Samuel Huston College," *New Handbook of Texas*, vol. 5, p. 790; "Tillotson College," *New Handbook of Texas*, vol. 6, p. 499; "Huston-Tillotson College," *New Handbook of Texas*, vol. 3, pp. 802–3; James W. Byrd, "John Mason Brewer," *New Handbook of Texas*, vol. 1, pp. 724–25.

WILEY COLLEGE

The Freedmen's Aid Society of the Methodist Episcopal Church, founded in 1866 for the purpose of setting up schools and colleges for formerly enslaved African Americans in the South, established Wiley College in Marshall, Texas, in 1873. Named for Bishop Isaac D. Wiley of Pennsylvania, a charter member and leader of the

Wiley College, Marshall. Courtesy Texas Historical Commission. Photograph by Andy Rhodes.

Freedmen's Aid Society and a missionary to China, the school received a state charter in 1882 and offered college and vocational courses. Initially run by a white administration and faculty, the school inaugurated its first black president, Bishop Isaiah D. Scott, in 1893.

Throughout its history, Wiley College has boasted a distinguished roster of presidents, faculty, and students. Its longest-serving president, Dr. Matthew W. Dogan, began his tenure in 1896 and led the college for forty-six years, during which time the institution experienced significant growth in academics, community involvement, and physical plant improvements. Among Wiley's notable alumni are acclaimed folklorist J. Mason Brewer and Heman M. Sweatt, the plaintiff in the landmark *Sweatt v. Painter* case that eventually led to the desegregation of state-supported law schools in Texas. Wiley students actively participated in the civil rights movement of the 1960s by leading sit-ins at the Woolworth's store in Marshall, helping to end segregation in local public facilities.

The Texas Historical Commission placed an Official Texas Historical Marker for Wiley College in front of the school's library in 1973 and in 1998 added a marker for James Leonard Farmer Sr. to the campus.

Sources: Wiley College, Travis County, THC marker files; Sallie M. Lentz and Gilbert Allen, "Wiley College," *Handbook of Texas Online,* www.tshaonline.org/handbook/online/articles/kbw17, accessed March 11, 2011; Richard Allen Burns, "Heman Marion Sweatt," *Handbook of Texas Online,* www.tshaonline.org/handbook/online/articles/fsw23, accessed March 12, 2011; James W. Byrd, "John Mason Brewer," *Handbook of Texas Online,* www.tshaonline.org/handbook/online/articles/fbrbb, accessed March 8, 2011; Michael R. Heintze, "Black Colleges," *Handbook of Texas Online,* www.tshaonline.org/handbook/online/articles/khb01, accessed March 10, 2011.

16

A Citizen with Work to Do

At the Texas State Capitol in March 1925, during the waning days of the regular session of the Thirty-ninth Legislature, members of the board of regents of the state normal schools (teacher colleges) sat in the senate gallery observing the proceedings. As they monitored the progress of legislation affecting public education and teacher training in the Lone Star State, one of the regents—the first woman ever appointed to that board—took a particular interest in the events unfolding on the floor below. Margie E. Neal had a thought that day that would affect her life and the lives of countless Texans for generations to come. As she remembered many years later, "That thought kept returning to my mind: 'If I had a vote down there, I might do more for education on the floor of the House or Senate than I am doing as a college regent sitting in the gallery.' That very thought was the determining factor in my later decision to run for the Senate."[1] The following year, with the overwhelming support of family and the constituents in her East Texas district, she became the first woman elected to the Texas senate.

Margie Neal's journey to a life of public service—one that included many firsts for Texas women of her generation—began in a log cabin on April 20, 1875, in the small Panola County farming community of Clayton. The daughter of Georgia natives William Lafayette Neal and Martha Ann Gholston Neal, she was christened Mary Elizabeth for the two women who attended her mother at her birth, but was immediately nicknamed Molly. "I was never called Mary," she explained, adding that when her young niece later mispronounced Molly as "Margie," her father adopted that name for her, as well, and from that time on she was known as Margie Elizabeth Neal.[2]

In addition to a prosperous eight-hundred-acre farm that employed several tenant farmers, William Neal also owned and operated a gristmill and a cotton gin from which he earned a comfortable living. Margie and her older sister and two younger brothers (one of whom died at age sixteen in an accident) attended the nearby Bethlehem School and the local Methodist church. She recalled a pleasant childhood of typical adventures and experiences. She loved to read, and her father strongly encouraged her to spend a great deal of time with her books.[3]

A strong desire for their children to receive a good education led William and Martha Neal to move their family to Carthage in 1884. They initially lived in a rented home while William Neal commuted back to the farm, but eventually he purchased more than fifty acres east of downtown (some of which later was conveyed for the Texas, Sabine Valley, and Northwestern Railway right-of-way) and established a new home in the county seat. Margie attended elementary classes at the Scruggs School and later received secondary instruction at Prof. O. P. Carswell's school in the local Masonic hall, where she studied bookkeeping in anticipation of assisting in her father's business interests. At Carswell's suggestion, in early 1891 she enrolled in Hill's Business College in Dallas, where her classmates included future Texas business and political leaders Jesse H. Jones, Houston financier and later a high-ranking official in Pres. Franklin D. Roosevelt's New Deal, and Howard Audrey, later mayor of Dallas.[4]

Neal returned to Carthage in the fall of 1891 and found that her father did not require her bookkeeping services after all. She enrolled in the newly established Panola Male and Female Academy and the following year, thanks to a scholarship procured for her by State Representative J. Ras Jones, she left home once again to study teaching at Sam Houston Normal Institute in Huntsville.

Although she did not ultimately earn a baccalaureate degree, she attained a first-class teaching certificate following her second year of study. She taught first at a small private school in Carthage, and in the ensuing years she held teaching positions at Mount Zion School (Panola County), Forney (Kaufman County), Scottsville (Harrison County), Marlin (Falls County), and Fort Worth, Texas, as well

Margie Elizabeth Neal as a young schoolteacher.
Courtesy Susanne Neal Golden.

as one year in Jacksonville, Florida. She attended summer normal school sessions to renew her teaching certificate as needed and found a fulfilling career in teaching.[5]

For much of Margie Neal's life her mother was in ill health, and when Martha Neal's condition worsened in late 1903, Margie agreed to resign from her teaching position in Fort Worth to return home to help provide care. At the same time, William Neal, acutely aware of the sacrifice being made by his daughter, negotiated a business deal that would propel her into a new career and the next phase of her life. Tom M. Bowers, owner of a local Carthage weekly newspaper, the *Texas Mule*, also was in ill health and agreed to sell the business. So in early 1904 Margie E. Neal became an editor and publisher. "When I bought the paper I planned to change the name," she later recounted. "I desired that the paper be progressive and tried to make it progressive."[6]

The inaugural issue of the renamed *East Texas Register* appeared on January 5, 1904. With a stated agenda to promote active citizenship and the well-being and progress of the community, Neal set about learning the newspaper business. She forged friendships and professional associations with colleagues in surrounding towns and became actively involved in the Texas Press Association. Working with two male employees, she quickly asserted her independence and authority. She raised a few local eyebrows when, as a staunch prohibitionist, she refused to carry liquor ads in the paper. A quick study in the ways of business, however, she tempered her position somewhat so that the paper did not suffer financially for her strongly held beliefs. As she explained, "Bowers carried whiskey ads. I didn't, except to carry out a few of his contracts for a short time."[7]

Although not the first woman at the helm of a newspaper in Texas, Neal was one of only a few in the early twentieth century. She quickly fulfilled her pledge to make the *East Texas Register* a progressive voice in the region, taking a stand in favor of prohibition, which she believed would benefit families affected by alcoholism and abuse, as well as strongly advocating business development, better roads, improvements in education, adequate water supply and fire protection, and promotion of various community-building projects such as parks, libraries, a county fair, and tree planting throughout Carthage. Politically, she strongly supported the Democratic Party, and the editorial pages of the *East Texas Register* reflected that position. As a former teacher, she took a particular interest in the community's young people, offering advice and not hesitating to chastise them in her editorial columns when they behaved in a manner she deemed unacceptable.[8]

Although she enjoyed her newspaper career immensely and flourished in her role as a community leader, Neal also retained the sensibilities of a traditional Southern woman whose primary allegiance and responsibility revolved around home and family. When Martha Neal's health deteriorated further in 1912, Margie Neal felt duty bound to sell the paper and devote all her resources to caring for her mother. Nevertheless, she maintained community ties through active participation in the Carthage Circulating Book Club, whose members wielded a fair amount of civic influence in the town.

By early 1916 Neal returned to a more active public life. She made her first public speech from the back of a pickup truck on the town square selling Liberty Bonds to support the World War I home front effort, and within a short time she enthusiastically embraced the cause of woman suffrage. Appointed to lead the effort in the second senatorial district by Texas Equal Suffrage Association (TESA) president Minnie Fisher Cunningham, she said, "I was doing what I could in a quiet way. Women were needed to assume citizenship responsibilities at home with the men in service, and with suffrage granted them, they were coming into their own, whether they realized it or not." Once woman suffrage was achieved, Neal led the effort to register voters in her district. Several accounts credit her as being the first woman to register to vote in Panola County, but in fact she did not achieve that distinction, although not for lack of trying. Setting the record straight, she wrote in 1954, "I was anxious to be the first woman to register here, but on arrival at the tax collector's office found that Mrs. Irwin Anderson was first, and I, second."[9]

The growing public profile she achieved in the region through her suffrage work, as well as her continued strong support of the

Democratic Party, led Neal to a new role as delegate to the State Democratic Convention in 1918. By the time the convention ended, she had added another achievement to her record: first woman appointed to the Executive Committee. Recalling the occasion, she revealed a sense of humor about her initial reaction to the idea when approached by several leading members of the committee: "Well, I laughed. I just didn't know what to say I was so embarrassed. I couldn't help but think they were joking. In turn I joked. I just said 'Well, will there be any opportunity for graft?' I don't know what their answer was, but they told me they were serious. Each senatorial district had its representation on the State Democratic Executive Committee and they wanted me. I told them I would accept the honor and do the very best I could with the responsibilities."[10] Her commitment to active citizenship would not permit her to do otherwise.

In May 1920, when the State Democratic Convention met to select delegates to the national convention, Margie E. Neal was one of four women delegates-at-large, along with TESA president Cunningham, Jessie Daniel Ames of Georgetown, and Jane Madden Spell of Waco. Meeting in San Francisco the following month, the National Democratic Convention nominated Ohio governor James M. Cox for president and Franklin D. Roosevelt of New York for vice president and selected Neal to travel to Hyde Park, New York, as a member of the committee that would officially notify Roosevelt of the nomination. A bit starstruck by the charismatic candidate, she remembered, "F.D.R. was an extremely handsome man then. Even to this date I can't ever remember seeing a more handsome man. As he appeared on the lawn that morning, dressed in white, young and vigorous, I felt that Apollo had nothing on him. It was just a year until he was stricken with polio."[11]

Returning to Carthage, Neal continued her civic and political activities, and in 1921 Gov. Pat Neff appointed her the first woman member of the State Normal School Board of Regents. As a member of the board's building committee, she actively participated in the evaluation and site selection process regarding the construction of new schools in Nacogdoches (Stephen F. Austin State Normal College, later Stephen F. Austin State University) in 1923 and Kingsville

(South Texas State Normal College, later Texas A&I University and Texas A&M University–Kingsville) in 1925. She traveled frequently to each of the normal school campuses in the state and took seriously her charge to promote professional teacher training in Texas. Along with her fellow regents, she attended legislative committee meetings and house and senate sessions to promote and monitor legislation affecting public education, an activity that led to the next phase of her long career in public service when she determined from her seat in the gallery to throw her hat in the ring as a candidate for the Texas senate.

As early as 1922 local newspaper editorials had promoted Neal as a possible senate candidate. Dubbing her "Margie E. Neal, Public Servant and Citizen," another publication hailed her accomplishments and said, "The measure of success that has come to her is not due to luck or special gift, but to hard work and noble resolve to do well her part."[12] In an episode that would foreshadow her legislative career, an issue quite separate from her work as a regent took her to the halls of the State Capitol in 1923. Her actions at that time, advocating on behalf of her fellow Panola County citizens, earned the lasting respect of both her supporters and detractors.

Senator J. G. Strong of Carthage and Rep. W. S. Crawford of Beckville both introduced bills to allow the manufacture of carbon black, a product made by burning excess gas from gasoline plants, a number of which were located in the Bethany gas field in rural Panola County. Along with a handful of fellow civic leaders, Neal went to Austin to lobby in favor of the measure in support of her rural neighbors, whom she believed would benefit financially if the legislation passed. Although the proposal passed in the senate, it encountered strong opposition by environmental conservationists in the house. Maintaining that the poor people of Panola County needed the anticipated financial boost the carbon black plant would provide, Neal was able to persuade enough senators to approve the measure, but it ultimately failed to pass the house by one vote. Newspaper editorials heralded her impressive showing at the Capitol, and, notwithstanding the final defeat of the bill, the citizens of Panola County welcomed her home with great fanfare.[13]

In March 1926—one month shy of her fifty-first birthday—Margie E. Neal announced her candidacy for the Texas State Senate to represent the second senatorial district comprised of Gregg, Harrison, Panola, Rusk, and Shelby counties. At a rally at the Panola County Courthouse in June, she laid out her four major goals. "I had a good platform—education, good roads, welfare, progress," she later recalled. She campaigned with seemingly boundless energy, personally visiting with people in all five counties of the district. She said, "The issue of the [political influence of the Ku Klux] Klan was quite hot. There were very strong partisans on both sides. I was very much opposed to it. My father and mother had an abhorrence to the Klan. It was a fireside topic of conversation from my cradle days. I went out into the cotton fields, the corn fields, etc. I saw the people. I carried four out of five counties. The campaign was interesting and a very rich experience."[14]

When the Fortieth Legislature assembled in Austin in January 1927, Margie E. Neal took her seat as the only female member and the first woman ever to serve in the senate.[15] (Dallas attorney Edith Therrel Wilmans, the first woman elected to the Texas Legislature, served in the house of representatives in the Thirty-eighth Legislature, 1921–25.)

Named to a number of committees, including that for educational affairs, where she served as vice-chair, she immediately set to work on her legislative agenda, particularly in the areas of education and welfare. She introduced or supported bills to strengthen professional requirements for teacher certification, increase state appropriations for rural schools, support Gov. Dan Moody's reform measures regarding judicial and prison systems, require physical education instruction as well as the teaching of the United States and Texas constitutions in Texas public schools, and provide for additional attendants and higher salaries for workers at state mental hospitals. She also introduced a resolution in support of prohibition in Texas, which passed, and a child support bill, which did not.[16]

While not entirely successful with legislation during her first term, she earned the respect of fellow legislators and the public by adhering to her principles, even to the point of ultimately voting against her own bill regarding teacher certification because of what she felt were unacceptable amendments tacked onto it by Sen. Thomas B. Love of Dallas. Although that action resulted in negative press coverage, with some political reporters and legislators contending her vote exhibited a lack of knowledge of parliamentary procedure, her firm but affable public explanation of her vote cemented her reputation as a capable and shrewd senator.[17]

Reelected by her constituents to serve three more terms in the senate, Neal continued to press her program of progressive legislation in the 1920s and 1930s. She headed the committee that oversaw the selection of "Texas, Our Texas" as the Texas state song. She supported expansion of the fledgling state parks system and offered a resolution calling for participation in a National Park Service survey of Texas with the goal of establishing national parks within its borders. She introduced legislation that established the Texas Centennial Commission and provided for its funding, resulting in a statewide celebration and a lasting legacy of buildings and monuments. In 1931 she called for a moratorium on cotton planting in Texas for the following year in response to an oversupply that threatened the economic livelihoods of farmers throughout the state. Her version of the bill failed by ten votes; a substitute measure limiting cotton planting in 1932 and 1933 to 30 percent of acreage cultivated in 1931 passed, but it later proved to be unconstitutional. She served on the board of the Texas Society for Crippled Children and sponsored legislation to aid people with disabilities. And in her continuing quest to support educational issues, as chair of the Senate Educational Affairs Committee she wrote the bill that established the State Board of Education.[18]

Senator Neal served during the administrations of three governors: Dan Moody, Ross Sterling, and Miriam A. Ferguson. She heartily supported Moody and had a cool but cordial relationship with Ferguson. "I didn't want to get tied in with Fergusonism," she later said, and although she chose not to support Ferguson in the Democratic primary, she explained that she "voted for her in the general elections because she was the gubernatorial nominee of the party." With Sterling, a well-known oilman and business leader, however, she had a sometimes contentious relationship. He had opposed Neal's version of the cotton bill and at the end of that session, in a comment clearly aimed at her, he told a reporter he wanted the legislators to "go home and tend to their knitting."[19]

The most serious and public altercation between Neal and Sterling came in the fall of 1931. Looking to increase state revenue from oil and gas leases, the governor called legislators back to Austin for a second special session to pass legislation for the leasing and drilling of state land in the Sabine River bed, almost all of which lay in Senator Neal's district. Her negative reaction to the proposal was immediate and widely supported by her constituents, particularly those living in Longview, which drew its water supply from the Sabine. Citing concerns that the drilling activities would pollute the water supply, she strongly opposed the measure in the senate, albeit against considerable odds. Having honed her knowledge about parliamentary procedures, she launched what she considered to be her only chance to defeat the riverbed drilling bill.

On the afternoon of September 28, 1931, one day before the scheduled end of the session, she began to speak against the measure on the senate floor. According to Walter E. Harris in his 1955 University of Texas thesis, "She had little more than begun when she realized that should she hold the Senate floor until six o'clock she could prevent a final vote on the bill. The rules of both the House and the Senate provided that no bill could receive a final vote within twenty-four hours of sine die adjournment, unless so ordered by a two-thirds vote of the chamber involved. This rule could be invoked at six p.m. The lady senator felt that she had no choice. This was her last opportunity to defeat an issue the injustice of which she was thoroughly convinced."[20] Rebuffing all efforts by her colleagues to interrupt, she completed her speech at the appointed time, thereby attaining her goal of derailing the bill. Sterling, furious at Neal's filibuster, threatened to call another special session if legislators failed to pass a concurrent resolution extending the date of adjournment in order to pass the riverbed drilling bill. Ultimately out-maneuvered by Sterling, Neal nevertheless held to her convictions. She maintained the support and admiration of her constituents, but newspapers throughout the state published editorials condemning her actions. The *Dallas Morning News* ran a political cartoon depicting the words "Talk-Talk-Talk" and "Shut 'er off!" emanating from the Capitol while Governor Sterling, holding a copy of the bill on the steps of the Governor's Mansion, exclaims, "I ask for oil and get GAS!"[21]

Throughout her senate career Neal maintained a prominent role in both state and national Democratic Party activities. A delegate to the national convention in 1932, she also served as cochair of the Texas campaign of presidential nominee Franklin D. Roosevelt and his running mate, Texas senator John Nance Garner. But by 1933, with the economic depression ravaging the country and affecting her own finances, she decided not to run for a fifth term in the senate. Instead, she sought employment with the federal government. With assistance from several of her Democratic Party friends, including US senators Tom Connally and Morris Sheppard and Cong. Lyndon B. Johnson, she obtained a position as chief of the women's section of the National Recovery Administration (NRA) and moved to Washington, DC. Although her new position began before the end of her final senate term, she made arrangements for a leave of absence from the NRA to return to Austin in the fall of 1934 for a special session of the legislature, saying, "The people of my district would be fully justified in saying I had left them in the lurch at the end, had I not come." Neal left the NRA for a position as information officer with the Social Security Administration in early 1936, and later that year she transferred to the agency's San Antonio office, where she remained until 1943. She worked for the War Manpower Commission in San Antonio and in Dallas during the latter years of World War II and finally retired and returned home to Carthage in 1945.[22]

Living once again in her hometown, Neal managed the substantial property interests she had inherited from her father and resumed an active community life. Her sense of citizenship remained strong, as evidenced by her involvement in numerous organizations and causes. She was instrumental in starting the local historical museum and in the founding of Panola General Hospital, and she led a years-long, although ultimately unsuccessful, fight to save the historic Panola County Courthouse. Designed by Irish architect J. J. E. Gibson, and almost identical in form to the Shelby County Courthouse in nearby Center, the 1885 structure was a landmark beloved by many in the county, and Neal's efforts to save it from the growing modernization movement garnered widespread news coverage. An editorial in the *Dallas Morning News* in July 1955 extolled "Miss Margie Neal, First Citizen of Panola County" and her preservation efforts, saying, "Carthage had better listen to Miss Margie." Sadly, they did not, and the building was razed.[23]

Still a strong supporter of the Democratic Party, Neal actively campaigned in local, state, and national elections but became increasingly dissatisfied with the policies of Pres. Harry Truman. In a marked departure from her long association with the Democratic Party, she supported the Republican ticket and served as co-chair of the Texans for Eisenhower committee in the 1952 presidential election. She also supported the conservative wing of the state Democratic Party and its standard bearer, Gov. Allan Shivers.[24]

In June 1952 the citizens of Carthage staged a Margie E. Neal Appreciation Day to honor the senator for her years of public service. Held in the high school athletic stadium to accommodate the large crowd, the event featured testimonial speeches by Governor

Shivers, US senator Lyndon B. Johnson, and Oveta Culp Hobby, who was house parliamentarian during Neal's Texas senate service, publisher of the *Houston Post,* head of the Women's Army Corps during World War II, and the first US Secretary of Health, Education, and Welfare. Looking out over the crowd, Shivers said,

> If there is anyone who could inspire such a heartfelt expression of affection and respect by people of all walks of life, it is the person whom we have come here to honor today. Miss Margie Neal to me is a symbol of those things that are noble and inspiring — tender, gracious, warmhearted, and yet possessed of a toughness of fiber and a clarity of mind that enabled her to see new horizons, to set her feet on new paths, and to follow them, without faltering, to the goal. . . . Yet for all her tenacity, her willingness to share in the give and take of legislative debate, she always retained her natural interests. Her sympathies were with the under-privileged and the handicapped. She started her career as a school teacher, and the cause of education was always closest to her heart. . . . She was a fine teacher, a maker of sound laws, an able public servant, but above all a great humanitarian.[25]

Johnson, who traveled from Washington to Carthage for the event, told the crowd he first met Neal when he was a young boy, when his father served with her in the state legislature. He said:

> Through the years, as I have gone through life I have learned to put a very high value on the attributes — unfortunately so rare — which are the hallmarks of Miss Margie. Everyone who knows Miss Margie knows that she is a woman of complete, solid, sincere integrity. Everyone who knows Miss Margie knows that she is a woman of fundamental courage. Everyone who knows Miss Margie knows that she is a woman of ability — the highest ability. . . . Miss Margie retired — far too early — from public life to live here in peace and quiet. But even though she is officially retired, her influence for good certainly did not end when she stepped out of the role of State Senator for this district.[26]

Indeed, Neal's influence for good did not end upon her retirement. She took a particular interest in the youth of Panola County, many of whom she personally assisted in their educational endeavors. As one former student remembered, "Entering my sophomore year (at the University of Texas) with only a few dollars, I hitchhiked from Carthage to Austin, and without Miss Margie's help then I might still be hitchhiking." Ann Morris, another Carthage citizen, remembered Neal's kindnesses to her family. In the 1960s, Neal arranged for Morris's aunt, a young widow struggling to raise three children on her own, to attend nursing school. Morris also recalled living with her grandmother across the street from Neal: "Miss Neal, bedridden or practically so, would have her maid/caretaker pick lovely flowers from her shrubs and bring them to my grandmother, a poor seamstress for the public."[27]

Remaining active for many years following the appreciation day staged in her honor in 1952, Margie E. Neal continued to exemplify a life dedicated to citizenship. As Walter Harris wrote, she was "a citizen with work to do." Revered as the elder stateswoman of Panola County, she was universally mourned by her fellow citizens upon her death at age ninety-six on December 19, 1971. Seventeen years later her nephew, John Neal, helped dedicate an Official Texas Historical Marker in her honor at Anderson Park in Carthage, on the site of the historic Panola County Courthouse she had worked so hard to save. Interviewed about his famous aunt that day, he related numerous stories about her distinguished public service career, but also remembered her lighter side. "She could always laugh and get others to laugh," he said. "When she was about 90 years old, I can remember her sipping her wine and saying, 'I guess I ought to go get in the closet with this. I think the preacher is coming.'"[28]

MARKER LOCATION: Anderson Park, intersection of US 59 Bus. and US 79 Bus., Carthage

Texas women, though given short shrift in many written historical accounts, claim many firsts that enliven the story of the Lone Star State. From the famous—such as Jane Long, known to generations of Texas public school students as "The Mother of Texas"—to the obscure—including Lallie P. Briscoe Carlisle of Greenville, the first woman to hold public office in Texas—women have shaped Texas history in myriad ways. Many women are commemorated in Official Texas Historical Markers, but others—such as the Native American woman Angelina, who served as a guide and interpreter for eighteenth-century French and Spanish explorers in East Texas and is the only woman for whom a Texas county is named—have yet to be memorialized in that manner.

On the other hand, stories of many Anglo pioneer women settlers appear on markers, including this very brief, politically incorrect, and almost comical text describing Candace Midkiff Bean in Cherokee County: "Wife of Peter Ellis Bean. Born near Nashville, Tenn. in 1802. Died near Douglass, Texas in December 1848. One of those pioneer women who braved the Indian menace and rocked the cradle of Texas liberty." (Although not mentioned on her marker, her husband also had another wife in Mexico to whom he returned in 1843 when he abandoned Candace and their three children. But that's another story.)

Texas women pioneered in a variety of ways, including in the realms of politics, education, medicine, civic affairs, business, and sports. Emma Grigsby Meharg of Plainview became Texas' first female secretary of state in 1925 when she was appointed to that office by the state's first woman governor, Miriam A. Ferguson. Annie Webb Blanton, a respected educator and the first woman president of the Texas State Teachers Association, also became the first woman elected to statewide office in Texas when, with the support of newly enfranchised women, she won a hotly contested race for state superintendent of public instruction in 1918.

Mollie W. Armstrong of Brownwood is recognized as the first

woman optometrist in Texas and is credited with helping to estab-lish optometry as a profession in the state in the early twenti-eth century. Hundreds of Texas public libraries were established through the efforts of women's literary societies or reading clubs in the late nineteenth and early twentieth centuries, including the Bronte Library, in Victoria, founded by Viola Shive Case. In 1912, Milam County resident Edna Westbrook Trigg founded the first Girls' Tomato Club, through which rural girls learned agricultural and food preparation techniques and financed college educations with the funds they raised by selling produce and canned goods. In addition, Trigg became the first home demonstration agent in Texas with the establishment of the Agricultural Extension Service in 1916.

Sarah Horton Cockrell of Dallas ran several successful busi-nesses along with her husband, Alexander, including a freight line, a brick factory, and a sawmill. Widowed in 1858, Sarah added to

"Miss Celie" Spoetzl was the only American woman owner of a brewery when she took over her family's Spoetzl Brewery operations in Shiner in 1950. Courtesy Texas Historical Commission, National Register of Historic Places files.

the family businesses with the construction of a hotel and a flour mill, and in 1872 she built the first iron bridge across the Trinity River, an enterprise that strongly influenced the economic growth of Dallas.

Two hundred fifty miles south and almost a century later, "Miss Celie" Spoetzl made history as the only woman in the United States to be sole owner of a brewery when she took over her family's Spoetzl Brewery operations in Shiner in 1950.

One of the greatest women athletes of all time, Mildred Ella "Babe" Didrikson Zaharias of Beaumont set world records and won two gold medals at the 1932 Olympic Games. She later became a golfer, winning scores of amateur and professional tournaments. In a ten-year span from 1940 to 1950 she won every title in professional women's golf, including world and US championships. The Associated Press named her Athlete of the Year six times and Woman Athlete of the Half-Century in 1950, the same year she and a group of other women golfers founded the Ladies Professional Golf Association.

Hundreds of historical markers tell stories of significant contributions by Texas women. As historian Ruthe Winegarten once said, "When you deprive people of their history, you deprive them of their power." Thanks to her work, as well as that of many who followed her, including historians at the Texas Historical Commission who are actively endeavoring "to address historical gaps, promote diversity of topics, and proactively document significant underrepresented subjects or untold stories," the power of Texas women will be recognized and their history conveyed in many more markers in the coming years.

MARKER LOCATIONS

Jane Long Boarding House: 200 block of N. 4th St., Richmond

Lallie P. Briscoe Carlisle: East Mound Cemetery, Marshall at Pine St., Greenville

Candice Midkiff Bean: Selman-Roark Cemetery, SH 21, Linwood

Emma Grigsby Meharg: Plainview Cemetery, 100 S. Joliet Street, Plainview

Miriam A. Ferguson: Sullivan Rd., 3 mi. east of SH 95, Sparks (birthplace); 518 N. 7th St., Temple (Ferguson Home)

Annie Webb Blanton: Blanton Elementary School, 5408 Westminster, Austin

Dr. Mollie W. Armstrong: Greenleaf Cemetery, 2701 US 377 S, Brownwood

Viola Shive Case: 302 N. Main St., Victoria (inside Victoria Public Library)

Edna Westbrook Trigg: Milam County Courthouse, Cameron

Sarah Horton Cockrell: S. Houston St., south side of Dealey Plaza, Dallas

Spoetzl Brewery: 603 E. Brewery Street, Shiner
Mildred "Babe" Didrikson Zaharias: 2232 Seventh St., Port
  Arthur (birthplace); Forest Lawn Memorial Park, Section C,
  5220 Pine St., Beaumont (gravesite)

Sources: THC marker files; Texas State Historical Association, *New Handbook of Texas;* Ruthe Winegarten Memorial Foundation for Texas Women's History, www .womenintexashistory.org.

17

Here I Am in Palestine

In the fall of 1944, during World War II, two mothers of US servicemen sent heartfelt letters of thanks to residents of Palestine in East Texas. The two women—one from the Midwest and the other from New England—acted independently but with shared appreciation for the hospitality shown their sons, whose troop trains had stopped briefly in the Anderson County seat. The mothers wrote to people they had never met and whose names they did not know, but to whom they were indebted for comforting their sons on their lonely trips away from home. One of the young men was en route to a training center in San Antonio, the other headed home following extended time overseas. The two soldiers were among thousands of military personnel who passed through Palestine during the war years, and they were also among those who came to revere Palestine with great fondness for the unselfish and unparalleled kindness of its citizens.

Addressing her letter to the chamber of commerce, Mrs. Alfred O. Peterson of Methuen, Massachusetts, wrote:

Gentlemen—

Recently my son, who is in the service, went thru your town on the way to San Antonio. He stopped at your USO and mailed me your circular letter from there—and written in the blank space—a little note from himself.

I am writing to tell you how much joy that letter gave me. He had not been feeling well and had to make a three day trip from Methuen, Mass., so when he wrote me of the kindness of your ladies—the drink of cold milk, the dainty sandwiches and cookies, I was so pleased.

Thank your ladies for their good wishes and tell them that their efforts *are not in vain*.[1]

From her home in Kalamazoo, Michigan, Mrs. Frank (Leona) Vorce addressed the following note to the "Ladies of Service Men's Club":

To one and all who made our son's stay in Palestine so enjoyable:

Our son P.F.C. Douglas A. Vorce USM.C. was on his way home from 27 months spent in the South Pacific. He is a veteran of many battles while being with the 1st Marine Div. Having time while in Palestine he visited your Service Men's Club. You can imagine how pleased he was when he found how welcome the boys were, also the good food, and pleasant talks, gave him a wonderful feeling of being home.

He told me, "Mom, be sure and write to those Ladies, they know just what to do to make a fellow feel at home." "Also they can sure make good coffee."

P.F.C. Douglas is now in the Naval Hospital in Philadelphia. He came down with a Malaria Fever contracted while overseas. However, he expects to recover soon and be back on duty.[2]

The Peterson and Vorce letters are only two examples of many received in praise of the good work of the Palestine Service Men's Club, which operated from 1942 to 1946. The original letters are now archived with photos and other mementos in the offices of the Anderson County Historical Commission, which makes its headquarters in the restored 1907 Federal Building in downtown Palestine only a couple of blocks from where the club operated. Today, the site of the O'Neill Hotel, which housed the club, is a vacant lot, save for the remains of one brick wall, painted years ago with a mural depicting in commemorative fashion the story of Anderson County's many contributions to military efforts through the years. Across busy Spring Street from the empty lot are still active rail lines that provide a strong visual reference for the countless troop trains that stopped at the Palestine passenger depot during the war years.

By the time of World War II, Palestine was a vital railroad center in East Texas through the significant role it played in the development and administration of the International–Great Northern Railroad, whose lines reached the area in the 1870s. With regard to the deployment of troops in wartime, it was a logical place for refueling and switching operations. When the trains stopped downtown, porters from the O'Neill Hotel made their way to the cars and personally invited the servicemen to the nearby club for refreshments, entertainment, or just quiet conversation and a chance to unwind. Many openly welcomed the invitation, but even those who remained on the train, whether too tired, shy, or homesick to join the others, soon found themselves the focus of local hospitality, as ladies boarded the cars to distribute fruit or homemade cookies and sandwiches and to sit and visit. Such scenes of unselfish outpouring of support for the troops played out daily as military trains stopped over in Palestine at all times of the day and night. None stopped over in Palestine without such attention. Thousands of soldiers and sailors, many of whom had never even heard of the Anderson County seat before the war, came to remember it with great fondness and appreciation throughout their lives. Some even returned to make their homes there after the war, so impressed were they with the friendly spirit of the small town.[3]

The strong feelings the servicemen felt are clearly evident in the letters they sent back to the Palestine ladies. Cpl. J. J. Foy wrote from Camp Polk, Louisiana, in 1944, addressing his words to Miss Katherine Ryan:

The reason for this communication goes back to Christmas Day. I was returning to my station at Ft. Sam Houston, when we were told there would be a stopover in your city. Shortly after alighting from the train, we (the members of the armed forces) were invited to enjoy a turkey dinner in the local USO. Let me tell you now that it was the bright spot of the entire trip.

Most of us, if they felt as I did, were out of sorts. Travelling away from home on Christmas Day is not a pleasant experience. You can appreciate how happy we were to receive the friendship extended to us. The meal was excellent and the hospitality beyond my expectations.

Interior photograph of the Palestine Service Men's Club. Throughout World War II, countless numbers of military men sat here to write letters back home, often describing their abiding appreciation for the hospitality and unselfish support of the local people. Courtesy Jimmy Odom and the Anderson County Historical Commission.

However, upon leaving, it was not enough that we should have had an excellent dinner, no we must have more. There was fruit enough for all. Over and above, each one of us was to select a present. I selected yours, because of the bright and pretty wrapping paper. In this were cheerful and practical articles. The shaving set and the playing cards. I might add that the latter proved to be of welcome financial assistance. It's not everyday that you receive lucky playing cards.

Therefore I have many things to be thankful for especially on that day. You brightened, considerably, a dark day, when I had to be away from my parents and family whom I love so much.

Sincerely,

Jack

P.S. If you care to, I would like to correspond.[4]

Chief Storekeeper Edw. R. Jucksch, US Naval Reserve, who served aboard the USS *General R. E. Callan* (AP-139), also wrote of his Christmas experiences in Palestine:

Dear Little Mothers:

Should you look back on your log of visitors of last Xmas you will find the name as written below and it is with the greatest of pleasure that my memory goes back to you today.

Many times in the past year have I told people about you all and what a wonderful dinner and the nice present that I received from you on Xmas day. The spirit of the ladies of Palastine [sic] will never be forgotten by the many service men that visited your center and received of your great and sincere hospitality.

Do not remember the lady's name that acted as the hostess that Xmas day but I would like to remember her as Mother. She was quite white of hair as I remember and her smile and kind thought and words will never be forgotten.

Please accept my sincere thanks for the memory.[5]

The Palestine Service Men's Club, so fondly remembered by countless soldiers and sailors who served in the war, originated in June 1942. While many referred to it as a USO (United Service Organizations) operation, it was in fact independent, established by and supported by volunteer citizens of Anderson County. The project was the idea of Zula Holcomb Hanks, the wife of local banker Clyde Walton Hanks. Born in 1884 at Troup, in Smith County, Zula Hanks was a leading citizen of Palestine at the time of World War II, and she had the connections, the vision, and the organizational skills to put her plan into action. The mother of two sons who would see service in the war, she knew firsthand the loneliness of a family's separation in time of war, and she hoped to do what she could on the home front to offer support and comfort to those servicemen who passed through the town. To assist her in that endeavor, she enlisted a large number of individuals who freely gave of their time as hostesses, cooks, carpenters, committee members, promoters, and fundraisers. One of the first to join her effort was M. A. Davey, owner of the O'Neill Hotel, who offered the group the use of a room off the lobby that had previously housed Red Cross activities. Volunteer workers painted the new club space and brought in furniture from their homes to make it feel comfortable and inviting.[6]

Initially, funding for operation of the Service Men's Club proved limiting, but Hanks persevered with the help of individual donations. Soon she set up committees to come up with innovative ways to secure broader financial support, and club members led scrap drives for such items as old keys, tin cans, and wax paper to raise cash. Among the more successful efforts were the glass scrap drives, which resulted in large amounts of cullet, or recycled glass. Palestine was fortunate in that it had a ready local market for the material through the Knox Glass Bottle Company, which had a major plant in the city. As the local newspaper noted in an appeal to the citizenry:

> Ever hear of cullet? Well, it's the definition glass manufacturers give to the reclaimed clear glass which they crush and use as an ingredient in making more clear glass containers. . . .
>
> A cullet salvage bin has been erected at the tiny triangle at Oak, Avenue A and Houston streets . . . (and) will be sold to the Knox Glass Bottle Company at the prevailing price. Every dime of the proceeds will go to the Service Men's Club.
>
> Mrs. Clyde Hanks, chairman of the Service Men's Club, emphasized the point that the bin was for cullet only, and that it would not become a public garbage depository, as happened in the tin can salvage effort.[7]

Significant amounts of money also came as a result of organized public appeals, most notably the regular showing of a special film at the Ritz and Texas theaters that raised several hundred dollars a month, a considerable amount for a town of fifteen thousand people still emerging from the economic depression of the 1930s. Produced locally in 1943 and funded by theater manager J. F. Jones, the short promotional plea featured commentary written by Franklin Bradford of the *Palestine Herald*:

> Ladies and Gentlemen—
>
> Need we remind you that in the jungled underbrush of the Solomons, on the Tundra of Attu, on the islands of the Mediterranean, and in the skies of Europe and Asia, American boys are driving doggedly ahead against the enemy?

In every battle zone, perhaps, there are Soldiers, Sailors, and Marines, who have been guests in our Community, guests of our Service Men's Club, the War-time monument to the hospitality of our citizens.

We glow with pride when a lad in Sicily or Constantine, Iran or Australia writes of an enjoyable time he spent in our mist [*sic*]. Maybe it was but an hour, maybe less, but he recalls clearly that he was treated like a King by the good women of the Service Men's Club.

American boys all over the world are thinking of home, and a reminiscence of a happy stay in Palestine, Texas, is indelibly stamped upon the minds of many. For this, we could have no greater honor. . . .

Once a month this Theater will take a free-will contribution to help meet the expenses of the Super-Deluxe-Home-Town-Service Men's Club. We do not ask you to give. Through this medium, we offer you the privilege of donating to the most worthy cause we know. If you wish to help, you will be extending the hand of love and fellowship to the men in uniform, men who are going out to die, perhaps, for you and me.[8]

Donations raised through these and other means went for such necessities as supplies and utilities but were also shared with a local organization set up to assist African American servicemen. In the 1940s, troop trains and Southern accommodations remained segregated, as did the military itself, and the Service Men's Club likewise reflected the custom of the time. Black servicemen generally rode in separate railroad cars, usually positioned at the rear of the troop trains, and at stops in Palestine local volunteers from the black community boarded them to provide food and hospitality to those men as well. Local church congregations and their leaders, including the Reverend S. H. Graham, the Reverend T. H. Moore, and the Reverend Taft Watts, were among those who provided leadership for the effort.[9]

Throughout its brief existence, the Palestine Service Men's Club remained an independent organization that depended on local donations and volunteer service for its continued operations. The club itself was not elaborate, but it provided adequate space for a wide variety of activities. Free food service was an integral part of the program; servicemen were not allowed to pay for their refreshments. While some sat and visited with their hostesses and reminisced about hometowns or wartime experiences, others listened to the local radio station, played games, read magazines, or danced with young ladies to the music of a record player. Writing letters to loved ones back home, a practice highly encouraged by Zula Hanks, was also a popular activity. For those who lacked ideas or inspiration for what to write, the club provided specially printed form letters that required the servicemen to add only the addressee's name in the salutation and their signatures at the bottom. Adorned with colorful graphics, the letters were brief and read more like boosterism brochures than heartfelt sentiments, but, as noted in Mrs. Peterson's letter to the chamber of commerce, they made a significant difference to those back home. "Here I am in Palestine," they began, "'way down in East Texas, and it's a swell town, believe me. I'm sending this letter from the Service Men's Club so you can know how they treat us here. This club is run entirely by local contributions, and the volunteer ladies in charge are the finest you can find anywhere. They made me feel at home by serving me with free food, drinks, magazines, real southern hospitality and friendliness." The text continued on with the briefest of historical and geographical references, and then mentioned the area's economic base of oil and gas, railroads, manufacturing, and small farms. As if to encourage future tourism or new residents, the letters added, "I surely would like to be here when the Dogwood is in bloom, for Palestine is the home of the Texas Dogwood Trails which in peacetime brought in more than fifty thousand visitors a year." And, they concluded, "I will be leaving Palestine soon now, but someday hope to come back and bring you with me, for there's much to be said for a mild climate like these people have—also for their good fishing lakes and hunting country—but most of all because I know the people in Palestine really wish me well."[10]

As the war came to an end in 1945, the club remained in operation briefly, providing continued assistance to troops returning home. By the end of the year, though, the community was ready to reflect on what it had accomplished in support of the war effort. In December the Palestine Rotary Club held a banquet at Meadowbrook Country Club to honor the ladies of the Service Men's Club. It was a time to honor Zula Hanks and her many volunteers, but also a time to think ahead about what an uncertain peace might require of the American citizenry. "Will you enter into an obligation with yourself," keynote speaker Brig. Gen. Don C. Faith implored, "that in these troublous times of peace you will do your civic duty—do your full civic job as a citizen and elect to public office only those men who will serve your community, your state and nation best, then follow them all the way through. I feel if you will do this," he added, "[your] son's sons may not have to go out and fight as your sons have done."[11]

On Christmas Eve in 1945, the local newspaper announced the pending end of the Service Men's Club: "Numerically, literally thousands of service personnel have visited the Palestine club. The club's scrapbook contains hundreds of letters from the men, their wives, mothers, sisters and fathers, all expressing appreciation for kindnesses shown here." On the first day of the new year, the last wartime troop train passed through town, and soon afterward the club members shut down their operation.[12]

It is significant that the newspaper article noted the collection of letters, which serve as the most complete record of the organization. In reality, there were two scrapbooks, which club member Rose Plaisance dutifully maintained through the war years, carefully adding the correspondence as well as photos and other mementos. Exactly what happened to the scrapbooks in the years immediately following the war is uncertain, but they may have remained in the hotel or in the possession of M. A. Davey. Regardless, they resurfaced years later after demolition of the O'Neill, which had fallen on hard times by the 1980s. Possibly through the influence of the Davey family or radio broadcaster Bill Laurie, the scrapbooks passed to Osjetea Briggs, a local writer, photographer, author, and history enthusiast. A native of Limestone County, Briggs moved to Anderson County in the 1950s and quickly became involved in numerous community activities, especially those of historical nature. Believed to be of Native American heritage, she wrote a weekly column in her *Elkhart Eagle* newspaper entitled "Walk in My Moccasins."[13]

In declining health by the late 1990s, Briggs was admitted to a Palestine nursing home. Many of the historical materials she had collected over the years subsequently passed through legal channels to two local organizations: the Anderson County Historical Commission and the Museum of East Texas Culture. With assistance from members of both groups, Jimmy R. Odom loaded his pickup truck to capacity with the documents and photographs and took them to a temporary location in a vacant building downtown. Soon after, representatives of the two groups met to go through the materials and determine what should be retained and by whom. In the process, the scrapbooks came into the possession of the commission, which secured them in acid-free boxes at the headquarters. There they remained for a few years until Odom came across them while searching for other records. Reviewing everything for the first time, he was captivated by the numerous heartfelt letters, and he set out to use them to document an application for a marker commemorating the story of the Palestine Service Men's Club. His efforts paid off when, on Armistice Day (November 11) in 2006, the commission dedicated the Official Texas Historical Marker against the backdrop of the hotel's remaining structural element—the brick wall that once formed the western edge of the club.

The event attracted a large crowd, including numerous veterans of the war, as well as many who had served on the Anderson County home front. Fittingly, Frances Hanks, the great-great-granddaughter of Zula Hanks (d. 1960), read the inscription to the crowd gathered for the ceremony.[14]

Although time has diminished many memories of the Palestine Service Men's Club, there are occasional firsthand reminders of the important role it played in countless lives. Not long after the marker dedication, Jimmy Odom had the opportunity to talk with Donald C. Laughmiller of Mount Vernon, Illinois, whose letters of thanks are included in the scrapbook collection. In one of them, dated May 23, 1944, the young Army Air Forces corpsman wrote, "It was utterly impossible for me to not write you and thank you humbly. A bunch of fellows get off a train, go into a Service Club,

Jimmy Odom, chair of the Anderson County Historical Commission, standing in front of the remaining wall of the Palestine Service Men's Club. In recent years local residents have adorned the wall with murals depicting the county's service in time of war. Photograph by Dan K. Utley.

are met by lovely young ladies and treated as if they were their brothers. It swept us off our feet. You should have heard the exclamations and praise as the train left Palestine. I, and I think I speak for the others, will not forget you for a long, long time." And, according to Odom, the memories remained as strong to Laughmiller in the twenty-first century as they did more than half a century earlier on his long route home from war.[15]

MARKER LOCATION: 400 block of West Spring St., Palestine

FROM COTTON FIELD TO FACTORY

When the glass scrap drives began in Palestine during World War II, the local plant of the Knox Glass Bottle Company had been in operation only a short time, although the corporation itself dated to the time of World War I. Roy R. Underwood opened a glass plant in Knox, Pennsylvania, in the northwestern part of the state, in 1917. The enterprise grew steadily in the early years and soon expanded its operations to other locales, including Mississippi. By the 1940s the company sought to establish a new plant farther west to serve new regional markets, and attention eventually focused on Palestine, Texas, perceived as an ideal location because of its available land, a natural gas supply, and key rail and highway transportation lines. Chester Underwood, Roy's younger brother, worked with company salesman Jim Keller, then operating out of Houston, to initiate the plans in cooperation with several bankers and other business leaders associated with the Palestine Chamber of Commerce. The enthusiastic response proved as promising as anticipated, and construction soon began on a forty-five-acre agricultural tract west of town in May 1941. Local gas suppliers Julian and Jack Meeker provided fuel for the plant operation, and the Missouri-Pacific Railway built a spur line to the site, where a construction sign boasted, "From Cotton Field to Factory in 95 Days."

Using both new and refurbished equipment run by local apprentice workers, as well as seasoned line crews from Mississippi and South Texas, the plant opened on July 5, 1941. The company dedicated most of its production to containers for sodas, pickles, wine, and peanut butter as well as some medicines. Local merchants supported the products with signs that encouraged consumers, "See what you buy, buy in glass." When the United States entered the war by the end of the year, the company at first faced an uncertain future. With special consideration by the War Production Board and the hiring of women employees, however, it managed to avert any downturn as a result of wartime labor shortages. As the operation boomed, so too did related local industries, in-

Examples of
Knox Glass jars
manufactured
in Palestine.
Photograph
by Jimmy and
Kathy Odom.

cluding the railroad and housing, as well as suppliers of raw materials and paper packaging products. At the war's end, the Knox
Glass Bottle Company remained relatively strong, and with several
hundred employees it was the most successful industrial concern
in the county.

In the years following the war, however, the company failed to
modernize its production capability sufficiently to meet increased
demands, and its market share began to decline. Another significant blow came in 1951 with the death of the company founder
and visionary, Roy Underwood. Renamed Knox Glass Company in
1956, the business became part of the Glass Container Corporation in the 1960s. Work at the Palestine plant continued under the
new corporate structure for a time, but in 1984 the company announced plans to shut down the operation. The last run occurred
shortly before Christmas of that year, when the No. 15 shop ran
continually for a twenty-four-hour period producing jars for the
Skippy Peanut Butter Company. Specially retooled molds marked
each of them as "The Last Jar Made in Palestine, Texas, Dec. 20,
1984," and extra copies became cherished mementos for those
who last worked the line. Among those who were there that last
day was Jimmy Odom, a thirty-year employee who in 2005, as a
member of the Anderson County Historical Commission, prepared

the application for an Official Texas Historical Marker honoring the site of the Knox Glass Company plant where he, his father, and his son had all worked.

MARKER LOCATION: Knox Street, south of W. Oak and north of W. Reagan, Palestine

Sources: Site of Knox Glass Company Plant, Anderson County, THC marker files; Bill Lockhart, Pete Schulz, Carol Serr, and Bill Lindsey, "The Knox Glass Bottle Co.," *Bottles and Extras* [publication of the Federation of Historical Bottle Collectors] 19, No. 3 (May–June 2008): 2–11.

18 The Three Graves of Judge Baylor

Few early figures in Texas history could match the depth of public service that marked the life of Robert Emmett Bledsoe Baylor. He was at various times in his life a lawyer, soldier, politician, jurist, preacher, and teacher. Born in 1793 to a successful merchant family in Lincoln County, Kentucky, in the center of the state, Baylor spent his formative years in Paris, Bourbon County, where he attended private schools. At the age of nineteen, during the struggle that became known as the War of 1812, he enlisted in the state militia and was among the troops who essentially fought their way into Fort Meigs, in northern Ohio, to relieve the besieged American forces. The actions of the Kentuckians helped turn the tide, causing the British eventually to cease their barricading action against the fort. When his enlistment ended, Baylor rejoined as a private and saw action in the US invasion of southern Canada.[1]

Returning to Kentucky after the war, Baylor studied law in the Lexington office of his distinguished uncle, Jesse Bledsoe, who saw service in both the US Senate and the Kentucky House of Representatives. Baylor passed the bar exam and opened his own office while in his early twenties, but in short order he, too, entered politics, first as a state representative in 1819. While the political field would come to define the early part of his career, his first venture proved to be short-lived. He resigned the position after only one year and moved south to Alabama. The reason for his abrupt departure, like many of his actions through the years, remains clouded in conjecture. Stories persist that it had something to do with the tragic death of his fiancée in a riding accident, or maybe with an unrequited courtship, but there are few details to substantiate either situation. Baylor kept no diary and wrote only occasionally about his early life, most commonly through letters to family and friends. Regardless of his reason for leaving his beloved home state, evidently never to return, he embarked on a path that kept him moving farther away over the next two decades. He also never married.

By the early 1820s Baylor practiced law in Tuscaloosa, Alabama, where he eventually reentered politics, again as a state representative. Once again he served only one term, but soon he won election to the US Congress, serving in the House of Representatives as a Jacksonian Democrat. As national politics became embroiled in emerging issues of states' rights, Baylor's support of Jackson perhaps worked against him back home, and in 1831 he faced defeat in his bid for reelection. He returned to his law practice in Tuscaloosa but was soon on the move again, first to Cahaba (Cahawba), the original state capital of Alabama, then to Selma, and eventually on farther south to Mobile. From there he again answered the call for military service, participating in the Creek Indian War in 1836.[2]

While in Alabama in the late 1830s, Baylor made two important decisions that dramatically altered the course of his life and unexpectedly placed him on a path that would redefine the last part of his career as well as his historical legacy. It is difficult to say which decision he faced first, and in a way they may have been intertwined from the beginning. Regardless, the decisions he made both came about in 1839. That summer he had the opportunity to attend revival services at a Baptist church in Talladega, where his cousin, the Reverend Thomas Chilton, preached. Also a lawyer and former politician, as well as a close colleague of David Crockett, Chilton enjoyed additional success as a minister. Baylor, viewed by various historians as a deist, Unitarian, atheist, infidel, or agnostic in his early years, nevertheless converted to Christianity while attending the revival, and soon afterward the Talladega Baptist Church sponsored his ordination as a preacher.[3] Still evidently dealing with the wanderlust that had marked the first part of his life, Baylor felt called to seek new opportunities in a place called the Republic of Texas. Like his conversion, it was not an easy decision for him to make, and his letters reveal he had thought about moving to Texas for years, even though he realized that by doing so he might never return home. As he wrote later about his migration outside the United States, he observed, "When I crossed the boundary line between the U.S. and Texas I did so with a sad heart . . . thinking I should never see my native land again which is literally true. But then I consoled myself," he added, "with the thought that Lafayette and others had come to the U.S. to assist a people struggling in the great cause of humanity for religious and civil liberty. Why might I not in a more humble way follow in their footsteps and do all I could to establish those great principles in Texas."[4]

Baylor's reference to Lafayette—Marie Joseph Paul Yves Roche Gilbert du Motier, Marquis de Lafayette, the French military leader who provided invaluable assistance to Gen. George Washington during the American Revolution—proved to be prescient if not providential. Arriving in Texas in 1839, Baylor settled in the newly created county of Fayette, named in honor of the military hero, at the county seat of La Grange, named for Lafayette's home in France. Located along the Colorado River in the southeastern part of the vast republic, La Grange was a promising young settlement, and Baylor chose it as the site of a new private school he established. For whatever reason, though, he refrained from announcing to his new neighbors that he was also a preacher. In fact, he was reluctant to admit that distinction even to himself, feeling instead at the time that he was more of an exhorter—someone who provided a compelling personal, experiential testimony to the power of Christian faith—than a trained minister. It was not until the noted Baptist frontier preacher Z. N. Morrell sought him out and urged him to be more involved in evangelical work that he committed to help foster struggling young churches in the republic. He began by assisting Morrell and other preachers in the immediate vicinity of La Grange.[5]

In the spring of 1840, peace negotiations in San Antonio between Anglo settlers and Comanches broke down, resulting in the deaths of numerous Indian leaders, as well as women and children, in what came to be known as the Council House Fight. In a series of deadly retaliatory raids that summer on Anglo settlements, Comanches swept down the Guadalupe River valley through Victoria, launching a particularly devastating attack on the small coastal

town of Linnville, in present Calhoun County. From there the war-
riors sought to return home with their plunder and captives, but
by then local militia forces, including R. E. B. Baylor, had formed to
block their escape. There were small but intense skirmishes along
the route, but the fighting culminated in an August battle along
Plum Creek, in the vicinity of present-day Lockhart, where Texas
forces successfully routed the Indians, pushing them, at least temporarily, outside the line of active settlement.

Following his participation in the Battle of Plum Creek, Baylor
returned again to La Grange, but the following year he left the
teaching profession to become justice of the Third Judicial Court.
His circuit included the counties of Bastrop, Fayette, Milam, Robertson, Washington, and Travis. As one of five district judges in the
republic, he was also part of the Supreme Court. As a pragmatic
jurist interested in the fundamental tenets of law, Baylor saw his
new assignment as an opportunity to make a significant difference in his adopted homeland, but he also viewed it as a call to
spread the gospel wherever he traveled. He saw no conflict in the
arrangement, traveling and administering justice on behalf of the
Republic of Texas during the day—always with his gun at hand—
and preaching, exhorting, and organizing churches in the evening.
As one writer noted, "He was a staunch advocate of separation of
church and state—yet no person ever merged the two with greater
skill." Perhaps the judge rectified the matter in his own mind by re-
fusing to take any pay for his ecclesiastical work. Regardless, it was
an arrangement he continued throughout his judicial career.[6]

By means of his evangelical work, Baylor became increasingly
involved in the early growth of the Baptist denomination in Texas.
At La Grange in 1840 he helped organize the Union Baptist Association to oversee church support efforts in the region, and at the
group's second meeting the following year he offered a proposal to
establish a Baptist college in Texas. As a result, the association formally established the Texas Baptist Educational Society to pursue
its success, both financially and legally, and named Baylor as president. Under his direction the society sought a congressional charter for the school, but ongoing concerns of the government about
possible armed conflict with Mexico in the early 1840s delayed the

implementation of their plan. In the fall of 1844, though, Baylor and his close friend William M. Tryon finalized the proposal for presentation to the Republic of Texas Congress when it convened at Washington-on-the-Brazos. Sen. George Alexander Pattillo, representing Jasper and Jefferson counties, introduced the bill, and as it made its way through the legislative process there were several informal deliberations on what to name the new school. San Jacinto and Milam, both evocative of the revolutionary era, received early consideration, but Baylor and Tryon also debated the issue, each unselfishly offering the other's name as a means of honoring significant contributions to the idea. In the end, though, the judge's name prevailed, and on February 1, 1845, Pres. Anson Jones signed the charter creating Baylor University.[7]

Historically, it was an uneasy time to establish such a university, given the fact that the unsettled and controversial "Texas question" still prevailed in the US Congress, but in short order the republic came to an end when Texas entered the union as the twenty-eighth state. Judge Baylor contributed to the success of that transition, offering his legal skills to help frame the new constitution required by statehood. Despite the uncertainties of the time, the Baylor University board of trustees, of which Baylor was a founding member, began meeting to plan the school's development. One of the most important decisions the board made came in October of that year when they selected the site for the institution. Carefully canvassing the proposals, the members considered four sites: the town of Travis, in Austin County; Huntsville, in what was then Montgomery County; the settlement of Shannon's Prairie, also in Montgomery County; and the small town of Independence, in Washington County. In choosing the last, the board hoped to place the university at the center of burgeoning development in Texas. Washington County offered great political, financial, and commercial promise at the time, and the Baptist leaders envisioned an educational institution that would grow in tandem as an integral part of the young state. Following their decision, work began immediately on a campus that would open the following year and include both male and female students.[8]

In the ensuing years, the Independence campus expanded as

planned with the completion of various new structures, the development of new courses of study, and a steadily increasing student body. Although Judge Baylor made one more effort soon after statehood to enter national politics as a congressman, his resounding defeat helped him refocus his judicial efforts. He successfully transitioned to serve as justice of the same district he had earlier served, and he continued in that capacity even after Texas joined the Confederacy at the onset of the Civil War. His decision to remain in service during the war years would later work against him when he petitioned in vain for a federal pension he felt he had earned as a War of 1812 veteran.[9]

In addition to his judicial duties, Baylor continued to serve as a trustee at his namesake university, where he taught classes in law, accepting no pay for his work. He also maintained his high level of involvement in Baptist programs. After 1851, when college president Rufus C. Burleson established separate institutions for male and female students at Independence, the judge taught classes at both campuses and served on both boards of trustees. He retired from the bench in the 1860s (sources differ on the specific year) and spent his remaining years in relative obscurity and near poverty at his Washington County home, Holly Oaks, in the Gay Hill community a few miles from Independence. He died there in 1873 and, according to his wishes, was buried in "Baylor soil" adjacent to the male college campus on a high elevation at Independence known as Windmill Hill. While the site fulfilled his instructions, it was not to be his final resting place, though. The wanderlust that had guided him throughout his life, it seemed, also guided the disposition of his earthly remains.[10]

Although the two branches of Baylor University had continued to show great promise, even during Reconstruction, by the 1880s it became clear that the state's center of growth had shifted considerably westward. As a result, a small rural settlement such as Independence no longer offered the early potential it once enjoyed, and that, school officials believed, was a key factor in declining enrollments and, thus, revenues. Rumors of plans to leave Washington County soon became reality, despite the 1882 completion of a new central main building, Tryon Hall, on the Windmill Hill cam-

The site of Judge R. E. B. Baylor's first grave, located at the original location of Baylor University on Windmill Hill, Independence. Photograph by Dan K. Utley.

pus. In 1885 the trustees of the two Baylors met to consider a resolution that states in part: "Whereas the changes wrought in the Providences of God by time, changes in population, centers of influence, accessibility, etc., it sometimes becomes necessary to remove institutions of learning to more favored localities . . . therefore be it resolved . . . that these institutions should be removed from Independence at as early a day as the preservation of their interest will admit. . . . Fealty to the mental interests of the rising ministry and to Christ require it."[11] While there were some final efforts to merge the two institutions before the move, Baptists meeting in state convention at Lampasas in 1885 voted to keep them separate. As a result, with the end of the 1885 school year the male department of the university moved to McLennan County, where it merged with Waco University, and the female department moved to Belton as Baylor Female College. In the 1930s, through the philanthropy of Burkburnett resident Mary "Mollie" Funk Hardin, it became known as Mary Hardin–Baylor College (now the University of Mary Hardin–Baylor).[12]

Although there were some legal complications to address, trustees of the two Baylors moved quickly to end their ties with Independence and to start the new chapters of their respective histories. The last formal action by the schools at their original site concerned the sale of three pianos. Rather than see the facilities completely abandoned, a small group of Baptists opened William Carey Crane College on the site in 1886, advertising it as a continuation of the Baylor program. The effort proved to be short-lived, as did the successor university started there by R. E. Binford. In 1890, much of the land transferred to the Guardian Angels Orphanage and Industrial School for Colored Boys, a Catholic organization headed by Father Francis M. Huhn. The institution struggled to stay open after his death in 1914, but it, too, soon closed, leaving the former university grounds completely abandoned. Time, erosion, fires, and neglect took their toll on the remaining structures, and local residents salvaged materials for building projects around the area. By the early twentieth century there were few physical reminders of the once promising institution except the lone grave of its founder, enclosed by a small metal fence.[13]

Even before the abandonment of facilities on Windmill Hill, rumors persisted about the condition of the judge's gravesite. In an attempt to dispel some of the more inflammatory stories amid recurring talk of removing the remains to the Waco campus, the *Dallas Morning News* ran an article in January 1900 by Harry Haynes that attempted to set the record straight. Specifically addressing an earlier article in the *Waco Telephone,* Haynes noted:

It has been stated with reference to this hallowed spot that it is being plowed over and planted in cotton; that it is a Catholic horse lot, and in a great variety of ways wickedly desecrated. These statements are made without a knowledge of the facts, and all are erroneous. It is true the old university property is now owned by a Catholic priest, but the grave of this good man is located 300 feet from his barn or horse lot, or any horse lot. The sod over this sacred spot has never been disturbed by a plow since the foundation of the world, and the only time it was ever broken was when Judge Baylor was placed beneath it. We wish to say, moreover, Father Huhn, who owns the property, evinces no kind of desire to have the remains removed from the campus, but on the contrary seems to entertain feeling of great veneration and respect for the place, and once when the iron railing was broken, unsolicitedly [sic], he replaced it with his own hands and with his own expense. Let these simple statements go on record. Their entire truthfulness will be attested by hundreds of living men.

Calling for a monument at Independence rather than for reinterment, the article concluded, "Rather than have his dust carted off, let that monument tower over the spot in the county he loved, and among the people who felt the ennobling and elevating of his life and service, and then the eternal fitness of things will be beautifully observed." Plans for both the monument and the relocation failed to materialize, however, but rumors of grave desecration continued.[14]

Years later, the Reverend George Washington Baines Jr. (d. 1923), son of the noted pioneer Baptist preacher and Baylor University president George Washington Baines Sr. (d. 1882), personally visited the grave of Judge Baylor only to learn that some of the rumors of its condition were, in fact, true. Finding it overgrown and isolated within an orchard where horses indeed grazed, he decided the time had come to find a more appropriate burial site for the revered jurist, preacher, and university founder. Relating his investigation first to a student gathering of the San Marcos Academy in Hays County, a Baptist institution run by his colleague, J. M. Carroll, he called on all Texas Baptists to support the effort. This time the reaction was quick and widespread, and at the meeting of the Baptist General Convention in Waco in 1916, delegates passed a resolution that, in part, read:

Whereas, The building and grounds of Old Baylor University at Independence, Texas, are now owned by Roman Catholics, the campus being used for a horse lot; and

Whereas, Within the said campus thus used is the grave of R. E. B. Baylor, the great and good man for whom our Baylors were named; therefore be it

Resolved, That it is the sense of this Convention, that the earthly remains of Judge Baylor should be removed from their present place of sepulchre and solemnly buried in some suitable place where they may have due attention and care from our Baptist people.[15]

The resolution further called for the formation of a committee to oversee the development of a plan for the grave relocation. With Carroll as the chairman, the committee moved quickly and presented a proposal to the Baylor University trustees at Waco in December. The board, which included Pat M. Neff, later governor of Texas and president of Baylor, declined the offer, noting:

Resolved, First. That Baylor will provide a suitable lot in Oakwood Cemetery in Waco for the interment of said remains, and will also provide a suitable place on the campus of the University for a monument to Judge Baylor, if the denomination should desire to erect one, and,

Resolved, Second. While we would be glad to have Judge Baylor's remains to rest in our cemetery, we do not think it advisable to inter them on the University campus.[16]

The board's recommendation did not meet with committee approval, however, since it failed to address the judge's express intent to be buried on Baylor soil. As a result, the committee withdrew its offer and made a new proposal to the board of Baylor Female College, Belton, which quickly accepted. Wasting little time, the oversight committee made arrangements for the exhumation at Independence. A 1917 article in the *Baptist Standard* observed: "The bones were in perfect preservation, and pronounced intact by a physician present, although not a sign of the coffin could be found, with the exception of one of the metal handles. One other article

Seniors from the class of 1959 placing flowers at the grave of Judge Baylor on the campus of Mary Hardin–Baylor College, Belton. Following destruction of the adjacent Wilson Administration Building by fire in 1971, rubble fell on the gravesite, breaking the slab cover and, in time, necessitating plans for reinterment at another site on the campus. Courtesy University of Mary Hardin–Baylor Museum Archives.

was found in the grave, a large Masonic emblem. The remarkable preservation of the bones seems almost miraculous." (In an odd twist of fate, the judge's remains moved to Belton, while the remnants of his coffin ended up at Waco, where they are now part of the university's Texas Collection.) On Sunday, May 5, 1917, following a grand memorial ceremony on the Belton campus, the remains of Judge Baylor were laid to rest in a lone grave immediately adjacent to the administration building and chapel. A white marble slab, simply inscribed, later marked what those in attendance that day believed would be the judge's final resting place.

Indeed, the grave became a well-visited landmark on the historic campus over the ensuing decades, the scene of an annual birthday ceremony in which graduating senior women, bedecked in their caps and gowns, filed reverently by to place flowers on the founder's grave. It was an honored tradition—a time of reflection about the past and of transition to the future.[17]

In February 1964, tragedy struck the small college campus when a fire began in the basement of the 1907 Wilson Administration Building (which housed the Alma Reeves Chapel) and spread rapidly throughout the structure, destroying the interior completely. Lost in the blaze were most of the school's original papers, including individual student records reaching back to the days at Independence. Only unstable charred walls of the three-story building remained after firemen fought valiantly to save the landmark, and out of concern for safety, school officials felt they had no alternative but to order full demolition. The resulting rubble from the fire and aftermath spread out from the footprint of the building, covering, among other things, Judge Baylor's grave. Within a month, workers cleared the site and, finding the marble tombstone broken into countless pieces, gathered three large stones from the debris to mark the grave. There it remained untouched until approval for a new building on the site necessitated another reinterment for the judge. This time it was only a few hundred feet away into a campus historical park that was the idea of Arla Ray Tyson, wife of college president Arthur K. Tyson. During her husband's tenure, Arla Ray Tyson championed campus beautification projects such as the new park, and her plan for a new burial site included the placement of an Official Texas Historical Marker to interpret Judge Baylor's rich history. The grave, now marked by a large gray granite slab incised only with the name R. E. B. Baylor, is part of a commemorative area that includes a perpetual flame, landscaped flower beds, and other historical markers. Not far away is Luther Memorial, the iconic symbol of the university that marks the site of the first campus building, also destroyed by fire. Several hundred feet to the north of the grave is the Walton Chapel, constructed on the site of the Wilson Administration Building and Alma Reeves Chapel—and Baylor's second grave.[18]

The serene setting of Judge Baylor's third—and perhaps final—grave befits the history of a Texas pioneer who lived an unselfish life rich in public service. It is also evocative of the stirring lines of

a poem called "Old Baylor" written by John Hill Luther, the transitional president when Baylor Female College moved from Independence to Belton. Later set to music by Herman J. Bal (ca. 1902) as a college hymn still performed by students and graduates, it concludes:

> Old Baylor, dear Baylor, on life's troubled sea,
> At home or abroad will our hearts cling to thee,
> And summoned on high at the end of our toil,
> We'll lie down to rest, on old Baylor's dear soil.[19]

MARKER LOCATIONS: The site of the first burial is marked at Baylor Park on Windmill Hill, Lueckemeyer Road, Independence; the site of the third burial is marked on the campus of the University of Mary Hardin–Baylor, Belton.

(opposite) *The current burial site of Judge Baylor on the campus of the University of Mary Hardin–Baylor. The chapel in the background is located on the site of the Wilson Administration Building, near which his remains were reinterred following their removal from Independence.* Photograph by Dan K. Utley.

A GIFT IN THE HOUR OF NEED

Who was Mary Hardin? She was not, as some assume, the wife of Judge R. E. B. Baylor, nor was she a member of his family, although she is considered part of the collegiate family that has bonded their names together in history. Born Mary Catherine Funk near Linville, Virginia, shortly before the Civil War, she became a rural schoolteacher in her home state. Later, however, for reasons known only to her, Mollie, as she was known to friends, headed to Texas and became a teacher in the small Wichita County community of Nesterville, present-day Burkburnett. There, she met a widower named John Gerham Hardin, a native of Mississippi, and they married in 1887. Their first years were typical for frontier families, and they lived in a dugout, worked hard, and lived frugally. The couple lost a daughter in childbirth but eventually adopted a son. John Hardin was an industrious person, and in addition to his farming he operated a store, loaned money, helped establish a bank, bought land, and made other investments, becoming a wealthy man in the first decades of the twentieth century. He was already a millionaire in 1919 when oil was discovered on his vast holdings around Burkburnett. Despite their prosperity, the Hardins continued to live modestly, carefully saving and investing their money. By the early 1930s, at the height of the Great Depression, the family wealth totaled more than five million dollars. It was then, as the couple reached their seventies in age, that they made the decision to give their fortune away to worthy causes. Being devoutly religious, they chose to give much of it to Baptist institutions of education, health care, and social service as well as to their adopted hometown of Burkburnett.

In the 1930s, many institutions of higher learning in Texas faced mounting debts, declining enrollments, and marginal endowments. A few, including Baylor College for Women at Belton, even considered closing. As circumstances headed quickly toward what appeared to be a point of no return, though, John and Mollie Hardin provided the timely assistance that allowed the historic

This portrait of Mary Hardin, showing the philanthropist in her later years, is located in the University of Mary Hardin–Baylor Museum. Photograph by Randy Yandell, courtesy University of Mary Hardin–Baylor Museum Archives.

school to continue. Their generous endowment, which eventually totaled more than $670,000, proved to be the turning point for the struggling college, and in appreciation the trustees renamed it Mary Hardin–Baylor College (now the University of Mary Hardin–Baylor) in 1934. Mary Catherine Funk Hardin passed away the following year, and John G. Hardin died in 1937. Both are buried in Burkburnett.

The Hardins succeeded in their efforts to bequeath the bulk of their estates, eventually disbursing almost six million dollars to such institutions as Baylor University, Buckner Orphans Home, Baylor University Hospital in Dallas, and Simmons College, Abilene (later renamed Hardin-Simmons in their honor). They also made substantial contributions to several churches in Wichita County, paid off debts of the Burkburnett school district, funded a city light plant, and set aside their original home place for what became Hardin Park. There, an Official Texas Historical Marker placed in 1970 reads in part, "Operating a store and owning extensive lands, [John G. Hardin] amassed a fortune that he left as a rich legacy for Texas children." Although Mary's name is not included in the philanthropy, the marker mentions several institutions, including Mary Hardin–Baylor College. She is also referenced, along with her husband, as a donor for Wichita Falls Junior College, now Midwestern State University, and for Hardin-Simmons University. Currently, though, there is no marker for her individual history and work. In a way, that befits her quiet and gentle life. There are more lasting testimonies to her generosity, as college president J. C. Hardy noted in a tribute to the Hardins entitled "Friends in Hour of Need": "Through the years to come, every young woman who receives her training in Mary Hardin–Baylor will have called to her attention the nobility of character, the beauty of womanhood, and the grace of generosity exemplified in the life of Mrs. Mary C. Hardin."

MARKER LOCATIONS

Wichita Falls Junior College: 1104 Broad Street, Wichita Falls

Hardin-Simmons University: Ambler and Simmons Streets, Abilene

John Gerham Hardin: Hardin Park, Burkburnett, at intersection of Davey and Williams Drives

Sources: J. C. Hardy, "Friends in Hour of Need," in "Mr. and Mrs. John G. Hardin: Stewards Who Administered Their Own Estates," an undated commemorative booklet published by the Baptist Foundation of Texas, copy included in the holdings of the University of Mary Hardin–Baylor Museum, Belton; *Life Story of John Gerham Hardin by His Own Pen* (Dallas: Baptist Foundation of Texas, 1939), also a commemorative booklet; Marg-Riette Montgomery, "A Life Sketch of Mary Hardin," unpublished manuscript included in the holdings of the University of Mary Hardin–Baylor Museum, Belton; "Funeral Services for Mrs. Hardin Scheduled Sunday: Educators to Laud Philanthropist Who Gave Millions to Colleges," *Dallas Morning News,* September 7, 1935, p. 5.

Notes

CHAPTER 1. A CHANCE ENCOUNTER
OF THE GREAT PROCESSION

1. E. H. Sellards, *Early Man in America: A Study in Prehistory* (Austin: University of Texas Press, 1952), pp. 17–18.

2. Sellards, *Early Man in America,* 18; Frederick W. Rathjen, "Floyd V. Studer," *New Handbook of Texas,* vol. 6, p. 135.

3. "Uncovers Evidence of Early Mammoth Hunters," *Science News Letter,* Feb. 4, 1935, p. 92.

4. Alex D. Krieger, "Elias Howard Sellards, 1875–1961," *American Antiquity* 27, no. 2 (Oct. 1961): 225–28.

5. Glen L. Evans, "E. H. Sellards' Contributions to Paleoindian Studies," in Vance T. Holliday, ed., *Guidebook to the Archaeological Geology of Classic Paleoindian Sites on the Southern High Plains, Texas and New Mexico* (College Station: Department of Geography, Texas A&M University, 1986), p. 9.

6. Sellards, *Early Man in America,* p. 24.

7. Ibid., p. 23.

8. Roberts County Historical Commission and Roberts County Museum, *The Miami Mammoth Kill Site* (Miami, TX: Roberts County Historical Commission and Roberts County Museum, 2005), pp. 9–16.

9. Ibid., pp. 17–19.

10. Krieger, "Elias Howard Sellards," p. 227.

11. Sellards, *Early Man in America,* p. 3.

12. Krieger, "Elias Howard Sellards," p. 227; Roberts County Historical Commission and Roberts County Museum, *The Miami Mammoth Kill Site,* p. 16; "Glen L. Evans," obituary, *Austin American-Statesman,* July 25, 2010, n.p.

13. Vance T. Holliday, C. Vance Haynes Jr., Jack L. Hofman, and David J. Meltzer, "Geoarchaeology and Geochronology on the Miami (Clovis) Site, Southern High Plains of Texas," *Quarternary Research* 41 (1994): 236, 239.

CHAPTER 2. JOHN BEN'S CRITTERS

1. Nancy Wells, Odessa Main Street Program, email to Cynthia J. Beeman, Sept. 29, 2010, copy in authors' files.

2. Walter Prescott Webb, *The Great Plains* (Lincoln: University of Nebraska Press, 1931, 1959), pp. 33, 38.

3. The Jackrabbit, Ector County, Official Texas Historical Marker files, Texas Historical Commission, Austin (hereafter cited as THC marker files).

4. John Ben Shepperd, Apr. 15–18, 1985, speech on the Odessa Jackrab-

bit, Box 109, Folder 2925, Item 77, John Ben Shepperd Papers, 91.01 Special Collections, J. Conrad Dunagan Library, University of Texas of the Permian Basin.

5. World's First Championship Jackrabbit Roping, Marker No. 12, Heritage of Odessa Foundation, 1990.

6. The Prairie Dog, Ector County, THC marker files.

7. Webb, *The Great Plains,* pp. 39–40.

8. "Anti–Prairie Dog Movement: Address to the People of Prairie Dog Infested Portions of Texas," *Dallas Morning News,* Nov. 15, 1898, p. 5; "The Prairie Dog Must Go," petition to the Twenty-sixth Legislature of Texas from the Citizens of Clay County, Memorials and Petitions to the Texas Legislature, Record Group 100, Texas State Archives, Austin; *General Laws of Texas, 1903–1905,* vol. 12, pp. 70–71.

9. "Killing Prairie Dogs," *Dallas Morning News,* Aug. 25, 1904, p. 10.

10. "Auto Exhaust Used to Kill Prairie Dogs on West Texas Ranch," *Dallas Morning News,* Mar. 21, 1923, sec. 1, p. 5; "Systematic Extermination of Texas Prairie Dogs Under Way," *Dallas Morning News,* Nov. 18, 1928, editorial, Amusement and Radio section, p. 12.

11. Stephen Harrigan, "New Dogs, Old Tricks," *Texas Monthly,* July 1977, p. 133; Kris Axtman, "The Prairie Dog: Pest or Pet?" *The Christian Science Monitor,* Aug. 13, 2002, p. 3.

12. The Mule, Bailey County, THC marker files; "Monument Due to Honor Mule," *Dallas Morning News,* Feb. 18, 1962, sec. 1, p. 7.

13. "Statue to Honor the Mule," *Dallas Morning News,* Nov. 19, 1964, sec. 1, p. 13; Frank X. Tolbert, "The 'Mule Lovers' Protest Old Pete," *Dallas Morning News,* Dec. 2, 1964, sec. 4, p. 1; Frank X. Tolbert, "Old Pete Accused of Being a 'Snide,'" *Dallas Morning News,* Nov. 24, 1964, sec. 4, p. 1.

14. Dedication Program, Mule Memorial Celebration, Muleshoe, Texas, copy in The Mule, THC marker file; Eddie S. Hughes, "Muleshoe Mule Will Greet Wanderers after July 3," *Dallas Morning News,* Mar. 15, 1965, sec. 1, p. 6; The Mule, THC marker file.

CHAPTER 3. A LIFE IN RAGGED TIME

1. US military registration card for Euday Louis Bowman, undated, but believed to be from 1916 or 1917, accessed through Ancestry.com, Nov. 15, 2010; photo of Bowman mausoleum, Euday Louis Bowman, Tarrant County, THC marker file.

2. US Federal Census, 1880, 1900, 1910, 1920, accessed through Ancestry .com, Nov. 14, 2010.

3. Landon Laird, "The 12th Street Rag Story," *Kansas City Times,* Oct. 23, 1942, reprinted in *Rag Times* 13, no. 1 (May 1979): 1–2.

4. Terry Waldo, *This is Ragtime* (New York: Hawthorn Books, 1976), p. 4.

5. Christopher Evans, "Rags to Rags: Man Who Wrote 12th Street Rag

Died Not Far from the Gutter," *Fort Worth Star-Telegram*, Dec. 20, 1992, n.p., accessed through Newsbank.com, Nov. 16, 2010.

6. Ibid.

7. Ibid.; US military registration card; US Federal Census, 1910, accessed through Ancestry.com, Nov. 14, 2010.

8. Peter A. Mustedt, "Kansas City Music Publishing," *American Music* 9, no. 4 (Winter 1991), pp. 353–83.

9. Evans, "Rags to Rags."

10. Dave Oliphant, *Texan Jazz* (Austin: University of Texas Press, 1996), pp. 29–33; Evans, "Rags to Rags."

11. Colin Larkin, ed. and comp., *The Encyclopedia of Popular Music*, 3rd ed., vol. 4 (London: Music UK Ltd., 1998), pp. 2638–39; Nicolas Slonimsky, ed. emer., *Baker's Biographical Dictionary of Musicians*, vol. 3 (New York: Schirmer Books, 2001), p. 1643.

12. Company history from Shapirobernstein.com, accessed Nov. 18, 2010.

13. Euday Louis Bowman, THC marker file.

14. From the *Fort Worth Observer*, June 1, 1978, quoted in the application narrative, Euday Louis Bowman, THC marker file.

15. Oliphant, *Texan Jazz*, p. 28.

CHAPTER 4. TURN EAST TO TEXAS

1. H. Bailey Carroll, ed., "The Journal of Lieutenant J. W. Abert from Bent's Fort to St. Louis in 1845," *Panhandle-Plains Historical Review* 14 (1941): 3–5; George W. Cullum, *Biographical Register of the Officers and Graduates of the U.S. Military Academy from 1802 to 1867*, vol. 2 (New York: James Miller, Publisher, 1879), p. 71.

2. Ferol Egan, *Frémont: Explorer for a Restless Nation* (Garden City, NY: Doubleday & Co., 1977), pp. 38–48.

3. William H. Goetzmann, *Army Exploration in the American West, 1803–1863* (New Haven: Yale University Press, 1959), pp. 66–69.

4. Egan, *Frémont*, pp. 17–20, 122–74, 274–79.

5. Goetzmann, *Army Exploration*, p. 117.

6. Ibid.

7. Ibid., pp. 117–18.

8. Egan, *Frémont*, pp. 275–76.

9. Ibid., pp. 276–77.

10. Carroll, "Journal of Lieutenant J. W. Abert," pp. 17–18.

11. Ibid., pp. 6, 20–21.

12. Frederick J. Rathjen, *The Texas Panhandle Frontier* (Austin: University of Texas Press, 1973), pp. 116–18; Carroll, "Journal of Lieutenant J. W. Abert," p. 5; Goetzmann, *Army Exploration*, pp. 109–11, 117.

13. Rathjen, *Texas Panhandle Frontier*, 117.

14. Carroll, "Journal of Lieutenant J. W. Abert," pp. 68–69.

15. Rathjen, *Texas Panhandle Frontier*, 121–22.

16. *Twenty-ninth Annual Reunion of the Association of the Graduates of the United States Military Academy at West Point, New York, June 19, 1898* (Saginaw, MI: Seeman & Peters, 1898), pp. 18–22.

17. Ibid., pp. 18–22.

18. Carroll, "Journal of Lieutenant J. W. Abert," p. 7.

19. Ibid., p. 6; Walter Prescott Webb, ed., "Texas Collection," *Southwestern Historical Quarterly* 45, no. 4 (April 1942): 376.

20. Goetzmann, *Army Exploration*, p. 127.

CHAPTER 5. ILLUMINED BY TRUTHFUL ARTISTIC IDEALS

1. Lloyd C. Engelbrecht and June-Marie F. Engelbrecht, *Henry C. Trost: Architect of the Southwest* (El Paso: El Paso Public Library Association, 1981), pp. 117–18; Troy Ainsworth, "Henry C. Trost: Architect of 'Arid America,'" *Journal of Big Bend Studies*, vol. 21 (Alpine, TX: Center for Big Bend Studies, Sul Ross State University, 2009), pp. 79, 81.

2. Ainsworth, "Henry C. Trost," pp. 73–74; Henry C. Trost, El Paso County, THC marker file.

3. Engelbrecht and Engelbrecht, *Henry C. Trost*, pp. 3–8.

4. Ibid., pp. 9–16.

5. Ibid., pp. 17–29; Ainsworth, "Henry C. Trost," pp. 83–90; Trost Thematic Resources, National Register of Historic Places (NR) file, El Paso County, Texas Historical Commission (hereafter cited as THC NR file); Mary A. Sarber, "Trost, Henry Charles," *Handbook of Texas Online*, www.tshaonline.org/handbook/online/articles/ftr12, accessed Jan. 16, 2011.

6. Engelbrecht and Engelbrecht, *Henry C. Trost*, p. 62.

7. Hotel Paso del Norte, El Paso County, THC marker file.

8. Hotel Paso del Norte, THC NR file.

9. Hotel Paso del Norte, THC marker file; Ainsworth, "Henry C. Trost," p. 89; Engelbrecht and Engelbrecht, *Henry C. Trost*, pp. 62–63.

10. Hotel Paso del Norte, THC marker file; Liz Carmack, *Historic Hotels of Texas: A Traveler's Guide* (College Station: Texas A&M University Press, 2007), pp. 27–29.

11. Hotel Paso del Norte, THC NR file; Hotel Paso del Norte, THC marker file.

12. Trost Thematic Resources NR file; Martin Donell Kohout, "Marathon, TX," *Handbook of Texas Online*, www.tshaonline.org/handbook/online/articles/hlm26, accessed Jan. 17, 2011; Clifford B. Casey, "Alpine, TX (Brewster County)," *Handbook of Texas Online*, www.tshaonline.org/handbook/online/articles/hfa05, accessed Jan. 17, 2011; Lee Bennett, "Marfa, TX," *Handbook of Texas Online*, www.tshaonline.org/handbook/online/articles/hjm04, accessed Jan. 17, 2011; Martin Donell Kohout, "Van Horn, TX," *Handbook of Texas Online*, www.tshaonline.org/handbook/online/articles/hgv01, accessed Jan. 17, 2011.

13. Ainsworth, "Henry C. Trost," pp. 94–96.

14. Gage Hotel, Brewster County, THC marker file; Martin Donell Kohout, "Gage, Alfred Stevens," *Handbook of Texas Online*, www.tshaonline .org/handbook/online/articles/fgapm, accessed Jan. 16, 2011; Ainsworth, "Henry C. Trost," p. 94.

15. Gage Hotel, THC marker file.

16. John Holland, Brewster County, THC marker file; Holland Hotel, Brewster County, THC marker file; "Army Asserts Murder Was Planned," *El Paso Times*, July 22, 1916, pp. 1, 5; "Spannells Were Life of Alpine; Tragedy Casts Pall over Town," *El Paso Times*, July 29, 1916, p. 9.

17. Holland Hotel, THC marker file; Carmack, *Historic Hotels of Texas*, pp. 24–25.

18. El Paisano Hotel, Presidio County, THC NR file.

19. El Paisano Hotel, Presidio County, THC marker file.

20. Ainsworth, "Henry C. Trost," p. 95; Pam LeBlanc, "Restored Hotel in Van Horn Again a West Texas Pit Stop," *Austin American-Statesman*, Mar. 28, 2010, sec. . G, pp. 12–13.

CHAPTER 6. HER LONELY WAY BACK HOME

1. Darragh Doiron, "Joplin's Childhood Home 'Marked,'" *Port Arthur News*, Jan. 20, 2008, p. 1; authors' recollections.

2. Kris Kristofferson, "The Pilgrim, Chapter 33," *The Silver-Tongued Devil and I*, Monument Records, 1971.

3. Laura Joplin, *Love, Janis: A Revealing Biography of Janis Joplin Inspired by Her Private Letters Home* (Petaluma, CA: Acid Test Productions, 1992), pp. 24–27; Alice Echols, *Scars of Sweet Paradise: The Life and Times of Janis Joplin* (New York: Owl Books/Henry Holt and Company, 1999), pp. 7–9.

4. Monteel Copple interview with Cynthia J. Beeman, Sept. 29, 2009, recording and transcript in authors' files.

5. Echols, *Scars of Sweet Paradise*, pp. 9–10; Joplin, *Love, Janis*, pp. 30–31; *Port Arthur News*, July 14, 1957, clipping in Janis Joplin vertical file, Port Arthur Public Library.

6. Yvonne Sutherlin interview with Cynthia J. Beeman, Sept. 28, 2009, recording and transcript in authors' files.

7. Echols, *Scars of Sweet Paradise*, p. 12.

8. Joplin, *Love, Janis*, pp. 45–47, 51–56; Myra Friedman, *Buried Alive: The Intimate Biography of Janis Joplin* (London: Plexus Publishing, 1972), pp. 17–18.

9. Joplin, *Love, Janis*, p. 58; Echols, *Scars of Sweet Paradise*, p. 37.

10. "The Dick Cavett Show," June 25, 1970, *The Dick Cavett Show: Rock Icons*, DVD, Daphne Productions, 2005.

11. Pat Sharpe, "She Dares to Be Different!" *The Summer Texan* [University of Texas at Austin newspaper], July 27, 1962, p. 5; Echols, *Scars of Sweet Paradise*, pp. 42–45, 66.

12. Echols, *Scars of Sweet Paradise,* pp. 89–90,128–31; Joplin, *Love, Janis,* pp. 129–32, 142–43.

13. "Soulin' at Monterey," *Time,* June 20, 1967.

14. Robert Shelton, "Janis Joplin Is Climbing Fast in the Heady Rock Firmament," *New York Times,* Feb. 19, 1968.

15. Michael Lydon, "The Janis Joplin Philosophy: Every Moment She Is What She Feels," *New York Times,* Feb. 23, 1969.

16. Ellis Amburn, *Pearl: The Obsessions and Passions of Janis Joplin* (New York: Warner Books, 1992), p. 276; Clive Seymour, "Janis Shows Up at Music Bash," *Austin American-Statesman,* July 11, 1970, p. 6.

17. Sam Monroe interview with Cynthia J. Beeman, Sept. 29, 2009, recording and transcript in authors' files.

18. "Blues Star Here for Reunion." *Port Arthur News,* Aug. 14, 1970, p. 1; Jeff Millar, "One Night in Port Arthur," *Houston Chronicle,* June 23, 1988 (reprint of article originally published in August 1970).

19. Echols, *Scars of Sweet Paradise,* p. 289.

20. Joplin, *Love, Janis,* pp. 309–10; Echols, *Scars of Sweet Paradise,* pp. 297–98.

21. *Port Arthur News,* Oct. 6, 1970, p. 1; *Houston Post,* Oct. 8, 1970; *Dallas Morning News,* Oct. 8, 1970; *Time,* Oct. 19, Nov. 16, 1970.

22. Copple interview with Beeman.

23. Dorothy Joplin to Sam Monroe, June 15, 1988, Janis Joplin Collection, Museum of the Gulf Coast, Port Arthur.

24. Monroe interview with Beeman.

25. "Janis Joplin," brochure, Museum of the Gulf Coast, Port Arthur.

CHAPTER 7. AND THE CARS KEEP ROLLING BY

1. Chester H. Liebs, *Main Street to Miracle Mile: American Roadside Architecture* (Boston: Little, Brown and Company, 1985), p. 4.

2. Ibid., pp. 95–96; Michael Karl Witzel, *The American Gas Station* (Osceola, FL: Motorbooks International, 1993), pp. 27–28.

3. Ibid., pp. 36–37; Liebs, *Main Street to Miracle Mile,* pp. 95–97.

4. Witzel, *The American Gas Station,* p. 59.

5. Bob's Oil Well, Motley County, THC marker file, narrative by Marisue Potts; "Bob Robertson Takes Own Life in Hotel Here," *Matador Tribune,* Jan. 16, 1947, p. 1. The 1900 US census shows Luther B. Robertson as a five-year-old boy living with his parents in Greenville, and it notes his place of birth as Texas. In the 1930 census, however, Robertson gave his birthplace as Oklahoma. Efforts to find his whereabouts in the intervening years proved inconclusive.

6. William R. Hunt, "Matador, Texas," *New Handbook of Texas,* vol. 4, p. 553; William M. Pearce, "Matador Land and Cattle Company," *New Handbook of Texas,* vol. 4, pp. 553–55.

7. Quoted in Liebs, *Main Street to Miracle Mile,* p. 21.

8. Ibid., p. 5.

9. Ibid., p. 43.

10. Ibid., p. 48; John A. Jakle and Keith A. Sculle, *The Gas Station in America* (Baltimore: The Johns Hopkins University Press, 1994), pp. 19–23.

11. US Patent Office application no. 93,134 (1934). Copies included in marker file.

12. Bob's Oil Well, THC marker file; Alice Gilroy, "Hubert Griffith Inducted into Clovis AFB Wall of Heroes," *Floyd County Hesperian-Beacon,* Feb. 15, 2007.

13. Corporate history accessed through www.conocophillips.com, Nov. 25, 2010.

14. Bob's Oil Well, THC marker file; "Bob Robertson Takes Own Life in Hotel Here," *Matador Tribune,* Jan. 16, 1947.

15. "'Bob's Cook Shack' Contrast to Name," *Matador Tribune,* Sept. 26, 1946, n.p.

16. "Bob Robertson Takes Own Life in Hotel Here, *Matador Tribune,* Jan. 16, 1947.

17. Ibid.

18. Ibid.

19. "Bob's Oil Well, Cook Shack Open after Tragedy," *Matador Tribune,* Jan. 23, 1947; "Wind Topples Tower Off Bob's Oil Well," *Matador Tribune,* Jan. 30, 1947; "Derrick on Station Is Restored," *Matador Tribune,* Oct. 27, 1949.

20. Bob's Oil Well, THC marker file.

21. 2004 Texas' Most Endangered Places files, Preservation Texas, Austin.

CHAPTER 8. "TO HAVE WHAT WE MUST"

1. Lady Bird Johnson. *A White House Diary* (Austin: University of Texas Press, 2007), p. 259.

2. Thad Sitton and Milam C. Rowold, *Ringing the Children In: Texas Country Schools* (College Station: Texas A&M University Press, 1987), p. 9.

3. Ibid., p. 198.

4. Gene Preuss, *To Get a Better School System: One Hundred Years of Education Reform in Texas* (College Station: Texas A&M University Press, 2009), pp. 77–92.

5. James Lindley, MD, interview with Dan K. Utley, Dec. 8, 2010, and Bernice Weinheimer, interview with Dan K. Utley, Dec. 8, 2010, notes and recording in authors' files.

6. Weinheimer interview; Bernice Weinheimer, "History of the Friends of the Gillespie County Country Schools," unpublished paper.

7. Weinheimer interview.

8. Andrew Gulliford, *America's Country Schools* (Washington, DC: The Preservation Press, 1991), p. 233.

9. Weinheimer interview; "Texas Amendment 13 (2001)," Ballotpedia,

http://ballotpedia.org/wiki/index.php/Texas_Amendment_13_(2001), accessed Dec. 31, 2010.

10. Crabapple School, Gillespie County, THC marker file; Crabapple School, Gillespie County, THC NR file.

11. Cherry Spring Schoolhouse, Gillespie County, THC marker file; Cherry Spring School, Gillespie County, THC NR file.

12. Lower South Grape Creek School, Gillespie County, THC marker file; Lower South Grape Creek School, Gillespie County, THC NR file.

13. Lindley interview.

CHAPTER 9. A JOURNEY BACK TO NATURE

1. Mark Odintz, "Taylor, Thomas Jefferson II," *Handbook of Texas Online*, www.tshaonline.org/handbook/online/articles/fta26, accessed Nov. 20, 2010.

2. Gail K. Beil and Max S. Lale, "Max Sims Lale and Longhorn Army Ammunition Plant," *East Texas Historical Association Journal* 45, no. 1 (2007), p. 33.

3. Historic American Engineering Record, Longhorn Army Ammunition Plant, TX-8, National Park Service, Department of the Interior, Washington, DC, pp. 2, 16–21, 29 (hereafter cited as HAER TX-8); Beil and Lale, "Max Sims Lale," pp. 33–34.

4. HAER TX-8, pp. 29, 32.

5. Ibid., p. 32; Beil and Lale, "Max Sims Lale," p. 34.

6. HAER TX-8, pp. 32, 34; Beil and Lale, "Max Sims Lale," pp. 35–37.

7. "Treaty between the United States of America and the Union of Soviet Socialist Republics on the Elimination of Their Intermediate-Range and Shorter-Range Missiles," US Department of State website, www.state.gov/www/global/arms/treaties/inf1.html, accessed Nov. 28, 2010.

8. Peter Applebome, "First U.S. Missiles Destroyed as Part of Nuclear Treaty with Soviets," *New York Times*, Sept. 9, 1988, n.p., accessed through www.nytimes.com, Nov. 18, 2010.

9. Beil and Lale, "Max Sims Lale," p. 38; Jay Jorden, "Last Pershing Destroyed; Elimination of Missile Fulfills Terms of Pact," *Dallas Morning News*, May 7, 1981, n.p., accessed through Newsbank.com, Nov. 18, 2010.

10. Beil and Lale, "Max Sims Lale," p. 39; Randy Lee Loftis, "Explosive Issue: Army, Environmentalists Debate Cleanup of Munitions Plant," *Dallas Morning News*, Sept. 26, 1994, n.p., accessed through Newsbank.com, Nov. 18, 2010.

11. Diane Jennings, "Henley's Caddo Lake Group Signs Lease on Bayou Land for Laboratory, Classrooms," *Dallas Morning News*, Oct. 5, 1996, p. A-33; Charles L. Dukes, "Don Henley: An Eagle's Eye View on Texas Wetlands Protection," *Texas Fish & Game*, Jan. 1997, pp. 111–15.

12. Terri Hahn, "Hundreds Attend Refuge Opening," and editorial, "Hard

Work Comes to Fruition in Refuge," both in *Marshall News-Messenger,* Sept. 27, 2009, n.p., accessed through Newsbank.com, Nov. 18, 2010.

13. Terri Hahn, "Thiokol's Impact Still Felt by Local Families," *Marshall News-Messenger,* Sept. 25, 2009, n.p., accessed through Newsbank.com, Nov. 18, 2010.

14. Jackson Browne, "Before the Deluge," *Late for the Sky,* Elektra/Asylum/Nonesuch Records, 1974.

CHAPTER 10. LIFT HIGH THE WATER

1. Alicia A. Garza, "Hidalgo, Texas," *The New Handbook of Texas,* vol. 3 (Austin: The Texas State Historical Association, 1996), p. 589; Hubert J. Miller, "Edinburg, Texas," *New Handbook of Texas,* vol. 2, p. 786; Valley By-Liners, *Roots by the River* (Mission, TX: Border Kingdom Press, 1978), pp. 9–14.

2 .Verna J. McKenna, "John Closner," *New Handbook of Texas,* vol. 2, p. 165; Valley By-Liners, *Roots by the River,* p. 103; J. Lee Stambaugh and Lillian J. Stambaugh, *The Lower Rio Grande Valley of Texas* (San Antonio: The Naylor Company, 1954), pp. 172–76.

3. Stambaugh and Stambaugh, *Lower Rio Grande Valley,* pp. 184–86; Louisiana–Rio Grande Canal Company, Hidalgo County, THC marker file; Lisa Brochu et al., *Getting Up Steam: The History of the Hidalgo Pumphouse* (Hidalgo: City of Hidalgo, 2000), p. 13.

4. Louisiana–Rio Grande Canal Company Irrigation System, Hidalgo County, THC NR file.

5. Ibid.

6. Ibid.; Brochu, *Getting Up Steam,* p. 20.

7. Robert Norton, Spurgeon Brown, and Walter Wisdom, recorded conversation with Dan K. Utley, Old Pumphouse Museum, Hidalgo, Texas, Apr. 26, 2010, notes and recording in authors' files.

8. Ibid.

9. Ibid.; Brochu, *Getting Up Steam,* pp. 23–27; Laurine Miller, "Restoring a Magic Maker in the Valley," *Houston Chronicle,* Jan. 2 (?), 1994, n.p.

10. Norton, Brown, and Wisdom recorded conversation.

CHAPTER 11. THE NORMAL ON CHAUTAUQUA HILL

1. Tommy Ruth Zarnow Ball, "The Administration of John Garland Flowers: Third President of Southwest Texas State College," MA thesis, Southwest Texas State College, May 1967, pp. 2–3; Joe B. Vogel et al., *Fifty Years of Teacher Education: A Brief History of Southwest Texas State Teachers College,* commemorative booklet, (San Marcos: Southwest Texas State Teachers College, 1951), pp. 2–3.

2. Ball, "Administration of John Garland Flowers," pp. 2–6.

3. Ibid., p. 6.

4. Ibid., pp. 6–7; Site of Coronal Institute, Hays County, THC marker file;

Old Main Building, Walker County, THC marker file; Nancy Beck Young, "Coronal Institute," *New Handbook of Texas,* vol. 2, p. 329.

5. Vogel et al., "Fifty Years of Teacher Education," pp. 2–3; Ball, "Administration of John Garland Flowers," pp. 7–8.

6. "Death of E. Northcraft," *San Marcos Record,* Nov. 21, 1919, n.p.; US Federal Census: 1850, 1860, 1870, 1880, 1900, and 1910, accessed through Ancestry.com, Dec. 1–12, 2010; "E. Northcraft, Pioneer Texas Architect, Is Dead," *San Antonio Evening News,* Nov. 20, 1919, n.p.; "State Orphan Asylum: Work Rapidly Advancing Toward Completion," *Dallas Morning News,* Dec. 15, 1888, n.p.

7. Willard B. Robinson, "Temples of Knowledge: Historic Mains of Texas Colleges and Universities," *Southwestern Historical Quarterly* 77, no. 4 (April 1974): 465; Old Main, Hays County, THC marker file; Hays County, THC NR files.

8. Ibid., p. 467 (floor plan illustration) and pp. 468–69.

9. "That San Marcos Visit: Governor Lanham and Party the Recipients of Many Attentions," *Dallas Morning News,* Feb. 15, 1903, n.p.; *Old Main Rededication,* commemorative booklet, (San Marcos: Southwest Texas State University, 1985).

10. Vogel et al., "Fifty Years of Education," pp. 4–7.

11. Ibid., p. 5.

12. Ibid., p. 7.

13. Ibid., pp. 6–8.

14. Ibid., p. 8.

15. "Death of E. Northcraft," *Dallas Morning News,* Nov. 21, 1919.

16. Old Main, Hays County, THC marker file and THC NR file.

17. "SWT's Old Main Gets Medallion," copy of undated newspaper article included in the Old Main THC marker file, newspaper source not noted.

18. Transcript of remarks delivered by Pres. Lyndon B. Johnson at Southwest Texas State University, Nov. 4, 1972, copy on file with the University Archives, Alkek Library, Texas State University–San Marcos.

CHAPTER 12. HISTORY ON THE GROUNDS

1. Wallace Stegner, "Sense of Place," *Where the Bluebird Sings to the Lemonade Springs: Living and Writing in the West* (New York: Random House, 1992), p. 202; David Glassberg, *Sense of History: The Place of the Past in American Life* (Amherst: University of Massachusetts Press, 2001), p. 8; David Thelen, *Memory and American History* (Bloomington: Indiana University Press, 1990), p. vii.

2. The Texas Capitol, Travis County, THC marker file; David C. Humphrey, "Austin, TX (Travis County)," *Handbook of Texas Online,* www.tshaonline .org/handbook/online/articles/hda03, accessed Jan. 27, 2011; William Elton Green, "Capitol," *Handbook of Texas Online,* www.tshaonline.org/ handbook/online/articles/ccc01, accessed Jan. 25, 2011.

3. *The Texas Capitol: A Self-Guided Tour,* and *The Texas Capitol Grounds: A Self-Guided Tour,* brochures (Austin: Texas State Preservation Board, n.d.).

4. Old General Land Office, Texas Secession Convention, Civil War Committee on Public Safety, and Confederate Texas Legislatures, THC marker files (all Travis County).

5. Tyler Rose, Smith County, THC marker file.

6. Ibid.

7. House Concurrent Resolution 53, 65th Texas Legislature, Regular Session, 1977, copy in The Texas Capitol, THC marker file.

8. Elora B. Alderman to Mrs. Dolph Briscoe, Mrs. John Connally, Mrs. Price Daniel, Mrs. Allan Shivers, Mrs. Preston Smith, July 26, 1976, in The Texas Capitol, THC marker file.

9. John Ben Shepperd, "State Capitol Building: The Gem of Texas," copy of speech in The Texas Capitol, THC marker file.

10. The Texas Capitol, THC marker file; Ali James, Curator of the Capitol, Texas State Preservation Board, to Cynthia J. Beeman, Feb. 22, 2011, email correspondence in authors' files.

11. Swedish Central Methodist Church, Travis County, THC marker file.

12. Saint Martin's Evangelical Lutheran Church marker file, Travis County, THC marker file.

13. Ibid.

14. The Archive War, Travis County, THC marker file.

CHAPTER 13. JUSTICE IS THE CORPORATE FACE OF LOVE

1. Kenneth Kesselus, *John E. Hines, Granite on Fire* (Austin: The Episcopal Theological Seminary of the Southwest, 1995), pp. 3–12.

2. Ibid., 13–39; John S. Spong, Bishop of Newark, "Farewell, My Treasured Friend," *The Voice of the Episcopal Diocese of Newark,* March 1997.

3. Kesselus, *John E. Hines,* p. 49.

4. Wolfgang Saxon, "John E. Hines, Episcopal Leader, Dies at 86," *New York Times,* July 22, 1997; John S. Spong, Bishop of Newark, "The Graceful Life of Helen Orwig Hines," *The Voice of the Episcopal Diocese of Newark,* May 1996; Kesselus, *John E. Hines,* pp. 61–70.

5. Kesselus, *John E. Hines,* pp. 83–100.

6. "Bishop Hines Consecrated at Houston," *Dallas Morning News,* Oct. 19, 1945, sec. 1, p. 3.

7. Kesselus, *John E. Hines,* pp. 142–48; Elizabeth Hayes Turner, "Episcopal Women as Community Leaders: Galveston, 1900–1989," in *Episcopal Women: Gender, Spirituality and Commitment in an American Mainline Denomination,* ed. Catherine M. Prelinger (New York: Oxford University Press, 1992), pp. 93–94.

8. "Connally Hails Texas Mark Being Left by Bishop Hines," *Dallas Morning News,* Dec. 12, 1964, sec. 1, p. 6; Kesselus, *John E. Hines,* pp. 149–50.

9. Kesselus, *John E. Hines,* pp. 165–76; Gardiner H. Shattuck, Jr., *Episco-*

palians & Race: Civil War to Civil Rights* (Lexington: The University Press of Kentucky, 2000), p. 41.

10. John E. Hines interview with Hugh Downs, Episcopal Television Network broadcast, 1981.

11. "Bishop Hines' Address to the 109th Annual Council, 1958," copy in John E. Hines vertical file, Austin History Center, Austin, Texas.

12. "Episcopal Bishops Urge End of Racial Disparity," *Dallas Morning News,* Nov. 11, 1958, sec. 1, p. 10.

13. Saul Friedman, "Bishop Hines on Big Issues," *Houston Chronicle,* Nov. 1, 1964, sec. 6, p. 5.

14. Kesselus, *John E. Hines,* pp. 228–29; Hines interview with Downs.

15. "Alabama: Death in the Black Belt," *Time,* Aug. 15, 1965; "Statement by the Rt. Rev. John E. Hines," Oct. 4, 1965, Episcopal News Service, Archives of the Episcopal Church, Austin, Texas.

16. "Vocal Church Role Seen by Top Cleric," *Dallas Morning News,* Sept. 21, 1965, sec. A, p. 7; Shattuck, *Episcopalians & Race,* pp. 147, 175–79; Kesselus, *John E. Hines,* pp. 272–96; "How to Carry Out a Conviction," *Time,* Sept. 29, 1967.

17. Kesselus, *John E. Hines,* pp. 364–66; Spong, "Farewell, My Treasured Friend," *The Voice of the Episcopal Diocese of Newark,* March 1997; Wolfgang Saxon, "John E. Hines, Episcopal Leader, Dies at 86," *New York Times,* July 22, 1997; Bob Banta, "Hines, Activist Episcopal Bishop, Dead at 87," *Austin American-Statesman,* July 21, 1997, p. B1; Statement by the Rt. Rev. John E. Hines, Feb. 10, 1972, reported by Episcopal News Service, digital archives of the Archives of the Episcopal Church, www.episcopalarchives.org/e-archives/ENS/, accessed Dec. 13, 2010; Hines interview with Downs.

18. "Episcopalian Backlash," *Time,* Oct. 15, 1973.

19. "Winners of 1999 John Hines Preaching Award Announced," Episcopal News Service, Mar. 9, 2000; "John Hines Chair of Preaching Established at ETSS," Episcopal News Service, Mar. 30, 2006.

20. C. FitzSimmons Allison, "John Elbridge Hines," in Samuel S. Hill, Charles H. Lippy, and Charles Reagan Wilson, *Encyclopedia of Religion in the South* (Macon, GA: Mercer University Press, 2005), pp. 376–77.

CHAPTER 14. A LIGHT ON THE PATH OF WISDOM

1. "Boys Mother Leads Camp Fire Girls," reprinted from files of *Sherman Daily Democrat,* Feb. 26, 1937, reprint comp. and ed. Ann Lowry in *Sherman Democrat,* Feb. 26, 1987, p. B6.

2. Hugh E. Hall, interview with Cynthia J. Beeman, Jan. 31, 2011, recording and transcript in authors' files.

3. Ibid.; Mita Holsapple Hall, Grayson County, THC marker file (application narrative written by Clyde H. Hall).

4. Jennifer Hillman Helgren, "Inventing American Girlhood: Gender and Citizenship in the Twentieth-Century Camp Fire Girls," PhD diss.,

Claremont Graduate School, Claremont, CA, pp. 2–3. As this volume was going to press, Helgren was preparing her dissertation for publication.

5. Award Honorees Luther and Charlotte Gulick, The Extra Mile—Points of Light Volunteer Pathway, Points of Light Institute, www.extramile.us/honorees/gulick.cfm; History, Camp Fire USA website, www.campfireusa.org/History.aspx; Helgren, "Inventing American Girlhood," p. 31.

6. Helgren, "Inventing American Girlhood," p. 89.

7. Mita Holsapple Hall, THC marker file.

8. Ibid.; "Sherman Party Back from Trip," *Sherman Daily Democrat*, July 6, 1925, n.p. (clipping in marker file).

9. William Kaszynski, *The American Highway: The History and Culture of Roads in the United States* (Jefferson, NC: McFarland & Company, 2000), p. 56; Phil Patton, *Open Road: A Celebration of the American Highway* (New York: Simon & Schuster, 1986), p. 42.

10. "Sherman Party Back from Trip," *Sherman Daily Democrat*, July 6, 1925, n.p. (clipping in marker file).

11. Hall interview.

12. Clyde L. Hall to Cynthia J. Beeman, Feb. 2, 2011, email correspondence in authors' files.

13. "Sherman Party Haled [sic] into Police Court in Salem Mass., at Request of Enterprising Newspaper Reporter," *Sherman Daily Democrat*, July 12, 1928, n.p. (clipping in marker file).

14. *New York Times*, Sept. 7, 1929, p. 17.

15. Hall interview.

16. Hall to Beeman, Feb. 2, 2011.

17. Hall interview.

18. Mita Holsapple Hall, THC marker file; Hall interview.

19. Mita Holsapple Hall, THC marker file; Hall interview.

20. Mita Holsapple Hall, THC marker file.

21. Martha F. Allen, National Director of Camp Fire Girls, Inc., to Dr. Clyde Hall, telegram, Feb. 5, 1965, copy in Mita Holsapple Hall, THC marker file.

22. *A Resolution in Memory of Mrs. Hugh Edward Hall,* Sherman Camp Fire Girls, Inc., copy in Mita Holsapple Hall, THC marker file.

23. "The Flame Burns," *Sherman Democrat,* Feb. 7, 1965, p. 2.

CHAPTER 15. TWO GENERATIONS STRIVING FOR CIVIL RIGHTS

1. *Bostonia,* Alumni Magazine of Boston University, Fall 1997; James Farmer, *Lay Bare the Heart: An Autobiography of the Civil Rights Movement* (Fort Worth: Texas Christian University Press, 1998), p. 35; Gail K. Beil, "James Leonard Farmer: Texas' First African American Ph.D." *East Texas Historical Journal* 36, no. 1 (1998); Gale K. Beil, "Looking for Dr. Farmer," paper delivered at the Texas State Historical Association conference, March 1998; James Leonard Farmer, Harrison County, THC marker file (application narrative written by Gail K. Beil).

2. Farmer, *Lay Bare the Heart,* p. 34.

3. Ibid., pp. 31–32, 37.

4. "Tillotson College," *The New Handbook of Texas* (Austin: The Texas State Historical Association, 1996), vol. 6, p. 498.

5. *The Foundation,* publication of Gammon Theological Institute, Atlanta, Georgia, July–August 1930, quoted in Beil, "Looking for Dr. Farmer."

6. Farmer, *Lay Bare the Heart,* p. 65

7. Ibid.

8. James Leonard Farmer, Harrison County, THC marker file.

9. Farmer, *Lay Bare the Heart,* pp. 115–20, 121–22.

10. Ibid., p. 89; Richard Severo, "James Farmer, Civil Rights Giant in the '50s and '60s, is Dead at 79," *New York Times,* July 10, 1999.

11. Raymond Arsenault, *Freedom Riders: 1961 and the Struggle for Racial Justice* (New York: Oxford University Press, 2006), pp. 106–9.

12. Ibid., 140–48; Henry Hampton and Steve Fayer, *Voices of Freedom: An Oral History of the Civil Rights Movement from the 1950s through the 1980s* (New York: Bantam Books, 1990), p. 79.

13. Arsenault, *Freedom Riders,* pp. 148–76.

14. James Leonard Farmer, Harrison County, THC marker file.

15. Ibid.; James Leonard Farmer, Jr., Travis County, THC marker file.

16. Farmer, *Lay Bare the Heart,* p. 76.

CHAPTER 16. A CITIZEN WITH WORK TO DO

1. Margie E. Neal Papers, Dolph Briscoe Center for American History, University of Texas at Austin (hereafter cited as Neal Papers). This collection consists of taped interviews with Margie E. Neal conducted by Walter L. Harris in 1952 and 1953 as well as transcripts handwritten by Harris and additional notes and statements handwritten by Neal.

2. Ibid.

3. Ibid.

4. Ibid.; Walter Lawrence Harris, "The Life of Margie E. Neal," MA thesis, University of Texas at Austin, 1955, pp. 9–12.

5. Neal Papers; Harris, "Life of Margie E. Neal," pp. 9–12.

6. Neal Papers.

7. Ibid.

8. Harris, "Life of Margie E. Neal," pp. 62–63.

9. Judith N. McArthur, *Creating the New Woman: The Rise of Southern Women's Progressive Culture in Texas, 1893–1918* (Urbana: University of Illinois Press, 1998), p. 135; Neal Papers.

10. Neal Papers.

11. Ibid.

12. Harris, "Life of Margie E. Neal," p. 86; *Who's Who of the Womanhood of Texas, Volume One* (Austin: Texas Federation of Women's Clubs, 1923–24), p. 117.

13. Harris, "Life of Margie E. Neal," pp. 88–89; "Miss Margie Neal Given Ovation by Panola County People," *Dallas Morning News*, Mar. 16, 1923, sec. 2, p. 14.

14. Neal Papers.

15. "Flowers Smother Margie Neal's Desk," *Dallas Morning News*, Jan. 12, 1927, sec. A, p. 2.

16. Harris, "Life of Margie E. Neal," pp. 101–4; Senate Bill 141, 40th Texas Legislature, Regular Session, Records of the Legislature, Texas State Library and Archives; Senate Bill 217, 40th Texas Legislature, Regular Session, Records of the Legislature, Texas State Library and Archives; "Efforts to Get More Help at Asylums Fail," *Dallas Morning News*, May 11, 1927, sec. 1, p. 7; Nancy Baker Jones and Ruthe Winegarten, *Capitol Women: Texas Female Legislators, 1923–1999* (Austin: University of Texas Press, 2000), pp. 82–83.

17. Harris, "Life of Margie E. Neal," p. 104; Jones and Winegarten, *Capitol Women*, p. 82.

18. Senate Journal, Forty-first Texas Legislature, First Called Session, p. 201; *General Laws of the State of Texas, Forty-first Legislature, Fourth and Fifth Called Sessions*, p. 281; *General Laws of the State of Texas, Forty-second Legislature, Regular Session*, pp. 220–22, 287–88, 884–85; Senate Journal, Forty-second Texas Legislature, Regular Session, pp. 97–98; *General and Special Laws of the State of Texas, Forty-third Legislature, Second Called Session*, pp. 164–69, Senate Bill 485, Forty-second Texas Legislature, Regular Session, Records of the Legislature, Texas State Library and Archives; James Wright Steely, *Parks for Texas: Enduring Landscapes of the New Deal* (Austin: University of Texas Press, 1999), pp. 8, 69; Kenneth B. Ragsdale, *Centennial '36: The Year America Discovered Texas* (College Station: Texas A&M University Press, 1987), pp. 20–21, 31–32 (Ragsdale wrote, "If the centennial had a patron saint, it was indeed Senator Neal" [p. 32].); Harris, "Life of Margie E. Neal," pp. 131–35; Senate Journal, 42nd Texas Legislature, Second Called Session, p. 88; *General and Special Laws of the State of Texas, Forty-second Legislature, Second Called Session*, pp. 2–9; *General Laws of the State of Texas, Forty-third Legislature, Regular Session*, pp. 400–402; *General Laws of the State of Texas, Forty-first Legislature, Second and Third Called Sessions*, pp. 12–17.

19. Neal Papers; Harris, "Life of Margie E. Neal," p. 136.

20. Harris, "Life of Margie E. Neal," p. 138.

21. Ibid., 138–41; "Sterling, Angry at Senate, Forces Session to Continue," *Dallas Morning News*, Sept. 30, 1931; "Disgusted Oil Man" cartoon by John F. Knott, *Dallas Morning News*, Oct. 1, 1931, sec. 2, p. 2.

22. Harris, "Life of Margie E. Neal," p. 155, 158–59, 162–63; Jones and Winegarten, *Capitol Women*, p. 83.

23. "Panola County Battle Rages Over Fate of Old Courthouse," *Dallas Morning News*, Mar. 31, 1955, sec. 1, p. 19; "Panola County's Courthouse to Go

on Block Friday," *Dallas Morning News,* July 13, 1955, sec. 3, p. 17; "Carthage as of Old," *Dallas Morning News,* July 18, 1955, sec. 3, p. 2.

24. "Democrats for Ike Set State Campaign," *Dallas Morning News,* Oct. 7, 1956, sec. 1, p. 2; "Miss Neal Named Nixon Introducer," *Dallas Morning News,* Oct. 27, 1952, sec. 3, p. 14.

25. Remarks of Governor Allan Shivers, Margie Neal Day Ceremonies, Carthage, Texas, June 16, 1952, Governor Allan Shivers Papers, Trip Files, Texas State Library and Archives, Austin, Texas.

26. Speech of Sen. Lyndon B. Johnson, "Miss Margie Neal Day," June 16, 1952, Carthage, Texas, Statements of Lyndon B. Johnson, Nov. 1951–1952, Box 11, LBJ Library.

27. James E. Walker, Chief Geophysicist, Shell Oil Company of Canada, telegram to Gov. Allan Shivers and Margie E. Neal Appreciation Day Program Committee, June 15, 1952, Shivers Papers; Ann Morris to Cynthia J. Beeman, email, May 4, 2010, copy in authors' files.

28. Harris, "Life of Margie E. Neal," p. 180; "Former Woman Solon Miss Neal Dead at 96," *Panola Watchman,* Dec. 20, 1971, sec. 1, p. 1; "Margie Neal, Suffragette, Dies in Texas," *Dallas Morning News,* Dec. 20, 1971, p. A-8; "Memories Cast Light on Activist's Life," *Panola Watchman,* Oct. 26, 1988, p. 1A.

CHAPTER 17. HERE I AM IN PALESTINE

1. Mrs. Alfred O. Peterson to Palestine Chamber of Commerce, Oct. 16, 1944. All letters referenced in this chapter are in the archives of the Anderson County Historical Commission, Palestine, Texas.

2. Mrs. Frank (Leona) Vorce to Ladies of Service Men's Club, Sept. 15, 1944.

3. Site of Palestine Service Men's Club, Anderson County, THC marker file.

4. Cpl. J. J. Foy to Miss Katherine Ryan, postmarked Jan. 21, 1944.

5. Undated letter from Edw. R. Jucksch.

6. *The Men and Women in World War II from Anderson County* (Dallas: Universal Publishing, 1947), n.p.; Site of Palestine Service Men's Club, THC marker file; US Federal Census, 1900 and 1930, accessed through Ancestry .com, Jan. 13, 2011.

7. "Service Men's Club Here Sponsors Cullet Salvage," undated newspaper article believed to be from the *Palestine Herald,* 1944, included in the Service Men's Club collection, Anderson County Historical Commission.

8. Typed and undated transcript of promotional film text, copy included in the Service Men's Club collection, Anderson County Historical Commission.

9. "Negroes Get $400 for Service Men," undated newspaper article believed to be from the *Palestine Herald,* August 1943; Statement by Mrs. C. W. Hanks, Mar. 3, 1944, typed copy in the Service Men's Club collection, Anderson County Historical Commission.

10. Sample form letter, copy included in the Service Men's Club collection, Anderson County Historical Commission.

11. "Home of Hospitality: Laud Patriotism of Service Club Women," *Palestine Herald,* Dec. 13, 1945, n.p.

12. "Service Men's Club to Close with Thanks from Many Men," *Palestine Herald,* Dec. 24, 1945, n.p.

13. Jimmy R. Odom phone conversation with the authors, Jan. 15, 2011; "Museum to Honor Briggs with Exhibit," *Palestine Herald,* Mar. 23, 2007, n.p.

14. Odom phone conversation with the authors, Jan. 15, 2011; Palestine Service Men's Club marker dedication program, Nov. 11, 2006.

15. Odom phone conversation with the authors, Jan. 15, 2011; letter from Donald C. Laughmiller, May 23, 1944.

CHAPTER **18.** THE THREE GRAVES OF JUDGE BAYLOR

1. Eugene W. Baker. *To Light the Ways of Time: An Illustrated History of Baylor University, 1845–1986* (Waco: Baylor University Press, 1987), p. 16; Thomas E. Turner, "R. E. B. Baylor: The Man behind the Statue" (first in a series of two articles), *Baylor University Report* 11, no. 10 (March 1982): 4–7.

2. Turner, "R. E. B. Baylor," pp. 4–7; Baker, *To Light the Ways of Time,* pp. 16–17; Thomas E. Turner. *Instruments of Providence* (Austin: Eakin Press, 2003), pp. 44–46.

3. Baker, *To Light the Ways of Time,* pp. 16–17; Thomas E. Turner, "Where is R. E. B. Baylor . . . ? And What's He Doing There . . . ?" *Discover Temple-Belton,* Feb. 1993, pp. 14–15; Turner, *Instruments of Providence,* pp. 45–46; Eugene W. Baker, James S. Belew, Ellen K. Brown, and Thomas L. Charlton, "R. E. B. Baylor, A Servant," marker application historical narrative, p. 5; Robert Emmett Bledsoe Baylor, Washington County, THC marker file.

4. Quoted in Thomas E. Turner, "R. E. B. Baylor: The Man behind the Statue" (second article in series), *Baylor University Report* 11, no. 11 (April 1982), p. 12.

5. Ibid., pp. 12–13.

6. Ibid., p. 13.

7. Ibid.; Lois Smith Murray, *Baylor at Independence* (Waco: Baylor University Press, 1972), pp. 23–24.

8. Murray, *Baylor at Independence,* pp. 44–45.

9. R. E. B. Baylor papers, Texas Collection, Baylor University; Baker, *To Light the Ways of Time,* pp. 16–18.

10. Baker, Belew, Brown, and Charlton, "R. E. B. Baylor, A Servant," p. 6; Turner, "R. E. B. Baylor," April 1982, p. 13; R. E. B. Baylor papers.

11. Murray, *Baylor at Independence,* p. 302.

12. Ibid., pp. 301–8.

13. Baylor University on Windmill Hill, Washington County, THC marker file (application narrative written by James S. Belew).

14. Harry Haynes, "R. E. Baylor's Remains: Some Misstatements Corrected by a Correspondent—A Bit of History," *Dallas Morning News,* Jan. 26, 1900, p. 6.

15. Coleman Craig, "An Eminent Baptist and an Historic Occasion," *Baptist Standard* 29, no. 20 (May 17, 1917), p. 1.

16. Minutes, Baylor University Board of Trustees, Dec. 8, 1916 (V-13 General Board Records 1905–1923), Texas Collection, Baylor University.

17. Craig, "Eminent Baptist," pp. 1 and 22; The Reverend Dayton Kelley, "Baylor's Founding Father," *Houston Chronicle Rotogravure Magazine,* Sept. 16, 1958, n.p.

18. "Fire Razes Building at College," *Dallas Morning News,* Feb. 10, 1964, p. 1; "Fire-Hit Girls' School Plans Recovery," *Dallas Morning News,* Feb. 11, 1964, p. 7; "Judge Baylor's Grave Restored at College," *Killeen Herald,* Mar. 30, 1964, n.p.; Thomas E. Turner, "Man of Action in Life, Judge Baylor Moves Again," *Dallas Morning News,* Mar. 27, 1966, p. 16.

19. John Hill Luther, *Old Baylor and Other Poems: A Gift to My Grandchildren* (Kansas City, MO: Hudson-Kimberly Publishing Co., 1900), n.p., retyped from a booklet (ca. 1900) entitled *Souvenir Verses* provided by Betty Sue Beebe, Museum Director, University of Mary Hardin–Baylor. Herman J. Bal, who composed the piece, was the director of music at the college from 1902 to 1908.

Index

Photo page numbers shown in italics

Abert, James William, 47–59, *49*, 60–61
Abert, John James, 47–48, 50–51
Adobe Walls (Bent's Trading Post), 55
African Americans, 36, 38, 52, 164, 206–207, 213, 233, 235–251, 277, 293
Ahrens, Charles F., 125
Ahrens, Martha, 125
Aikin, A.M., 117
Alamo (TX), 153
Alamo, the, 184, 194
Alderman, Elora B., 190
Alibates Flint Quarries, 54
Allen, Martha F., 230
Allin, John M., 215
Allred, James, 94
Alpine (TX), 67–69, 71
Amarillo (TX), 6, 60
Ames, Jessie Daniel, 257
American Baptist, 214
American Legion, 107–108, 111
Anahuac (TX), 20
Anders, Dave, 30
Anderson County, 271, 273, 275, 279–280
Anderson County Historical Commission, 272, 280, 284
Anniston (AL), 243–244
archeology, 5–18
Archer County, 68
architecture, 63–77
Archives War. *See* Eberly, Angelina.
Arkansas River, 52
Armstrong, Louis, 40

Armstrong, Mollie W., 266–267
Audrey, Howard, 253
Austin (TX), 84, 165, 177, 184, 191, 194, 199, 201, 208, 215, 237–239, 248, 259, 261
Austin College, 178–180
Austin County, 290
Austin, Moses, 197
Austin, Stephen F., 184, 197
automobile age/travel, 99, 104, 112–114, 223, 232–234

Bailey, F.M., 116
Baines, George Washington, Jr., 294
Baker, Carroll, 72
Baker, Daniel Oscar, 113
Baker, Jess, 113
Baker-Rylee Building, 112–114
Bal, Herman J., 299
Baptists, 287, 289–290, 292, 294, 300
Basie, Count, 40
Bassett, Charles, 68
Bastrop County, 289
bats, 32–34
bat roost, 32–34, *33*
Baylor, Robert Emmett Bledsoe, 286–297, 300; graves of, *292*, *296*, *298*
Baylor Female College. *See* University of Mary Hardin-Baylor.
Baylor University, 70, 209, 290–295, 302
Baytown (TX), 210
Beaumont (TX), 91, 93
Bean, Candace Midkiff, 266

Bean, Peter Ellis, 266
Beckville (TX), 259
Belton (TX), 293, 295–296
Belvin, Robert Hixon, 176
Bend (TX), 146
Bent's Fort, 50–53, 57
Bent's Trading Post (Adobe Walls), 55
Benton, Thomas Hart, 48
Big Brother and the Holding Company, 84–85, 92
Binford, R.E., 293
Birmingham (AL), 244
Bishop, W. R., 15
Blake, Isaac E., 106
Blake, James Herbert "Eubie," 42
Blanton, Annie Webb, 266, 277
Bob's Oil Well, 104–110, *105*, *107*
Boogie Kings, 90
Bowers, Tom M., 255
Bowman, Euday Louis, 35–43, 44–45
Bowman, Geneva Morris, 40
Bowman, George, 35, 37
Bowman, Isaac Gatewood, 37
Bowman, Junius, 36
Bowman, Mary Margaret, 36, 38, 40–41
Bowman, Olivia Marguerite Graham Este Lembin, 36–37
Bowman, Ruth Emma Thompson, 41
Boy Scouts, 221, 225
Brady (TX), 69
Branch, Mary Elizabeth, 248
Bratherich, H., 123
Brewer, J. Mason, 248, 251
Bridge City (TX), 94
Briggs, Osjetea, 279–280
Brown, J.S., 169
Brown, Mamie E., 169
Brown, Spurgeon "Spud," 155
Brown & Root Construction Company, 137

Browne, Jackson, 144
Browning, Edmund, 215
Bryan, J.P., 69
Bryan, Mary Jon, 69
Burkburnett (TX), 293, 300
Burke, William, 198
Burleson, Lucy Northcraft, 163, 165, 167
Burleson, Rufus C., 291
Burnet (TX), 19
Burnett, Samuel Burk, 41
Bush, George H.W., 138
Butler, M.C., 71

Caddo Indians, 134, 141
Caddo Lake, 134, 139
Caddo Lake Institute, 140–141
Caddo Lake National Wildlife Refuge, 139, 141, *142*, *143*
Caldwell (TX), 19
Calhoun County, 289
Camino Real Hotel. *See* Hotel Paso del Norte.
Camp Fire Girls, 220–231
Camp Howze, 230
Campbell, Charles A.R., 32–34, *33*
Campbell, Henry H. "Hank," 101
Canadian (TX), 6
Canadian River, 6, 51, 54, *55*, 56, 60
Canyon (TX), 6, 108
Carlisle, Lallie P. Briscoe, 266
Carr, Waggoner, 30
Carroll, H. Bailey, 53, 57–58
Carroll, J.M., 294
Carson, Kit, 49, 51
Carswell, O.P., 253
Cass County, 140
Carthage (TX), 253, 255–257, 259, 263–264
Caruso, Enrico, 67
Case, Viola Shive, 267
Catholics, 294–295
Cave Creek School, 127
Cavett, Dick, 83

Center (TX), 263
Chapman, R.M., 217
Charnquist, Carl, 192
Chautauqua (NY), 162
Chautauqua or Chautauqua Hill.
 See Texas Chautauqua.
Cherokee County, 266
Cherry Mountain School, 132
Cherry Spring School, 123, 128
Chicago (IL), 44
Chilton, Thomas, 287
Christ Church Cathedral, 207, *208*,
 217–219, *218*
civil rights, 206–213, 235–248
Civil War, U.S., including memori-
 als, 56, 176, 179, 184–185, 190–191,
 198, 217, 291
Clarendon (TX), 26
Clark, Doug, 89
Clayton (TX), 252
Clayton, Nicholas J., 64, 180
Clifton (TX), 19
Clinton, Bill, 246
Closner, John, 150
Clovis (NM), 7, 12–14
Cocke, Fred, 164
Cockrell, Alexander, 267
Cockrell, Sarah Horton, 267–268
Coke, Richard, 176
Cold War, 136, 138
Coleman, Thomas, 213
Colorado River, 146, 184, 288
colonias system, 150
Columbian elephants (*Mamma-
 thus columbi*), 9–10
Comfort (TX), 32, 34
Commack, William R., 108
Common School Movement, 116
Congress of Racial Equality (CORE),
 241–242
Connally, John, 209
Connally, Tom, 262
Conoco, 106
Cooke County, 230

Copple, Monteel, 79, 89
Coronal Institute, 164, 174, 176–178;
 cornerstone, *175*
Corsicana (TX), 165
Cowan, Charles Ross, 5
Cowan Ranch archeological site,
 6–10, *10*, 12, *12*, 13–14
Cox, James M., 257
Crabapple School, 121–123, *122*, *124*,
 128
Crawford, Helen Hornsby, 170
Crawford, W.S., 259
Crockett, David, 287
Culberson, Charles, 41
Cumby, Robert H., 176
Cunningham, Minnie Fisher, 256–
 257
Cuthrell, George, 224
Cypress Creek (Henderson County),
 15

Dallas (TX), 64, 232–234, 263
Dallas County, 233
Dana, Napoleon J.T., 48
Danevang (TX), 19
Daniels, Jonathan, 213
Davey, M.A., 275, 279
Davis, Jefferson, 217
Dean, James, 72
Delco, Wilhelmina, 190
Democratic Party, Texas, 256–257,
 262–263
Denman, Vernon and Paul, 159
Denton (TX), 164
Dibrell, J.B., 164
Doctorman, V.C., 15
Dogan, Matthew W., 251
Dorris, George Preston, 232–233
Doss School, 133
Doubleday, Abner, 48
Downs, Hugh, 210
Dublin (TX), 19
Dubose, Horace M., 162
Dumas (TX), 59

Duncan, Joe, 74–75
Duncan, Lanna, 74–75
Dust Bowl, 5

East Mound Cemetery, 107–108,
   111–112, *112*
Eberly, Angelina, 194
Edinburg (TX), 149
education, 115–133, 252–253, 257, 261
El Paisano Hotel, 68, 72, *73*, 74, *74*
El Paso (TX), 63, 65, 67–68, 76
El Paso High School, 76, 77
Elementary and Secondary Educa-
   tion Act, 115
Elgin (TX), 19
Ellington, Duke, 40
Ennis (TX), 19
Episcopal Church in the U.S., 205–
   209, 211–217
Escandón, José de, 149
Evans, C.E., 168–169
Evans, Glen L., 8–13
Evant (TX), 146

Faith, Don C., 279
Falls County, 253
Farmer, James Leonard, Jr., 235–
   246, *246*
Farmer, James Leonard, Sr., 235–
   239, 245, 248, 251; house, *237*
Farmer, Nathaniel, 238
Farmer, Pearl Houston, 235–236,
   242
Farwell (TX), 102
Fayette County, 288–289
Fellowship of Reconciliation, 240–
   241
Ferber, Edna, 72
Ferguson, Miriam A., 261, 266
Ferlinghetti, Lawrence, 82
First Christian Church, San Marcos,
   172
First United Methodist Church, San
   Marcos, 172, *173*, 177

Fischer, 167
Fisher, Bernice, 241, 246
Fitzpatrick, Thomas, 52
Floydada (TX), 102
Folsom (NM), 7, 10
Ford, Henry, 99
Forney (TX), 233, 253
Fort Davis (TX), 74
Fort Hood, 145
Fort Worth (TX), 36–37, 39, 41,
   45–46, 64, 253, 255
Foy, J.J., 273
Franz, John David, 155, 159
Frazier, Johnny, 141
Frazier, Milton (Mit), 141
Fredericksburg (TX), 19, 118, 201
Fredericksburg Independent
   School District, 119
Freeman, Dorothy, 223
Frémont, John C., 48–52, 57–58
French, John L., 233
Friends of Gillespie County Coun-
   try Schools, 120–121, 123, 126–127
Friona (TX), 19
Full Tilt Boogie Band, 86, 88

Gage, Alfred S., 68–69
Gage, Edward, 68
Gage, Seth, 68
Gage Hotel, 68–69, *69*, *70*
Galveston (TX), 46, 64, 180–181, 236
Gandhi, Mohandas, 240–241
Garner, John Nance, 262
gas stations, 100–101, 103, 112–114
Gatesville (TX), 146, 165
Gateway hotel chain, 68, 72, 74
geography, 50
geology, 7, 9, 12
Giant, 72
Gibson, J.J.E., 263
Gillespie County, 116–120, 126
Gilmer, Claud, 117
Gilmer-Aikin Laws, 117–118, 123
Ginsberg, Allen, 82

Gittinger, Mrs. L.J., 198
Gladewater (TX), 20
Goetzmann, William H., 58
Gordon, Bill, 220, 223, *224*
Gordon, Jack, 38
Gordon, William M., 220
Gore, E.B., 151
Graham, S.H., 277
Granbury (TX), 112–114
Granbury Town Square Service Station. *See* Baker-Rylee Building
Grant, Ben Z., 141
Grapetown School, 133
Gray, Glen, 40
Gray, William Fairfax, 217
Gray County, 56
Grayson County, 220, 225, 228–230
Grayson County Historical Commission, 230–231
Green, Edward H.R., 232
Green, Hetty Robinson, 232–234
Green, Mabel, 234
Greenville (TX), 101, 266
Greenwood, Caleb, 52, 55
Gregg County, 259
Grote, Henry, 122
Guadalupe River, 288
Guderjan, Thomas H., 16
Gulf Coast Music Hall of Fame, 92
Gulick, Charlotte, 221–222
Gulick, Luther, 221–222

Hall, Clyde, 221, *221*, 225, 228
Hall, Hugh Edward, 221, 227
Hall, Hugh E., Jr., 221, 223, 225, 228–230
Hall, Mita Holsapple, 220–231, *221*, *224*, *229*
Hamilton, John, 107–108
Hamlisch, Marvin, 42
Hanks, Clyde Walton, 275
Hanks, Frances, 280
Hanks, Zula Holcomb, 275–276, 278–280

Hardin, John Gerham, 300–301
Hardin, Mary "Mollie" Funk, 293, 300–302, *301*
Hardin-Simmons College, 302
Hardy, J.C., 302
Harlow, Mabel, 232
Harris, Thomas G., 167–168
Harrison Bayou, 140
Harrison County, 137, 140–141, 259
Harvey, Paul, 188–189
Hatcher, John, 52, 55
Hawkins (TX), 19
Haynes, C. Vance, Jr., 13
Hays County, 162, 164, 294
Helms, Chet, 84
Hemphill, Dan, 24
Hempstead (TX), 164
Henderson County, 15
Hendricks, Grace, 20, *21*
Hendrix, Jimi, 85
Henley, Don, 140–141, 144
Henry, Reeve, 233
Heritage Foundation of Hidalgo County, 155, 158
Hershey, Tom, 146
Hidalgo (TX), 148–149, 151, 153–156, 158–159
Hidalgo County, 149, 155
Hidalgo County Historical Commission, 154, 158
Hidalgo County Historical Society, 158
Hidalgo Pumphouse, 148–159, *152*, *156*, *157*, 158–159
Hilderbran, Harvey, 120
Hill College, 199
Hillsboro (TX), 199
Hilton Hotel (El Paso; Plaza Hotel), 67
Hines, Edgar A., 205
Hines, Helen Orwig, 207, 215
Hines, John Elbridge, 205–216, *212*, 219
Hines, Mary Woodbury Moore, 205

Hispanics, 213
Hobby, Oveta Culp, 264
Hofman, Jack L., 13
Holland, Clay, 69, 71
Holland, Crystal. *See* Spannell,
    Crystal Holland.
Holland, John R., 69–71
Holland, Mary, 69–70
Holland Hotel, 68–71
Holliday, Vance T., 13
Hollingsworth, Orlando Newton,
    164, 174, 176–177
Hollingsworth, Ruth Grace
    Katherine Platner, 176
Holsapple, J.W., 220
Holsapple, Merle, 223, *224*
Hood County, 113
Hopper, Dennis, 72
Hotel Cortez, 67
Hotel El Capitan, 68, 74–75
Hotel Paso del Norte (Camino Real
    Hotel), 64–67, *67*
Houston (TX), 210, 219
Houston, Sam, 184
Houston, Temple, 184
Howard, Edgar B., 7
Hudson, Rock, 72
Huhn, Francis M., 293–294
Hunt, Walter "PeeWee," 40–41
Hunt County, 101
Huntsville (TX), 164, 178–179, 181,
    290
Huston, Samuel, 248
Huston-Tillotson University (also
    Samuel Huston College and
    Tillotson Collge), 209, 237, 242,
    246, 248–249, *249*
Hutchison, W.O., 163
Hutchinson County, 56
Hygieostatic Bat Roost, *33, 34*

Independence (TX), 290–291, 293–
    295, 297
industry, 148–159

Intermediate-Range Nuclear
    Forces (INF) Treaty, 138–139
Iokovos, Demetrios, 212
irrigation, 149–150, 153–159, 160–
    161

jackrabbit, 20, *21*, 21–22, *23*, 24–25
Jackson, Jack (Jaxon), 84, 86
Jasper County, 290
jazz, 37, 39
Jefferson County, 93, 290
Jefferson County Historical Com-
    mission, 78, 80
Jenkins, John Wesley, 38
J. W. Jenkins' Sons Music Company,
    38
Jester, Beauford, 117
Johnson, Claudia Alta Taylor (Lady
    Bird), 115, 134
Johnson, Lyndon Baines, 67, 115,
    134–135, 171, 262, 264
Jones, Anson, 290
Jones, J.F., 276
Jones, J. Ras, 253
Jones, Jesse H., 253
Joplin, Dorothy East, 79–80, 89
Joplin, Janis, 78–92, 95, *91*
Joplin, Laura, 79, 82, 90
Joplin, Michael, 79, 90
Joplin, Scott, 39, 42
Joplin, Seth, 79–80
Jucksch, Edw. R., 274
Junction Schoolhouse, 115

Kansas City (MO), 36–38, 44
Karnack (TX), 135–136, 139
Kaufman, County, 232, 235
Kearny, Stephen W., 56
Keller, Jim, 283
Kempthorne, Edith, 223, 230
Kenedy (TX), 20
Kennedy, Robert F., 244–245
Kerouac, Jack, 82
Kerr, Alfred B.F., 172

Killeen (TX), 146
King, Martin Luther, Jr., 212
Kingsville (TX), 169
Knox City (TX), 19
Knox Glass Bottle Company, 276, 283–285; photo of jars, *284*
Korean War, 136, 145
Kozmic Blues band, 85
Krieger, Alex D., 7, 11
Kristofferson, Kris, 79, 92
Ku Klux Klan, 243–244, 259
Kyle, Fergus, 164

La Grange (TX), 288–289
LaCroix, Jerry "Count Jackson," 90
Lafayette, Marie Joseph Paul Yves Roche Gilbert du Motier, Marquis de, 288
Lamar University (Lamar State College of Technology), 83, 209
Lamb, Gil, 29–30
Lambie, R.C., 167
Lafayette (LA), 91
Lake Charles (LA), 91
Lale, Max, 138
Lampasas (TX), 146, 292
Lampasas County, 145–147
Lampasas River, 146
Langdon, Jim, 82
Lanham, S.W.T., 167
Latimer, Truett, 189, 198, 200
Laughmiller, Donald C., 280, 282
Laurie, Bill, 279
Ledbetter, Huddie "Leadbelly," 82
Lehman, II, Ronald F., 139
Lewis, J.E., 65
Lewis and Clark Expedition, 49
Limestone County, 279
Limpia Hotel, 74
Lincoln, Abraham, 61
Linden (TX), 44, 140
Lindley, James, 126
Linnville (TX), 289
Lions Club, 93, 107

Llano (TX), 19
Lockhart (TX), 19, 289
Lometa (TX), 145
Loney, Kate Deadrich, 115
Long, Jane, 266
Longhorn Army Ammunition Plant, 134, 136–141, *137, 142, 143,* 144
Longhorn Ordnance Works, 135, *135*
Longstreet, James, 48
Longview (TX), 261
Lorenzo de Zavala State Archives and Library Building, 194, *195*
Louisiana Purchase Exposition, 1904, 150
Love, Thomas B., 260
Lower South Grape Creek School, 119–120, 123, 125–126, *125,* 128
Lubbock (TX), 26, 28
Lubbock Lake Landmark, 17, *18*
Lucas, Mattie, 228–229
Luckenbach (TX), 123
Luckenbach School, 128
Luther, John Hill, 299

Malakoff (TX), 15
Malakoff Fuel Company, 15
Malakoff Men, 15–17
Malaria, 32
Mann, Horace, 116, 163
Mansfield (TX), 37
"Maple Leaf Rag," 44–45
Marathon (TX), 67–68
Marcy, Randolph B., 60
Marfa (TX), 67–68, 72, 74
Marlin (TX), 253
Marshall (TX), 136–139, 236, 239, 246, 248, 250–251
Mary Hardin-Baylor College. *See* University of Mary Hardin-Baylor.
Matador (TX), 101–102, 104, 106, 109
Matador Hotel, 107

Matador Land and Cattle Company, 111
Matador Masonic Lodge, 107–108, 111
Matador Ranch, 101, 111
May, Hazel, 223
McAllen (TX), 158
McClintock, Christy, 93–94
McLennan County, 11, 292
Mead, John A., 5–6
Meadows Foundation, 155
Meeker, Julian and Jack, 283
Meharg, Emma Grigsby, 266
Meltzer, David J., 13
Mesquite (TX), 233
Methodist Episcopal Church, South (also Methodist), 164, 177, 235–238, 240, 248, 253
Meusebach Creek School, 128
Mexican War, 56
Miami (TX), 7–8, 11, 14, 17
Midland (TX), 20, 25
Midwestern State University, 302
Milam County, 289–290
Mineo, Sal, 72
Mission San Francisco de la Espada, 160; aqueduct, 160, *161*
Mission San Joaquín del Monte, 149
Monroe, Sam, 86–87, 89–90
Monsanto Chemical Company, 135–136
Monterey International Pop Festival, 85
Montgomery County, 290
Moody, Dan, 260–261
Moore County, 54, 56
Moore County Historical Commission, 59, 61
Moore, T.H., 277
Moriaty, Dave, 82
Morrell, Z.N., 288
Morris Ranch School, 132
Morris, Ann, 265

Morrisroe, Richard F., 213
Motley County, 101, 104, 107, 111
Motley County Historical Commission, 109
mule, 28–29, *29*, 30
Muleshoe (TX), 28–29, *29*, 30–31, 102
Muller, Arthur, 165–166, 180–182
Museum of the Gulf Coast, 92
Myers, Elijah E., 184

National Association for the Advancement of Colored People, 248
National Country School Association, 120
Native Americans, 54, 56, 66, 134, 160, 222, 279, 288
Navasota (TX), 19
Neal, John, 265
Neal, Martha Ann Gholston, 252–253, 255–256
Neal, Margie (Mary) Elizabeth, 252–265, *254*, *258*
Neal, William Lafayette, 252–253, 255
Nebgen School, 128
Neches River, 82, 93
Neff, Pat M., 257, 295
Newman, Paul, 42
Nicollet, Joseph Nicolas, 48–49
Nieman, Hugh R., Jr., 199, 201
Nimitz, Chester W., 201
normal schools, 163–164, 168
Norton, Robert, 154–156, 159
Northcraft, Edward S., 162–166, 169–170, 172, 174, 177, 181
Northcraft, Mary Elizabeth Donalson, 165
Nuevo Santander, 149

Oakwood Cemetery (Fort Worth), 41–42, *42*, 46
Odessa (TX), 20, 22, 24–25

Odetta, 83
Odom, Jimmy R., 280, *281*, 282, 284–285
Old Main, Sam Houston State University, 166, 178–182, *179*
Old Main, Texas State University, 162, 165, *165*, *166*, 167, 169–171, 172, 181
Oldham County, 54, 56
Operation Long Horn, 145–147
Orange County, 93–94

Paducah (TX), 102
paleontology, 5–18
Palestine (TX), 271–284
Palestine Service Men's Club, 272–282, *274*
Palmer, John, 89
Panhandle-Plains Historical Museum, 6
Panola County, 252–253, 256, 259, 264–265
Paris (TX), 19
Parmelee, Deolece, 29, 188–189, 200
Patterson, John, 244
Pattillo, George Alexander, 290
Pecan Creek School, 128
Peck, William G., 52, 54, 56–57
Pedernales Rural School, 133
Perrin Field, 230
Perry, Rick, 121
Pershing, John J., 67
Peterson, Mrs. Alfred O., 271
Pharr (TX), 153
Plainview (TX), 102, 266
Plaisance, Rose, 279
Polk, James K., 52
Polk, Leonidas, 217
Port Arthur (TX), 78–84, 86, 89–92, 93
Port Arthur College (Lamar State College-Port Arthur), 83, 89
Potter County, 54, 56, 60
Potts, Janie, 146–147

prairie dog, 25–28
Prairie View (TX), 164
Prairie View A&M University, 164, 209
Presbyterian Church (USA), 180
Preservation Texas, 109
Progressive Era, 116, 222
Public Works Administration, 93
Puckett, Charles, 5, 14
Pue, Ronni, 119

Quin, Clinton S., 207, 209, 219

Raggedy Ed, 36
ragtime music, 36–40, 42–43, 45
railroads, 150, 232, 234, 253, 272–273, 277, 283
Rainbow Bridge, 82, 93–95, *94*
Red River, 50–51, 55–56
Redford, Robert, 42
Regency (TX), 146
Republic of Texas, 53, 184, 194, 287, 289–290
Rheingold School, *129*, 132
Rice University, 209
Riley, Crockett, 121
Rio Grande, 148–149, 151, 153, 158–159
roadside architecture, 103–107, *105*
Roberts County, 6, 10, 56
Roberts County Museum, 14
Robertson County, 289
Robertson, Luther Bedford (Bob), 101–104, 106, 111
Robertson, Olga Cunningham, 101, 107–109, 111
Robertson, Reatha Rayne (Bobbie), 101, 108
rock and roll music, 78, 85–86
Roesener, F.G., 193, *193*
Rogers, Will, 67
Roosevelt, Franklin Delano, 135, 253, 257, 262
Roosevelt, Eleanor, 67

Rusk County, 174, 176, 249
Russia, 138–139
Rylee, Jefferson Davis, 113

Sabine River, 261
Sample, J.H., 101
Sam Houston State University
(Sam Houston Normal Institute),
163, 178–180, 209, 253
Samuel Huston College. *See*
Huston-Tillotson University.
San Angelo (TX), 26, 145
San Antonio (TX), 176, 263, 271, 288
San Antonio Missions National
Historical Park, 161
San Antonio River, 149
San Juan (TX), 153, 155
San Marcos (TX), 162–165, 169–170,
176, 177, 181–182, 294
San Marcos River, 169
Sanderson (TX), 19
Sayers, Joseph D., 164, 167
Scarlett, William, 206–208
Schmidt, Mathias, 121–122
Scottsville (TX), 253
Seale, Carl, 158–159
Sedalia (MO), 44–45
Seigenthaler, John, 245
Segal, Ben, 241
Sellards, Elias Howard, 7–13, 15–17
Sewell, S.M. "Froggy," 169
Shabalin, Nikolai, 138
Shackelford County, 68
Shannon's Prairie (TX), 290
Shapiro, Bernstein, and Company,
41
Shelby County, 259
Sheppard, Morris, 262
Shepperd, John Ben, 20, 22, 24–25,
28, 30–31, 190–191
Sherman (TX), 180, 220, 223–231
Shivers, Allan, 20, 117, 209, 263–264
Sibley, H.H., 45
Simpson, James Hervey, 60

Slaughter, John B., 41
Smith County, 188, 275
Smith County Historical Survey
Committee, 188
Smith, Bessie, 83
Smith, Howard K., 244
Smith, Ima, 191
Smith, Jedediah, 52
Smith, John Peter, 45–46
Smith, Ogden, 94
Smith, Preston, 191
Social Gospel (social justice) move-
ment, 205–207, 210–211, 215
Southwest Texas Normal School
(Institute, College), 164, 169, 174,
181–182
Southwest Texas State Teachers
College, 169
Soviet Union, 145
Snyder (TX), 26, 28
Spannell, Crystal Holland, 69–71
Spannell, Harry J., 70–71
Spell, Mrs. W.E. (Jane Madden), 257
Spoetzl, "Miss Celie," 268; Spoetzl
Brewery, *268*
St. John, Powell, 84
St. Louis (MO), 44, 211, 232–233
St. Martin's Lutheran Church (St.
Martin's German Evangelical
Lutheran Church), Austin, 192,
192, 193, 194
Stanley, J.S., 108
Starks, Judy, 119
Stephen F. Austin State University,
209, 257
Sterling, Ross, 261–262
Stevens, George, 72
Steves, Albert, Sr., 34
Stonewall (TX), 118, 126
Stonewall Heritage Society, 119
Stotts, John, 108
Strackbein, Christian, 123
Strong, J.G., 259
Studer, Floyd V., 6–7

Sullivan, Louis, 64
Sutherlin, Yvonne, 80–81
Swanson, Gloria, 67
Sweatt, Heman M., 251
Swedish Central Methodist
  Church, 192

Tarrant County, 37
Taylor, Elizabeth, 72
Taylor, Frances, 223
Taylor, Thomas Jefferson, 134
Taylor, Tom, 22, 24
teacherage, 121, *122, 124*
Terrell (TX), 232–234
Texarkana (TX), 44, 236
Texas A&I College (Texas A&I University, Texas A&M University-Kingsville), 169, 258
Texas A&M University, 209
Texas annexation, 50, 54
Texas Centennial, 228–229, 260
Texas Chautauqua (also Chautauqua Hill), 162–164, 167, 171, 182
Texas Clay Products Company, 15
Texas Court of Criminal Appeals, 197
Texas Highway Department, 22
Texas Historical Commission, 20, 34, 59, 61–62, 69, 71–72, 111, 113, 134, 155, 158, 170, 181, 183, 185, 189, 198, 231, 251, 269
"Texas, Our Texas," state song, 260
Texas Parks and Wildlife Commission, 201
Texas Rangers, 191
Texas State Capitol, 165, 184, 190–192; monuments on grounds of, 184–196, *186–187;* markers on grounds of, *186–187, 189,* 194, *195,* 197–199, 252, 258
Texas State Historical Survey Committee, 17, 20, 24, 46, 170, 185, 188, 200
Texas State Parks Board, *193,* 194

Texas State Preservation Board, 191, 197
Texas State University, 162, 172. *See also* Southwest Texas State University (Normal School, State Teachers College).
Texas Supreme Court, 197
Texas Tech University Museum, 17, *18*
Thiokol Chemical Corporation, 136–139, 141
Thomas, Henry, 172
Thomas Jefferson High School (Port Arthur), 80
Thoreau, Henry David, 239–241
Thornton, Willie Mae "Big Mama," 83
Threadgill, Kenneth, 84, 86
Tillotson College. *See* Huston-Tillotson University.
Tobey, Nathaniel W., Jr., 180
Tolbert, Frank X., 24, 26
Tolson, Melvin B., 239–240
Torian, Jack, 25
Travis, William B., 194
Travis (TX), 290
Travis County, 289
Travis County Historical Commission, 190–191
Trigg, Edna Westbrook, 267
Trinidad (TX), 15
Trinity River, 233
Trost, Adolphus Gustavus, 64
Trost, Ernst, 64
Trost, George Ernst, 64
Trost, Gustavus Adolphus, 64, 71
Trost, Henry Charles, 63–66, 68, 71, 74–75, 76
Trost & Trost architectural firm, 64–65, 67, 71–72, 76
Troup (TX), 275
Truman, Harry, 263
Tryon, William M., 290
Tutu, Desmond, 214

"12th Street Rag," 36, 38–39, *39*,
    40–41, 43, 45
Tyler, John, 50
Tyler (TX), 188
Tyson, Arthur K., 297
Tyson, Arla Ray, 297

Underwood, Chester, 283
Underwood, Roy R., 283–284
United Church of Christ, 214
United Methodist Church, 214
United Presbyterian Church, 214
United States Army Corps of Engi-
    neers, 60
United States Army Corps of Topo-
    graphical Engineers, 47–48, 52,
    57, 60
United States Environmental Pro-
    tection Agency, 139, 141
United States Fish and Wildlife
    Service, 139, 141
Universal Match Corporation, 136–
    137, *137*, 141
University of Houston, 209
University of Mary Hardin-Baylor,
    293, 295–297, *296*, *298*, 300–302
University of North Texas, 164
University of Texas at Austin, 7, 13,
    84, 209, 248, 265
    Bureau of Economic Geology, 8
    Texas Memorial Museum, 8,
        11–12, 16
    Vertebrate Paleontology Labora-
        tory, 14
University of Texas of the Permian
    Basin, 25
US Highway 70, 102
USS *Patoka*, 93
USS *Texas*, 199–201, 224

Van Dorn, Earl, 48
Van Horn (TX), 68, 74
Vandale, Earl, 57
Vander Lyn, Robert, 119

Varnier, J.E., 111
Vera, Joe, 155
Vernon (TX), 102
Victoria (TX), 288
Vietnam War, 137
Villa, Pancho, 67
Vorce, Mrs. Frank (Leona), 272

Waco (TX), 70, 145, 199, 293–296
Waco Mammoth site, 11
Waco University, 293
Waggoner, W.T., 41
Walker County, 178
Walker County Historical Commis-
    sion, 181
Waller, Fats, 40
Waller Creek Boys, 84
Warner Brothers film company, 72
Washington County, 289–291
Washington, George, 288
Washington-on-the-Brazos (TX),
    290
Watts, Taft, 277
Waxahachie (TX), 19
Webb, Catherine, 223
Webb, Water Prescott, 21, 26, 58,
    193–194
Weddington, Sarah, 191
Weinheimer, Bernice, 119–120
Wentworth, Jeff, 120
Weslaco (TX), 19
West (TX), 19
West Tawakoni (TX), 20
Weston, Frank A., 64
Wharton County, 69
Wheeler County, 56
Whipple, Amiel Weeks, 60
White, Zach T., 65
Who, The, 85
Wichita County, 300, 302
Wiggins, Lanny, 84
Wilbarger County, 102
Wiley College, 236, 239–240, 246,
    248, 250–251, *250*

Wiley, Isaac D., 250
William Carey Crane College, 293
Williams, Walker, 44
Williams, Will, 44
Williams Creek (Albert) School,
  130–131, 132
Williamson, Billy, 188–190
Willow City School, 132
Wilmans, Edith Therrel, 259
Wilson, A.J., 181
Wilson, George Henry, 181
Wisdom, Rufus Lee, Sr., 156
Wisdom, Rufus Lee, II, 156
Wisdom, Walter, 156
woman suffrage, 256–257
Wood, W.D., 162–163

Works Progress Administration, 9,
  13, 16
World War I, 101, 220, 224, 256, 283
World War II, 104, 106, 116–117, 134–
  136, 229–230, 240, 271–284
World's Columbian Exposition,
  1893 (Chicago World's Fair), 44,
  64
Wrede School, 132
Wright, Frank Lloyd, 64

Yellowley, Charlton, 176
Young, Lester, 40

Zaharias, Mildred Ella "Babe" Did-
  rickson, 268–269